THE 10-POUND SHRED

THE 10-POUND SHRED

FROM FLAB TO FIT IN 4 WEEKS

TOMMY EUROPE

Collins

Published by Collins, an imprint of HarperCollins Publishers Ltd.

First edition

HarperCollins books may be purchased for educational, business, or sales promotional use through our Special Markets Department.

HarperCollins Publishers Ltd
2 Bloor Street East, 20th Floor
Toronto, Ontario, Canada, M4W 1A8

www.harpercollins.ca

Library and Archives Canada Cataloguing in Publication is available.

ISBN 978-1-55468-997-2

RRD 9 8 7 6 5 4 3 2 1

Printed and bound in the United States

To everyone who has decided to improve their lives through fitness and healthy living. My hope and wish is that this book can help everybody achieve their own goals, improve their quality of life and take control of their lives.

And to Team T. A. M., I love you; this is for you.

CONTENTS

THE 10-POUND SHRED

INTRODUCTION

Have a seat. I'm going to give you the straight goods. Unless you're already sitting down, that is. Maybe you're in the bookstore right now, wondering whether this really is the first step toward where you want to be. Or maybe you're sitting on the couch, munching away on a bowl of chips, thinking that sooner or later you're going to have to work out some better habits, particularly if you're ever going to fit into that old pair of jeans again.

Whatever the case, you're probably going to be sitting down a lot less in the coming weeks, but grab a seat right now, because we're going to get a few things straight. As hard as it may be to believe right now, a lot is going to change over the next month.

Over the next 31 days, you are going to lose inches and pounds. That's right: At the end of this month, you're going to see the difference, and so will everyone else.

Over the next 31 days, you are going to find you have less and less body fat, and more lean muscle mass. You're going to feel different.

Over the next 31 days, you are going to gain the knowledge and the confidence to get the results that have escaped you up to this point. You see where this is going, don't you? You are actually going to be different.

At the end of the month, you are definitely going to fit into those old jeans again. You're going to look great at that upcoming event, whether it's a wedding, graduation, family function or anything else. You're going to run that race, make that team or just kick your buddies' butts in golf. Just as important, you're going to set a great example for your peers, your friends and your family.

Are you okay with all that?

If you are, then keep reading. Because we're going to stop making excuses, blast through your comfort zones and have a great time along the way.

I'm not going to lie to you, though. It's not going to be easy. If it were, you would have done it already and you wouldn't be reading this book. I'm sure you've already tried. But, for some reason, your good intentions have tailed off. Maybe you didn't know how to keep going. Maybe you didn't even really know where to begin.

I'm going to show you exactly where to begin. It's called Day 1, and we're going to get to that in a minute. As for how to keep going, we've got that taken care of, too: Day 2, Day 3, Day 4 and so on to 31. You don't have to worry about anything except knowing what day it is. Oh, and one more thing: putting everything you've got into your workouts.

Now, that probably sounds like a lot of sweat and a lot of pain. And if you thought sweat and pain were fun, you might not be trying to lose 10 pounds right now. Well, guess what? Those things are fun. I know, it sounds more than a little crazy. But look around. Why do you think people compete in triathlons, or climb mountains, or lift weights, or even play ultimate Frisbee with their friends? Because trying hard feels good, and if you end up with a few aches and pains at the end, even that feels all right.

You may already know this, of course. But if you have to take my word for it, I might as well tell you that I've had my share of aches, too, and I know what it feels like to push myself hard. Fitness has always been a part of my life. I've been very active since I was a kid. I was always playing one sport or another . . . soccer, track, rugby, baseball, football and hockey—yeah, that's right, I said hockey. That was the first sport I truly loved. Then football took centre stage. I played four years at Bishop's University, then went on to play as a pro in the Canadian Football League for 11 years.

If you like to play sports, doing it for a living is a lot of fun. But it's a lot of work, too. I mean a *lot* of work. Playing at that level required me to spend some serious hours in the gym, and an equal amount of time on a physiotherapist's table. After all, sometimes I was the hammer, but every once in a while I was the nail, too! But that's the thing: The fun and the work go together.

So trust me: When you're feeling like it's getting tough, remember that I've been there and I've gotten through it. You will, too.

But I don't want to make the 10-Pound Shred sound like a month of suffering and sacrifice! Do you remember when you were a kid and could just run and play all day long, learning new athletic moves as if it was the most natural thing in the world? That's why it was fun—because you always got to do something different and learn something new. No one has to tell a kid to suck it up and do one more set. Just the opposite—you have to tell kids to *stop* playing. Well, if you're exercising right, you should be having that kind of fun yourself, especially once you're back in shape.

You may not notice it when you're sitting on the couch, but your body likes to move. It may or may not like to do sets of bench presses, but unless you're an offensive lineman or a body builder, those particular movements and muscle groups are probably not all that important to you. Not many people find the ability to push 350 pounds off their chests an especially useful talent. Maybe that's why people eventually get bored of working on that skill. Or sit-ups. Anyone like sit-ups? I didn't think so. No one wants to do something hard just for the sake of doing something hard. But don't worry: The 10-Pound Shred is not just a hardcore version of high-school phys. ed. class.

It's way more fun than that.

I appreciate the different movements different sports require, so I incorporate the principles of these movements into my High-Intensity Training Zone (HITZ) functional training system. Fitness is about work, but it's about play, too.

What do I mean by "functional training"? I mean I lot of things, but most important, I mean that we're going to be working on the muscles you use in everyday life—even if you didn't know you had them. And no, I don't mean your already Olympic-calibre

TOMMY TIP

beer-drinking arms or BlackBerry thumbs.

More than anything else, functional training means working on what you'll keep hearing me call your *core*. What exactly is your core? Well, the technical answer is your transverse abdominus, your internal and external obliques, your quadratus lumborum and your diaphragm. If working on these muscles doesn't sound like a real priority to you, I'll add that they're the ones we use in important activities—like breathing, for example. They also work together to give you stability and strength in whatever you do. I don't care whether you're working on your tennis serve, your tee shots in golf or your wrist shot in hockey—or ballroom dancing, ultimate fighting or carrying your kid around in the mall. Your core is where you get your power.

Now, I don't know about you, but doesn't having more power—and therefore more energy—seem like a great reason to train your body the way it was meant to be trained?

That's what we're going to do.

But it's not just your core we're going after. It's your whole body—and your long-forgotten cardio, too. And wherever you're weak, that's what's going to get hit first. It's going to be a whole-body workout, so there will be nowhere for the weak muscles to hide. We'll find them sooner or later. Probably sooner. The 10PS is going to come at you from all angles and bring out that inner athlete in you. The saying "Work smarter, not harder" cannot be more true. As we roll through the 10PS, we will be addressing the physical, mental and nutritional aspects of maintaining a healthy lifestyle.

Don't start worrying, though. My HITZ functional training system is going to make things easier for you, not harder. Think about it: By hitting all the necessary muscles, using a wide variety of exercises, you'll find you're not getting bored. It's a lot easier to get creative with your workouts when you're doing something different every day.

Each week, you will have three HITZ Resistance days, two HITZ Cardio days and two "active rest" days. Each day is laid out for you so you'll know what to expect, along with what you will eat on that particular day. Take notes as you go along and pay attention to the exercises, so that you will have it all figured out once your 31 days are successfully completed.

Following a fitness plan is really more about leading than following. I can bark at you all day, or offer words of encouragement until I'm out of breath and you're sick of listening to me. But unless you take responsibility, nothing is going to happen. You can't just talk about it. You have to be about it.

And I'm not just talking about Days 1 through 31. I'm talking about Day 32 especially. My goal for you at the end of the 10-Pound Shred is not just that you'll be fitter, happier and better-looking (though those aren't bad goals). It's that you will have more than a new body—you'll have a new lifestyle. You'll see the results, you'll have all the tools to push yourself in a safe and efficient way, and Day 32 will be the start of the new you!

I'm an athlete and a trainer, so you are welcome to take things with a grain of salt when I talk about changing the world. But I'd like you to keep in mind that the decision you've just made is about more than just looking and feeling better. Take a look around at the people who haven't made the same decisions. Our society is getting unhealthier by the day. For those who choose to hold off on healthy lifestyles, health issues such as cancer, heart disease, hypoglycemia and Type 2 diabetes are on the rise. It is up to people like you and me to reverse this dangerous trend. Living a long life is only a blessing if you are healthy and able to enjoy the amazing things that life has to offer.

That is one of the reasons I wanted to write a book. I've been blessed to be working in a field that genuinely helps people change their lives in a positive, healthy fashion and I want my daughter, Makayla, to see the benefits of living a healthy lifestyle. I've managed to learn a few things from moms and dads, from regular fitness enthusiasts, from weekend warriors and from athletes and entertainers in training sessions. I have had the opportunity to work with thousands of men and women who have started with goals like yours, wanting to lose weight once and for all, wanting to have a health makeover.

Some of the success stories blow even my mind. Out of all of the people I've worked with, one who really stands out is my boy Nathan. Nathan was a strapping fellow and a world-class beer drinker. I mean, this guy could put away eight pints before most people could finish their first. Needless to say, that kind of beer intake is not consistent with a healthy lifestyle, and Nathan was seriously out of shape.

But he had something that all winners have. Nathan had drive. When he decided to make some changes, it was as good as done. At the end of a month of training five days a week, this guy had lost 32 pounds and 14 inches. Yeah, that's right: *in one month*. But he wasn't done. A year later, Nathan ran the Vancouver Marathon in 2:58:42, which put him 11th in his division and 51st overall, which means he beat a whole lot of serious runners. Right now, he's training for the Boston Marathon, which was one of his goals when he started out. Nathan proves that it's not where you start but where you finish that matters. All it takes is a goal, and a never-give-up policy until you reach that goal.

Of course, I've witnessed some pretty mediocre results over the years, as well. If you want to fall into the "amazing transformations" category, just do what the successful ones do: Stick to the plan. You will definitely get out of this what you put into it. It's what you do when nobody's looking that will mean the most. I need you to bust your butt for the next 31 days, which is all I can ask of you.

I'll be with you each and every day. If, for some reason, you mess up, don't beat yourself up. You just have to dust yourself off and get back up again. It's not as though you don't know where to begin. Just open up the book and get back at it. You are capable of anything you put your mind to, so put the "Tommy Talk" in the back of your head and don't "save it for the next workout," because I'll be watching.

Before you go any further, you need to know your goal. So what is it? It could be weight. It could be inches. Is it a dress you want to wear? Then keep it in front of you. Do you want to run a 10K? Cycle to the next town down the road? Swim across the lake? Dazzle old classmates at a high-school reunion? Whatever it is, you can do it. But you can't make much progress without a goal. That goal is what you are going to be all about for the next 31 days.

All it takes is that goal. Plus a month of hard work. Sound fair?

Then let's get the 10-Pound Shred started.

DAY 1
Planning for Success

TOMMY RULE #1: DON'T TRY—DO!

Today is a great day!

It's also probably the toughest one of the whole 10-Pound Shred. After all, this is the day you've been putting off for so long. So even though most of what we're doing today is getting ready for the weeks that follow, I'm going to count this as part of the 10PS. Maybe even the most important part.

You are about to embark on a 31-day journey that will act as a preview of your lifestyle change. That's right. You're not just signing up for 31 days. What we have in store is permanent, and today is the first day of that new life.

So let's get at it. Do you have your goals in place and written down?

Seriously, write them down.

The next 31 days are going to be challenging, and you may wonder every now and then why you are doing what you're doing. I can even tell you when those moments will come. Will it happen when your alarm goes off and you struggle to summon the willpower to haul your aching body out of bed for an early-morning workout? Absolutely.

Will it happen when the devil on one shoulder tries to seduce you into stuffing a bacon double cheeseburger into your mouth, while the angel on the other shoulder reminds you that lentils and spinach salad are what's on the menu? Guaranteed.

Will it happen when you're blasting off a few more reps and your lungs and muscles are burning? If it doesn't, you're not working hard enough.

But this isn't meant to be easy. It's meant to work. And it's meant to be worth it. So when you want to quit, and flop onto the couch with a beer and a bag of cheesies, just remember what you wrote down.

You *have* written your goals down by now, haven't you?

Maybe you're not sure what they are, and you just want to be healthier. In that case, take a look in the mirror, and I can just about guarantee you'll come away with a goal worth writing down. Seriously, guys, can you even see your belt? Then maybe your beer gut is the name for your goal. Or do you have what I call a "back ass"? (That's a word I use to refer to cleavage on your back. Front cleavage is one thing, but in the *back*? Come on, man!) Girls, don't laugh. Maybe your goal is what I call your pouch. A pouch is the female equivalent of the male beer belly—if a look in the mirror reminds you to pick up a box of muffins, then you've got something to target. You don't even have to be fat to have a pouch—you could be slim, yet soft and doughy and what I call "skinny fat." Just because you are a size 0 or extra-small doesn't mean you are fit—or even healthy.

Great, then. You've got goals. But your goals shouldn't just be a list of things you don't like. Focus on what you *want* to be, and *how* you want to be. Self-criticism is great if it gets you off your ass, but I don't want anyone beating themselves up over some bad habits they used to have. Today is the day you start your new, life-affirming habits. So take one last look at your old self, then fix your eyes on the new self you have just taken the first step toward creating. Let that be your inspiration.

Ultimately, you're going to blow past your goals. When you see the results, and feel how great it is to have your strength and stamina back, you're not going to be satisfied with just fitting into an old pair of jeans or walking a golf course rather than riding in a cart. But your goals are what will see you through a few tough mornings and a few confrontations with cheeseburgers, lattes and beers.

I know, I know. It's starting to sound grim. Trust me, though—it's not. It's going to be rewarding, and you will have tons of fun along the way. But it *has* to be challenging to work—if it's not challenging, there's no point doing it. And if you don't wanna put in the work, you'll be cheating only yourself.

There's no way around that. The workouts in the 10PS are progressive in nature, so as you make your way through them, they'll become increasingly challenging. I know that you're not afraid of a challenge, so let's do this thing!

GETTING THE GEAR TO GET IN GEAR

Every successful mission requires a plan, so today you and I are going to lay the foundation for your 31-day lifestyle change. Give this process your full attention and effort, because your results will mirror your effort and dedication. We are going to work your entire body and utilize more than 60 different HITZ Resistance exercises and eight different HITZ Cardio workouts. I want to make sure that you are fully prepared, so here is the list of equipment you will need to complete the 10PS:

Stability Ball (SB). Get a medium-sized SB and do not overinflate it. The SB should be neither rock hard nor so soft it flops around. You want something firm.

Dumbbells (DBs). At a minimum, you should have four sets of DBs: 5, 10, 12 and 15 pounds for the ladies, and 12, 15, 20 and 25 pounds for the fellas. If you are at home, you can work out with a handled 1-gallon (4 L) water jug, filled with water or sand to the weight you want. If you will be training in a gym, all the DBs you require will be racked up neatly and alluringly. Stronger exercisers will want heavier weights (30 to 50 pounds) toward the last few weeks of the program. I've suggested weights throughout, but trust your own body—you're aiming for your muscles to be fatigued at the end of a set. If you can't make it to the end, lighten up a bit, but if you're not tired, go heavier.

Resistance Bands (RBs). Grab two of them—one with a medium tension (red handles) and one with a stronger tension (black). I prefer RBs that are in a sheath, just in case the band snaps.

Skipping Rope. Choose a "speed rope," which you can pick up at any retailer. You will want to ensure that it is adjustable. In a pinch, grab a classic playground skipping rope or even bounce on the spot. Just work hard!

Mat. Or you can just use the floor if you don't mind getting your back dirty. It's not the end of the world.

Pull-Up Bar. If you are in a gym, use one of the bars on a squat rack or Smith machine. If you are exercising outdoors, many parks will have a bar to do pull-ups on. There is also a Lebert Equalizer pull-up bar that you can buy if you need to. At times I have even used a bar and two chairs.

Stopwatch. Your repetitions will be set by time, so you will make your life much easier if you have one. You should like this piece of equipment, since it tells you when you get to stop.

Attire. I know, it's kind of obvious, but you're going to need something to wear while you work out. Running shoes, shorts, tights and so on will come in handy.

Now, the expensive stuff. Most of the HITZ Cardio workouts in the 10PS are best done on a treadmill or elliptical machine. If you plan to hit the gym for the 10PS, you're good to go. They'll have the gear. And if you have a few thousand dollars lying around, by all means, go out and buy these machines. But if you're not going to the gym or the fitness machine superstore, don't worry.

You can also opt for Bootcamp-style cardio outdoors. Real running, stair climbing, swimming, biking and cross-country skiing give you a complete workout and will probably be more interesting—and therefore more motivating, as well. So don't think you need a lot of gear to get active.

What you do need, though, is to make sure you do it right. Let's get to that next.

HOW HARD IS TOO HARD?

You're going to get out of this exactly what you put in, so I want you going hard. But that doesn't mean pushing yourself to the brink of collapse every time you lace up your running shoes or pick up a dumbbell. We're trying to train your body, not punish it. When exercising, it's important to monitor your intensity to make sure you're working at a pace that is challenging enough to help you reach your goals, but not so hard that you blow a lung. If any part of the 10PS feels bad, it's time to start doing something differently.

So how do you tell the difference between challenging and bad? I find that the Perceived Exertion Scale (PES) is the best way to monitor your intensity levels as you work through your cardio days. And looking down the road to Day 32, you'll see that the PES is a great way to switch up one cardio exercise for another. Also, if you're substituting a brisk swim for a session on the elliptical machine, or you want to go canoeing on a glorious afternoon rather than get on a rowing machine in a sunless gym, go for it—but make sure you're doing the right amount of work. The PES will help you do that.

The PES is a numbered system that describes the intensity of a workout on a scale of 1 to 10. Generally speaking, for most HITZ Resistance workouts, you want to be working at an intensity level somewhere between 5 and 8. HITZ Cardio is all about intervals (intense bursts followed by moderate levels of activity), so you will have to adjust the speeds accordingly and match them to the PES level you want to be at. That is, I'm not going to tell you how fast to go—I'm going to tell you how hard to work. As you get fitter, and things get easier, you just go faster in order to work harder.

So what does the scale look like?

Level 1. You're probably at Level 1 right now. If so, it's a PES level you're all too familiar with. Watching TV, playing video games, sitting on the back deck with a bag of snacks— that's the kind of exertion Level 1 demands of you.

Level 2. Now you're moving. You're comfortable and could maintain this pace all day long. Let's call it a stroll.

Level 3. You're still comfortable, but breathing a bit harder. Now it starts to feel like exercise.

Level 4. Okay, now you're beginning to sweat a little. But you feel good and can carry on a conversation effortlessly.

Level 5. You're just above comfortable. The sweat is really starting to come now, but you can still talk easily.

Level 6. You can still talk, but you're slightly breathless.

Level 7. You can still talk, but you don't really want to. You will likely be sweating like a pig.

Level 8. You can grunt (and make other strange sounds) in response to questions and can keep this pace only for a short time period. If you've ever seen my TV shows, you'll recognize Level 8—this is when recruits start swearing at me! This is the highest I want you going in your HITZ Cardio.

Level 9. You feel like you're probably going to die. Have you ever seen a competitive cross-country skier cross the finish line and collapse after wringing the very last bit of strength out of his or her exhausted body in the final sprint? Well, that's Level 9. Elite athletes push themselves to this level, but it's not a whole lot of fun.

Level 10. Forget about it. Level 10 is not an option, unless you're from another planet. We're not even going to talk about it. In fact, if you hit Level 9, gear down before you do your best impersonation of the aftermath at a beer-drinking, hot dog–eating contest. That's right—Level 9 almost always ends the same way: with your lunch on the floor.

◆ ◆ ◆

When you're going hard, think Level 7 or 8. When you're recovering after a burst of effort, or you're doing your active rest weekend workout, think Level 4 or 5. All this will be laid out carefully each day, so don't worry about memorizing PES levels right now. I just want to make clear that the real measurement here is what your body is capable of. We're going to push that every day, but we're not going to push too hard.

So please use caution when you're exercising. Listen to your body. If you feel light-headed or dizzy, your day is over. Find a wall and lean against it, head up and eyes open. If you're not about to keel over, you can always bring your heart rate down by working at a slower pace until you feel ready to continue. The thing is, you're not doing yourself any favors by going to Level 9 or by punishing yourself so cruelly that you make yourself miserable. This isn't *Rocky XXIII.*

And remember, whether you're out for a walk in the woods or pumping iron in the gym, you're supposed to be enjoying this. Pushing yourself feels good. Punishing yourself doesn't. You've got 31 days to do this (including today). No need to rush. The point is to get it right, and to be consistent.

THOUGHT FOR FOOD

The same thing goes for your nutrition. This is not a crash diet we're getting you on; it's just healthy eating. And that is crucial. In order to make it through the next 30 days, you will have to fuel your body effectively, so sticking to the meal plan is just as important as sticking to the fitness plan. So let's go over what's in store for you nutrition-wise.

You will be working hard, and burning a lot of calories, so we need to make sure that what you put into your mouth is going to keep you moving forward. That means no junk, I'm sorry to say. No sweets. Nothing refined. (Refining pretty much means that a factory somewhere has taken out much of the stuff in the food that slows down the digestion process, which means that the calories go straight to your bloodstream, leaving you hungry.) And, nothing that calls itself "enriched." Nothing needs to be enriched—either it's good food, or it isn't. Just stick to your daily plan. It works. Trust me.

◆◆◆

So much for what not to eat. What *will* we be eating? Your 10PS meal plan has been put together by Maria Thomas, who is a registered dietitian and owner of Urban Nutrition.

Maria is a colleague and friend; we shot the pilot to *The Last 10 Pounds Bootcamp* together. Every success story you've seen on TV was a direct result of my HITZ functional training system and Maria's meal plans. I like to call her the mastermind behind the scenes. Maria has put together an amazing 31-day plan for the 10PS that will make the difference between so-so results and a full shred—so stick to it!

◆◆◆

Take a look at your meals for the week (on page 35) and get to the grocery store. The foods are listed by food group. If you don't like the foods in your daily plan, you can exchange them for other foods using the chart. Two rules, though. First, make sure that you swap foods within same group. No swapping out your broccoli in order to get seconds of steak! Second, pay close attention to your portion sizes. If you want to change up chicken for turkey, for example, keep the portion size the same. I've given you some portion-size guidelines, but in general, a lunch-sized portion should be swapped for another lunch-sized portion; the same goes for breakfast, dinner and snacks. If you still feel lost, keep mixing up your menu simply by swapping one lunch for another, or one dinner for another.

TOMMY TIP

As a rule of thumb, try to make sure that you have a snack about an hour to an hour and a half before your workout. The closer you are to your workout, the less you should eat. Everyone is a little different, so you will have to experiment a little bit to find the optimal time for your pre-workout meal. By the way, protein shakes and high-fibre bars are not a good idea right before you start exercising, as they take longer to digest, and the last thing you want is for your stomach to be full of food while you're going hard. Keep it light in order to keep it "tight"!

Maria's menus add up to about 1,600–1,800 calories per day, which is typical for the average beginner exerciser looking to lose weight. If you're quite petite or a big guy, though, you'll need to tweak the menus based on your appetite. Be honest with yourself—if you're following the menus and feeling stuffed, you can remove the mid-morning snack and double your fruit intake at breakfast (you still need the fruit servings, so don't drop those!). If you're honestly feeling starved (and we're not talking starved for cookies here!), try doubling the size of one of your snacks, either the morning or the afternoon depending on when you're feeling hungriest. No one menu is suitable for every person, but the meals Maria has provided are a great place to start. Maria suggests that you listen to your own body, pay attention to your appetite, and use the menu as a guide—but be conscious of the fact that the first few days will involve a natural adjustment of your appetite. If you have food allergies or dietary restrictions, or if you are a vegan or a vegetarian, please make the necessary adjustments to your meal plan.

SUGGESTED PORTION SIZES

GRAINS	DAIRY and CALCIUM	EXTRAS	PROTEIN	FRUIT	VEGETABLES
1 package instant oatmeal (plain) or 1/2 cup raw	1 cup skim milk or soy milk	1 to 1-1/2 cups soup (look for one that has about 150 to 200 calories per serving)	1/4 cup nuts or seeds, like whole almonds, walnuts or sesame seeds	dried cranberries	spinach
1/3 cup All-Bran Buds with psyllium	1 Mini Babybel Light cheese			apples	mixed greens
1/2 cup Kashi GOLEAN™ cereal			1/3 cup hummus	mangoes	onions (red and white)
1 small whole-wheat fajita wrap	3/4 cup low-fat yogurt (preferably plain or vanilla)	1 tbsp. Miracle Whip Light dressing or light mayonnaise	8 to 10 prawns	strawberries	grape tomatoes
1/2 whole-wheat English muffin	1/4 cup low-fat (2%) cottage cheese	1 tsp. non-hydrogenated margarine	3 to 4 oz. lean meat, poultry or fresh fish	nectarines	red peppers
1 small whole-wheat roll		salsa	2 oz. canned fish	oranges	mushrooms
1 slice whole-grain bread (look for a brand that's high in both fibre and protein—at least 5 grams of each)	1 oz. part-skim mozzarella cheese	balsamic vinegar	1 to 2 eggs	grapes	cucumbers
1/2 cup brown rice		soy sauce	2 tbsp. natural peanut butter	grapefruit	baby carrots
3 RYVITA crackers (sesame rye)				bananas	garlic
1/2 cup whole-wheat spaghetti					broccoli
1 granola bar (the Kashi Seven Whole Grain and Almond bars are ideal, but look for a whole-grain bar with 5 grams each of fibre and protein)					
3 to 4 small potatoes (or 1/2 cup equivalence)					
1/2 cup yams					

Now, the last thing we want you to do is stress about what you eat. The 10PS is about lifestyle change, and peering through a magnifying glass at nutritional tables and boxes of food is no lifestyle I'd want.

I'm sure you feel the same way. Eating should be the most natural thing in the world. You want to be healthy? Eat healthy food. It should be as simple as that.

The trouble is, there is just so much garbage out there—and confusing garbage, too. It's not just the stuff that's downright bad, though there is plenty of that, like certain milk-shakes that contain more than 2,000 calories and 68 grams of saturated fat—the equiva-lent of nearly six dozen strips of bacon. But there is lots of food out there that claims to be healthy yet just isn't. And nothing is healthy if you eat too much of it. Stuffing your face with "healthy" snack foods when you're not really hungry is no way to eat. The same goes for so-called low-calorie snacks. I don't care that there are only 100 calories in that cookie if you don't need those calories, especially if you eat five cookies.

So, while I don't want to turn you into an obsessive calorie-counter, I figured I'd at least give you a few tips to make sense of the nutritional data that looks so much like the small print on your credit card statements.

Have a look at this example of a nutri-tional information box. A simple scan of the ingredients could tell you whether or not you should be consuming the food in question— if only you knew how to interpret the thing.

SERVING SIZE

All the nutrition information is based on whatever serving size is stipulated, whether

Nutrition Facts	
Serving Size 1 cup (228g)	
Servings Per Container 2	
Amount Per Serving	**% Daily Value**
Calories 250	
Fat 12 g	18%
Saturated Fat 3 g	15%
Trans Fat 3 g	
Cholesterol 30 mg	10%
Sodium 660 mg	20%
Total Carbohydrate 660 mg	10%
Dietary Fiber 0 g	0%
Sugars 5 g	
Protein 5 g	
Vitamin A	4%
Vitamin C	2%
Calcium	20%
Iron	2%

or not that is how much you actually eat. If you eat twice the stated serving size, you will need to multiply all the calories, fat, protein and so on by two. Some foods packaged to appear as a single serving may actually contain two or three. Tricky, no? A granola bar, for example, may weigh 200 grams, even though a "serving" is listed as 100 grams on the box. In other words, there are twice as many servings as there are granola bars. Watch out!

CALORIES

Note the number of calories the food contains. Remember that if you are trying to lose one pound per week, you need to have a deficit of 3,500 calories for the week. That doesn't mean you're going to be counting those mysterious calories (don't worry—that's already been done), but it does mean you're going to have to take in fewer than you used to. Have a look at the example. One "serving" contains 250 calories, and one package is actually two servings, so eating that mysterious food will set you back 500 calories. That's 500 more to burn, or 500 fewer to eat at another time. So ask yourself: Is it really worth it?

FATS

The first number you see indicates the total amount of fat (in grams); indented under that, you will see a breakdown by type of fat. Try to choose foods with less than 2 grams of saturated fat per serving. Avoid products that contain trans fats. This example contains three times as much as you want—six times if you consider that you're likely to eat two "servings."

DIETARY FIBRE

This is something you'll want to pay attention to when you're investigating a grain product like pasta, rice, bread, crackers or something along those lines. Look for foods that are high in dietary fibre—that contain at least 3 grams per serving. This example contains zero. Not a good sign.

SODIUM

Try to keep your daily sodium intake under 2,300 milligrams (about 1 teaspoon of salt) per day. Foods that contain less than 140 milligrams of sodium are considered low-sodium foods. So the example, which weighs in at 660 (or 1,320 if you eat both "servings"), is not exactly low-sodium.

PERCENT DAILY VALUES

The Percent Daily Values (% DV) are another confusing part of the food labels. These are the recommendations for nutrients based on a 2,000-calorie diet. If your calorie budget is 1,500 or 2,500 calories per day, these percentages will not apply to you.

◆ ◆ ◆

Yawn.

Are you still with me? I know it's a little dry—maybe more than a little. But don't worry, there won't be a test on nutritional charts. We're going to keep it simple, and the 10PS plan is going to lay out exactly what's on the menu, so don't stress. My point was just that it's not what's on the front of the box that tells you what you're eating—it's what's on the side. But if you're buying natural foods and fresh produce and controlling your portions, you won't have to puzzle over those charts at all.

YOUR FIRST WORKOUT

The next step for us is to get you ready for action.

You're about to get smaller. That means that this is the last moment of the time "before" you got fit. So if there is going to be a set of before and after measurements, now is the time to get out your tape and a pen to write down the numbers you're going to be seeing for the last time.

First, record the following measurements:

Chest/Bust. Stretch the tape around your back and your nipples.	88 cm 90
Waist. Use your belly button as the centre point. Ladies, do not measure the smallest part of your "waist." That may work for clothes, but not for the 10PS.	79 cm 77
Hips. Measure around the widest part of your hips.	92 cm 89
Weight. Now, finally, step on the scale your with your shoes off.	125

The numbers don't lie. But that's going to work in your favour in just a few weeks, when you pull out the same tape and step onto the same scale. Next time you do this, 14 days from now, the news is going to be good and you're going to be feeling amazing. If you're a daily scale watcher, you will drive yourself (and your family) crazy, so don't do it! Your overall weight changes from day to day with water retention, and I don't want you getting thrown off course by minor fluctuations. Wait until Day 15 for your next weigh-in, and then Day 31 for your final weigh-in. Just stick to the plan and remember your long-term goal. If you do this, I promise you that on Day 31 you will be healthier and feel better then you have in a very long time, and you will look fantastic!

Now grab a friend, partner or relative and get them to take a picture—unless you're a "solo shot" expert. Save it to your computer, but don't agonize about what it may look like. In fact, don't even look at it until Day 32!

In the meantime, it's time to punch in your time card . . . we've got a lot of work to do.

As you begin the 10PS, you will see two different workout levels. Level 1 is for beginners and Level 2 is for intermediate exercisers. How do you know which one is right for you? Well, let me show you, because right about now it's time to start the first day of your 31-day success plan . . .

Pull out your stopwatch. We're going to time your first workout to see what kind of shape you're in.

I've got seven exercises on deck for you, and this test isn't finished until all the repetitions of all seven of them have been completed. The goal is to finish as quickly as you can, using proper form and remaining under control. Take a moment to read through the entire plan, then set up your seven stations before you start your warmup so that you're ready to go.

A warmup is essential, and as such it's something you will do every day throughout the 10PS. Do not train without warming up—you may get done a little more quickly, but it will only be a matter of time before you hurt yourself by exercising cold.

We are going to start with a 10-minute warmup, using the cardio equipment of your choice (including the sidewalk or running path right outside your door). Just go at a nice comfortable pace.

Once you are finished, we will move on to the following three dynamic stretches. We're going to be doing a lot of these, so I'll say a few words about them now.

Dynamic stretching is just a kind of stretch you do with movement, rather than sitting still. You're getting your muscles moving, pushing them to the limits of their ranges without pushing past them. Stretching this way before exercising increases blood and oxygen flow and gets muscles ready for physical exertion and athletic performance. Coaches, trainers and athletes are using dynamic stretching more and more to improve performance and reduce the risk of injury. It's your turn.

Got it? Now stretch.

DYNAMIC QUAD STRETCHES

1. Stand tall (shoulders back), with your feet shoulder width apart. Lift your left foot behind you and grab your ankle (or foot) with your left hand.

2. Gently push your left hip forward, while keeping a straight line with your body and maintaining your balance on your right heel. Hold for 3 seconds, then release your left ankle.

Repeat this sequence with your right leg. Perform 5 repetitions on each leg.

DYNAMIC CHEST AND BICEP STRETCHES

1. Stand tall (shoulders back), with your feet shoulder width apart. Slowly move your arms out to the sides, slightly behind you, with your thumbs up (just like The Fonz).

2. As your arms go back, rotate your thumbs down and back until they are pointing to the wall behind you. Pause, then return to the starting position. You should feel this one in your chest and biceps.

Perform 10 repetitions.

DYNAMIC SUMO SQUATS

1. Stand tall (shoulders back), with your feet close together. Take a large lateral step to the right and drop into a deep squat (think of a sumo wrestler). Pause, then return to the starting standing position.

2. Now take a large lateral step to the left and drop into a deep squat. Pause, then return to the starting position.

Perform 5 repetitions on each side.

Now you are really ready for some action. Are your seven stations all set up? Have you checked out the exercises to make sure you're not wasting time figuring out what to do?

Good. Then you're about to go as fast as you can, under control. Remember to use proper form. If anything hurts, stop!

Ready.

Get Set.

GO!

HITZ FITNESS TEST	REPS	MEN'S EQUIPMENT	WOMEN'S EQUIPMENT
Skipping (Double Jump Rotations)	30		
Prisoner Squats	30		
Ab Crunches with Dumbbells	30	10 lbs.	5 lbs.
Walking Lunges	30 Steps		
Resistance Band Lat Pull-Downs	30	Strong	Medium
Dumbbell Plié Squats	30	40 lbs.	20 lbs.
Bench Push-Ups	30		

SKIPPING

Ever wonder how boxers get so ridiculously fit? Well, skipping is a big part of it. By the end of the 10PS you, too, will be able to go the distance. But today, it's just 30 rope revolutions, jumping with both feet.

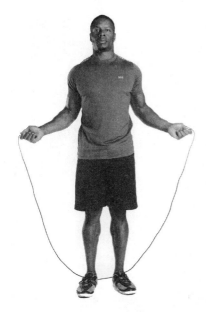

1. Place your skipping rope on the ground and stand in the middle of it. Grab the handles, which should reach about 6 inches below your collarbone when you pull the handles straight up.

2. Start to rotate the rope. The rotation should come from your wrists. To increase the speed of the rotations, increase the tightness of the circles that your wrists are making.

Skip 30 revolutions.

PRISONER SQUATS

The prisoner squat requires you to engage your entire body. It forces you to keep your head up, your shoulder blades back and your core engaged.

1. Stand tall, with your feet slightly wider than shoulder width. Place your hands on your ears and pull your elbows back. Engage your core and pull your shoulder blades together.

2. Bend at your knees and hips, then push your hips backward as if trying to sit on a chair that's behind you. Drop until your knees are at 90 degrees, while keeping your back straight and your weight on your heels.

3. Now return to your upright standing position.

That's 1—now you just have 29 more.

TOMMY TIP

Do not let your lower back become rounded. As you return from your squat position, remember to initiate the push through your heels. This squat is a great tool and just the tip of the iceberg of what I've got in store for you.

AB CRUNCHES WITH DUMBBELLS

This one will test your core.

1. Start by lying down on your back, with your legs out in front of you, knees bent and feet shoulder width apart. Hold a 5- or 10-pound DB slightly above your belly button, while your palms cup each end of the dumbbell.

2. Curl your shoulder blades while pressing the DB with arms extended straight up toward the ceiling.

3. Pause, then return to the starting position (DB above your belly button).

Repeat 30 times.

TOMMY TIP

Make sure that you look straight up and do not tuck in your chin. Keep your heels on the ground. If the weight begins to feel too heavy, just put it on the side and continue with the ab crunches for the remaining time.

WALKING LUNGES

Don't sacrifice form for speed!

1. Stand with your feet shoulder width apart. Raise your left leg and right arm, keeping your abs tight.

2. Take a large lunge step forward with your left leg, while at the same time bending both knees so that your left thigh is parallel to the ground and your right knee is pointing down toward the ground. Keep 70% of your weight on your left (front foot) heel, and stay balanced with 30% of your weight on the front of your right foot.

3. "Step" forward, repeating the same sequence with your right leg.

Keep on walking for 30 steps total (15 steps with each leg).

TOMMY TIP

Contract your glutes (butt) and engage your core throughout the movement. Your spine should always be in a neutral (straight) position. Avoid pushing your body forward as you descend.

RESISTANCE BAND LAT PULL-DOWNS

Focus on your lat muscles (the "wings" of your upper back) to feel the burn. Keep your back flat and your core engaged.

1. Attach your resistance band to an elevated bar or other solid structure and hold on to the handles with a wide overhand (thumbs-down) grip. Drop into a squat position—you should be leaning forward at a 45-degree angle.

2. Using your lats as the primary mover, shrug down and then pull your elbows down toward your hips.

3. Pause, then fully extend your arms.

Repeat this action 30 times.

TOMMY TIP

Use a slow, steady speed and feel the burn. Keep your weight on your heels and *do not* round your back. If you don't have a resistance band, you can use a cable machine.

DUMBBELL PLIÉ SQUATS

Yes, more legs, this time with a dumbbell (DB) in your hand.

1. Stand tall, with your feet wider than shoulder width and your toes turned out. Engage your core and pull your shoulder blades together. Cup your hands and hold a 20-pound DB between your legs.

2. Begin the movement by bending at your knees and hips, then push your hips backward as if trying to sit in a deep imaginary basket behind you.

3. Bend your knees to 90 degrees, while keeping your back straight and your weight on your heels. Pause for 1 second, then return to your upright, standing position.

Repeat 30 times.

TOMMY TIP

Do not let your back become rounded. Think of literally sitting on a pole (ouch—yeah, I know). As you return from your squat position, remember to initiate the push through your heels.

BENCH PUSH-UPS

Last exercise of the fitness test.

1. Place your hands on a bench or step, shoulder width apart, and step your feet back so that you are in an upright plank position.

2. Lower yourself into a push-up position, bending your arms and keeping your elbows as close to your sides as possible.

3. Engage your core, maintain a flat back (neutral spine) and push your body up until both arms are extended.

After 30 repetitions you're done!

TOMMY TIP

Your back should never sag throughout the movement. Keep your head neutral (so that your neck is flat) and focus on lowering your chest to the bench, not your chin. If you cannot complete a push-up from your feet, try it from your knees, or stand up and use a wall.

Woo-hoo, you're finished!

What was your time? _____

Write it down and remember it, because you will be doing the same test on Day 31! In the meantime, let's put those numbers into action.

If your fitness test time was over five minutes, you are a beginner. Don't worry—it's only temporary. And if Level 1 starts to seem too easy, guess what: you get to jump to Level 2.

If your time was under five minutes, you are an intermediate exerciser. Good for you, but this means I'll be pushing you even harder!

Congratulations! You are now one day closer to *shredding* away your last 10 pounds. Take some time right now to perform the following four static stretches (these are more like reach-and-hold positions) to set you up nicely for HITZ Resistance #1 tomorrow.

HIP STRETCHES

1. Lie down and cross your left foot over your right knee.

2. Clasp your hands behind your right knee. Gently pull your right leg toward you, keeping your back straight.

Hold the stretch for 30 seconds.
Repeat with the left leg.

HAMSTRING STRETCHES

1. Lie down on your back, with a slight bend in both legs.

2. Lift your right leg straight up and grab it behind your calf. If you are flexible enough, grab your ankle (or even your toe). Gently pull your right leg toward you, keeping your back straight.

Hold the stretch for 30 seconds. Repeat with the left leg.

QUADRICEPS/HIP FLEXOR STRETCHES

1. Starting in a standing position, take a big step forward with your left leg, then place your right knee on the ground.

2. Maintaining this posture, shift the entire body slightly forward from the hip. You should feel this stretch down the front of your quad and hip flexor. Exhale and hold the stretch. Don't arch your back.

Hold for 30 seconds, then gently release and switch legs.

SPINAL TWISTS

1. Lie on the floor, with your arms extending outward in a T position. Put your right foot on your left knee.

2. Using your left hand, gently pull your right knee toward the floor, twisting your spine and keeping your left arm straight out, hips and shoulders on the floor. Hold for 30 seconds.

Repeat, using the right hand and left knee.

That's it. You should be cooled down, clear-headed and ready for the real action on Day 2. Great job today. Now go and get some rest. Tomorrow is a new day, and we are gonna hit the streets running!

Your meal plan also starts tomorrow: Organize things ahead of time so that you are not scrambling to fit in your meals. Each week, I'll give you an overview of your meal plan that you can use as a guide to help you shop and prepare for the days to come. But don't think this is a free-for-all buffet! I'll give you specific quantities and instructions at the end of each day. What are you waiting for? Get shopping!

MEAL PLAN #1

DAY 2	DAY 3	DAY 4	DAY 5	DAY 6	DAY 7	DAY 8
Breakfast	**Breakfast**	**Breakfast**	**Breakfast**	**Breakfast**	**Breakfast**	**Breakfast**
Toast with almond butter, orange and a glass of milk	Oatmeal, cottage cheese, strawberries and a glass of milk	Scrambled eggs with mozzarella, English muffin, apple and a glass of milk	Low-fat yogurt with granola, All-Bran cereal, mango and a glass of milk	Toast with natural peanut butter, banana and a glass of milk	Mushroom and red pepper omelette with toast, watermelon and a glass of milk	Oatmeal with slivered almonds and dried cranberries and a glass of milk
Snack	**Snack**	**Snack**	**Snack**	**Snack**	**Snack**	**Snack**
Strawberries and yogurt	Grapes and walnut halves	Banana and yogurt	Apple or mango with cottage cheese	Orange and cottage cheese	Plum or orange and yogurt	Watermelon and cottage cheese
Lunch	**Lunch**	**Lunch**	**Lunch**	**Lunch**	**Lunch**	**Lunch**
Butternut squash soup with tuna on crackers and baby carrots	Chicken pita	Butternut squash soup with tuna on crackers and baby carrots	Leftover turkey pasta	Chicken-salsa wrap	Leftover beef and broccoli spaghettini	Grilled cheese sandwich with baby carrots
Snack	**Snack**	**Snack**	**Snack**	**Snack**	**Snack**	**Snack**
Granola bar and almonds	Yogurt with granola	Hummus with grape tomatoes and red pepper	Granola bar and walnut halves	Yogurt with granola	Granola bar and almonds	Hummus with rye crackers
Dinner	**Dinner**	**Dinner**	**Dinner**	**Dinner**	**Dinner**	**Dinner**
Curry chicken breast with sweet potato and asparagus	Honey-lemon salmon with brown rice and salad	Turkey pasta	Chicken quesadilla with mixed-green salad	Beef and broccoli spaghettini	Turkey breast with potatoes and spinach salad	Chicken teriyaki stir-fry with brown rice

DAY 2
HITZ Resistance #1

TOMMY RULE #2: PROPER FORM IS THE RULE, NOT THE EXCEPTION. SQUEEZING OUT ANOTHER REP OR TWO WITHOUT PROPER FORM WILL LIKELY END UP IN INJURY, SO PLAY SAFE AND TRAIN SMART!

Remember the first day of school? You used to show up in your new clothes, meet the teacher, find out what you were going to be learning about—maybe check out the hotties and figure out who's who in class. You didn't do much the first day of school, did you? The second day was when the work started. So forget about the hotties for now, and let's get to work.

Just two more things before we start. I'll be reminding you of the first one throughout the month, but I'm going to mention it now so that you can start off on the right foot: Whatever effort you put in each day will be rewarded accordingly. If you take a half-assed approach to the 10PS, guess what your results are going to look like. We never settle for average, so let's really go after it and start this off with a bang.

The second thing is just a good habit—we're going to be mixing the exercises up from day to day. So you should familiarize yourself with the exercises before you begin each workout in order to keep a constant flow. You'll have them pretty much memorized before long, but, at least at the beginning, make sure you know what each movement is so that you can keep up the pace and the rhythm. Just walk through each one a couple of times so you're not puzzling over things in the middle of your workout and so that you can be sure you have the right equipment at hand.

If you plan things right, you should be completely hydrated and fuelled before your workout! And this is the last time I'm going to ask: Have you got your goals written down? This is your last chance.

Now, let the shredding begin.

TODAY'S WORKOUT

FOCUS	EQUIPMENT	REPETITIONS	SETS
Core and upper body.	Two dumbbells (DBs)—5 to 10 pounds for beginners, 12 to 20 pounds for intermediates—and a resistance band (RB).	For beginners, your reps will be 20 seconds long; for intermediates, 40 seconds.	Three—that means you're doing all eight exercises three times.

HERE'S WHAT I'VE GOT FOR YOU TODAY:
Warmup
Dynamic Stretches
HITZ Resistance #1

• **BURPEES** • **DUMBBELL ROWING**
Take a 45-second rest. Your juices should be flowing now. Very nice start, but keep up the pace!

• **CORE HEEL SCRAPERS** • **DUMBBELL LUNGE CURLS**
Another 45-second rest. You are halfway through the circuit! Stay the course—you can do this. Grab some water.

• **DUMBBELL PUSH-UPS** • **HIGH-KNEE RUNNING**
One more 45-second rest. You're three-quarters of the way through this set.

• **RESISTANCE BAND GLUTE EXTENSIONS** • **CORE SLIDERS**
That's it for the set. Grab some water and take a minute to catch your breath.

Cool-Down
Static Stretches

TOMMY TIP

This is an important one, and I'm going to keep coming back to it. Again and again over the course of the 10PS, I'm going to tell you to keep a "neutral spine." This is the proper alignment of the body between postural extremes. It means that your shoulders are back and your core is engaged. What this means for you is that you have far less chance of being injured, your body will be in the strongest position and the overall stress on your muscles, joints and vertebrae will be minimized. Don't worry, now; I'm not going to let you forget. But keep this in mind!

WARMUP

Keep your water and towel close by, because here we go.

Training indoors today? Then jump on a bike or treadmill for your 10-minute warmup. If you are training outdoors, you should be jogging or riding a bike.

For the first five minutes, work at an intensity of Level 4 on the Perceived Exertion Scale (PES). You should be sweating a little, but feeling good and still able to carry on a conversation effortlessly.

For the last five minutes, work at an intensity of Level 5. You should be just above comfortable, sweating more and still able to talk easily.

DYNAMIC STRETCHES

After your 10-minute warmup, perform the following three dynamic stretches:

DYNAMIC GLUTE AND HAMSTRING STRETCHES

1. Stand tall (shoulders back), with your feet shoulder width apart. Lift your left foot and grab just below your left knee with both hands.

2. With both hands, gently pull your left knee up, while maintaining your balance on your right heel. This will activate your butt and the backs of your legs. Hold for three seconds, then release your left leg.

Repeat this sequence with your right leg. Perform 5 repetitions with each leg.

DYNAMIC CHEST AND BICEP STRETCHES

1. Stand tall (shoulders back), with your feet shoulder width apart. Slowly move your arms out to the sides, slightly behind you, with your thumbs up (just like The Fonz).

2. As your arms go back, rotate your thumbs down and back until they are pointing to the wall behind you. Pause, then return to the starting position. You should feel this one in your chest and biceps.

Perform 10 repetitions.

DYNAMIC BACK SWINGS

1. Stand tall (shoulders back), with your feet shoulder width apart. Lift and hold both arms up to the side at shoulder height. Twist as far as you can to the right, so that you can feel a good stretch in your mid- to lower back.

2. Pause, then twist to the left (you should resemble a propeller as you twist).

Repeat for 10 revolutions.

HOW ARE YOU MAKING OUT? YOUR FIRST WARMUP, INCLUDING YOUR DYNAMIC STRETCHES, MAY SEEM LIKE A WORKOUT ON ITS OWN, BUT NOW IT'S TIME TO HAVE SOME FUN. GO GET SOME WATER AND GET READY TO TACKLE HITZ RESISTANCE #1. REMEMBER TO READ THROUGH ALL THE DESCRIPTIONS OF THE EXERCISES FIRST, SO THAT YOU CAN MOVE SMOOTHLY AND QUICKLY FROM ONE TO ANOTHER, KEEPING THE PACE THE WORKOUT CALLS FOR.

BURPEES

The burpee is a fitness dinosaur, but its benefits far outweigh its age. It's a full-body exercise that's perfect for all fitness levels.

1. Stand tall with your feet shoulder width apart.

2. Bend at your knees and hips while placing both hands on the floor.

3. Step (beginner) or thrust (intermediate) both feet back so you are in a push-up position. Then reverse what you just did, kicking both feet back in, tucking your knees and standing up (beginner) or jumping (intermediate).

Repeat for your allotted time: beginners, 20 seconds; intermediates, 40 seconds.

TOMMY TIP

When you kick your feet back, do not let your back sag! Breathing is an essential part of this exercise, so don't forget to breathe throughout the movement! Beginners should shoot for 10 or more burpees in 20 seconds: intermediate exercisers should shoot for 15 to 25 burpees in 40 seconds.

DUMBBELL ROWING

Dumbbell rowing is a great upper-back exercise that really targets the "lats," also known as the infamous "back ass" (that soft, fleshy part of your back that looks like cleavage when you're wearing something tight). Your DBs should be heavy enough that as a beginner you cannot complete more than 16 repetitions in 20 seconds, or if you're an intermediate you can't do more than 30 in 40 seconds.

1. Stand up straight, holding a pair of 10- to 20-pound dumbbells in your hands. Brace your abdominals and slightly bend your knees (20 degrees). In your half-squat position, bend at the waist to a 45-degree angle. Now you're leaning forward, with your legs slightly bent.

2. Keep your elbows tight to your body and, with a rowing motion, lift both DBs up to your hips. As you pull, think of pulling with your back (lats) instead of your biceps. Always keep your back flat. You will have the urge to round it as you fatigue, but be strong and stay strong!

3. As the DBs reach slightly above your hips (your elbows should be at a 90-degree angle), pause for 1 second, then return to the starting position. Maintain a constant speed (2 seconds pulling the weight up, pause, 2 seconds bringing the weight down) thoughout your repetition time. No jerking or heaving.

 45-SECOND REST

TOMMY TIP

If it seems too easy, it probably is. You're here to challenge yourself, so grab something heavier. You don't need to go to complete failure, but make sure that you push yourself.

CORE HEEL SCRAPERS

It's time to target your lower abdominals (also commonly known as the beer belly or pouch).
The slower you perform this exercise, the harder you will force your abdominals to work.

1. Lie flat on your back (use your mat if you have one). Without tucking your chin, raise your head off the ground and look up at the ceiling. Then lift your heels off the ground while bending your knees, so that your thighs are at a 90-degree angle to the mat.

2. Lower both legs from the hip until your heels graze the ground.

3. Now push your heels out until both legs are straight. As you extend your legs, push your lower back into the ground for support. Beginners, you can have a slight bend in the knees—for now. Pause, then return your legs to the starting position.

Beginners, keep going for 20 seconds; intermediates, 40 seconds.

TOMMY TIP

Once you start, your legs should never touch the ground. The most important (and hardest) part is bringing your legs back to the starting position. The slower you go, the more your lower abdominals are engaged. So slow down!

DUMBBELL LUNGE CURLS

This is a compound exercise (that means it uses multiple muscle groups). It targets your legs (quads and hamstrings), butt and biceps. Contract your glutes (butt) and engage your core throughout the movement.

1. Stand with your feet shoulder width apart, while you hold a pair of 5- to 20-pound DBs.

2. Take a large lunge step forward with your right leg, while bending both knees until your right thigh is parallel to the ground and your left knee is pointing down. At the same time, curl both DBs up and ensure that your weight is supported on the heel of the right (front) foot while balancing on the left (rear) toe.

3. Push off your right heel to return to standing starting position. As you stand up, slowly lower both DBs down to your side.

Repeat the sequence, stepping with your left leg. Alternate lunge steps for 20 seconds if you're a beginner, 40 seconds if you're an intermediate.

 **45-SECOND REST**

TOMMY TIP

Use a dumbbell weight that you can actually curl at least 15 times in your allotted time—probably 5 to 20 pounds.

DUMBBELL PUSH-UPS

Push-ups are one of the most popular exercises around because they force you to move your own body weight—which means they work well because big people get a heavy weight and small people get a lighter one. They are a great way to gauge your overall strength. These in particular will target your triceps, chest, forearms and core.

1. Start in a plank position, with each hand on a DB under each shoulder. I'm demonstrating from my knees here, but if you're an intermediate, you should be up on your toes.

2. Engage your core, maintain a flat back (neutral spine), bend your elbows and drop your chest to about 2 inches above the DB. Keep your elbows as close to your sides as possible.

3. Pause, then push your body up until both arms are extended.

Repeat this sequence for your allotted time: 20 seconds if you're a beginner, 40 seconds if you're an intermediate.

TOMMY TIP

Never let your back sag. The closer your elbows are to your sides, the more you will work your triceps muscles; the wider you have them, the more you will work your chest. If you cannot do a push-up from your knees, then stand up and use a wall.

HIGH-KNEE RUNNING

This little bit of HITZ Cardio will push your endurance while targeting your core in the fat-burning process. The higher you lift your knees, the more effective the exercise.

1. Stand tall, with your feet shoulder width apart. Run on the spot, lifting your knees as high as possible and pumping your arms vigorously. Ideally, your knees will be coming up to waist height.

2. You must remain tall at all times. Do not slump.

Keep going for 20 seconds if you're a beginner, 40 seconds if you're an intermediate.

 **45-SECOND REST**

RESISTANCE BAND GLUTE EXTENSIONS

This is a great exercise that will target your glutes (butt), hamstrings and lower back. Use a medium-tension resistance band for this exercise. It's also your first step toward building a nice, toned booty.

1. Begin on all fours (hands and knees). Place a resistance band around the middle of your right foot and hold on to the handles. Keep your right toe pointed down. The further forward you place your hands, the more resistance there will be on your right leg.

2. With a smooth, steady and slow movement, extend, push, then lift your right leg straight back.

3. Pause, then return to the starting position.

Repeat with your right leg for your allotted time (beginners, 20 seconds: intermediates, 40 seconds), then switch to your left leg.

TOMMY TIP

For safety's sake, do not look down and back (make sure the band is in the middle of your foot—trust me, it doesn't feel good to be on the receiving end of that slingshot). As always, engage your core and do not let your back sag.

CORE SLIDERS

This is a great exercise to really attack those "love handles" and overall core.

It's a simple exercise that yields fantastic results.

1. Lie on your back, with your feet on the ground and your knees bent. Put your hands flat by your sides and raise your head 3 inches or so off the ground, while looking up toward the ceiling.

2. Keep both hands in contact with the mat at all times, and reach and slide your left hand forward toward a spot between your feet. Make sure you slide far enough to challenge yourself.

3. Pause and repeat the same slide with your right hand.

Follow the same action for your allotted time: 20 seconds for beginners, 40 seconds for intermediates.

THAT'S IT FOR THE SET. TAKE A 1-MINUTE BREAK, GRAB SOME WATER, CATCH YOUR BREATH, THEN START THE NEXT SET.

TOMMY TIP

Do not tuck your chin to your chest; look straight up to the sky. And no breaks between sides—once you've started, keep your head lifted for the full time period. If your neck gets too sore (and it will), you can rest it on the mat.

COOL-DOWN

Great job. You made it!

Ready to flop onto the couch without taking the time for a cool-down? Better think again, because this is one of the most important and most overlooked facets of training. Let's have a look at the benefits of a proper cool-down.

- It helps your heart rate and respiration gradually slow down.
- It helps you avoid dizziness or fainting. Don't laugh; that happens a lot, especially when you stop exercising suddenly. You don't want your heart racing when you're sitting still.
- It makes the recovery and repair transition easier between workouts.
- It helps your muscles remove lactic acid. In other words, a good cool-down will mean you're less sore tomorrow. That should be reason enough right there.

Now, *those* are some benefits that will definitely pay dividends in the long run. Finish off Day 2 with a bang. Get on a bike or treadmill and ride or walk for 10 minutes at an intensity of Level 3 on the PES. You should be relatively comfortable. This exercise is designed to slowly bring your heart rate down, so go easy with it.

STATIC STRETCHES

Once you have finished your 10-minute cool-down, it's time for you to stretch. Perform the following four static stretches and hold each one for 30 seconds per side:

CHEST COMPLEX TRIPLE STRETCHES

The chest complex involves several stretches. They should just be gentle stretches—I don't want any pain.

1. For the first stretch, stand next to a wall or door frame. Extend one arm and bend at the elbow, so that your arm forms a right angle, with your upper arm parallel to the ground and your forearm sticking straight up. Place your forearm against the wall or door frame. Now, twist your whole body away from the wall, with a special emphasis on pushing your chest through the turn. Hold this for 10 seconds.

2. For the next stretch, step away from the wall so that, instead of your forearm, only your hand is on the wall. The arm still forms a right angle from your body, but this time your hand and shoulder are at the same level. Make the same twist, pushing your chest into the turn, to stretch the chest in the new position. Hold this for 10 seconds.

3. For the third and final variation, step further from the wall and extending your arm straight, so that the entire arm is parallel to the ground. Place your hand on the wall, then twist again into the stretch. You should feel the tension on your chest. Hold this for 10 seconds.

Switch arms and repeat this same sequence.

SPINAL TWISTS

1. Lie on the floor, with your arms extending outward in a T position. Put your right foot on your left knee.

2. Using your left hand, gently pull your right knee toward the floor, twisting your spine and keeping your left arm straight out, hips and shoulders on the floor. Hold for 30 seconds.

Repeat, using the right hand and left knee.

QUADRICEPS/HIP FLEXOR STRETCHES

1. Starting in a standing position, take a big step forward with your left leg, then place your right knee on the ground.

2. Maintaining this posture, shift the entire body slightly forward from the hip. You should feel this stretch down the front of your quad and hip flexor. Exhale and hold the stretch. Don't arch your back.

Hold for 30 seconds, then gently release and switch legs.

HAMSTRING STRETCHES

1. Lie down on your back, with a slight bend in both legs.

2. Lift your right leg straight up and grab it behind your calf. If you are flexible enough, grab your ankle (or even your toe). Gently pull your right leg toward you, keeping your back straight.

Hold the stretch for 30 seconds. Repeat with the left leg.

AND THAT'S IT—YOU'RE DONE! GREAT WORK ON YOUR FIRST TRAINING DAY. CAN'T WAIT FOR TOMORROW! ONE THING, THOUGH: YOU'VE GOT TO BE FUELLED PROPERLY. THAT DOESN'T JUST MEAN YOU NEED *ENOUGH* FOOD. IT MEANS YOU NEED THE *RIGHT* FOOD.

DAY 2 MEAL PLAN

If you want to maximize your weight-loss results and make your new body permanent, nutrition will be a major factor. So be diligent in following both the fitness plan and the meal plan. If you do, prepare to be surprised by the results.

BREAKFAST 2 slices whole-grain toast with 2 tbsp. natural almond butter; 1 orange; 1-1/2 cups skim or soy milk.

SNACK 1 cup strawberries; 3/4 cup low-fat yogurt.

LUNCH 1 cup butternut squash soup (choose one that's stock-based, not cream-based); 2 oz. canned light tuna mixed with 1 tbsp. light mayonnaise, onion and celery, spread on 3 light rye crackers; 1/2 cup baby carrots. **Cook-ahead option:** Mix up an extra portion of both the soup and the tuna and pop them into the fridge for Day 4's lunch.

SNACK Granola bar; 10 almonds.

DINNER **Curry chicken breast:** pan-fry 4 oz. of chicken with 1 tsp. curry paste, spices; 1/2 cup baked sweet potato; 1 cup grilled asparagus. Use up to 1 tsp. (combined) of olive oil for cooking. **Cook-ahead option:** Cook an additional 2 oz. of chicken breast and set aside for tomorrow's lunch.

DAY 3
HITZ Cardio #1

TOMMY RULE #3: HARD WORK IS THE ONLY WAY TO SUCCESSFULLY REACH YOUR GOAL. NOBODY ELSE CAN DO IT BUT YOU. BUT IN RETURN, YOU GET THE SATISFACTION OF ACCOMPLISHMENT.

All right, here we go with your first session of High-Intensity Training Zone (HITZ) Cardio. Let's just say that this is probably not going to provide you with your fondest memory of the 10PS. If you are a beginner, extremely out of shape or obese, this is where the "no pain, no gain" philosophy is really going to start to make sense to you. Whether you're on a treadmill or elliptical machine in the gym, don't worry too much about speed or incline—I want you focused on the Perceived Exertion Scale (PES), instead. (And if you cannot run or you have any health conditions, talk to your doctor first and then use the PES as your guide. I didn't say do *nothing*, though. I just said stay within your limits.)

This initial workout will take you less than 30 minutes to complete, so *don't* pace yourself. Just get after it. Working at high intensity is going to require your full attention, so listen to your body. If you get light-headed or dizzy, stop what you are doing immediately. Find a wall and take a break. Keep your head up and your eyes open. Nobody needs to be a hero.

TODAY'S WORKOUT

FOCUS	EQUIPMENT	TOTAL TIME
Fat-burning intensity.	Treadmill, bike or just your running shoes and a good route.	Just over 40 minutes.

HERE'S HOW IT'S GOING TO PLAY OUT:
Warmup
Dynamic Stretches
HITZ Cardio #1
Cool-Down
Static Stretches

All right, then, time for your warmup.

WARMUP

For five minutes, work at an intensity of Level 4 on the Perceived Exertion Scale (PES). You should be sweating a little but feeling good, and you should be able to carry on a conversation effortlessly. Remember that this can be any type of activity you like—it's the level of exertion that matters.

DYNAMIC STRETCHES

After your warmup, perform the following three dynamic stretches:

DYNAMIC GLUTE AND HAMSTRING STRETCHES

1. Stand tall (shoulders back), with your feet shoulder width apart. Lift your left foot and grab just below your left knee with both hands.

2. With both hands, gently pull your left knee up, while maintaining your balance on your right heel. This will activate your butt and the backs of your legs. Hold for 3 seconds, then release your left leg.

Repeat this sequence with your right leg. Perform 5 repetitions with each leg.

DYNAMIC QUAD STRETCHES

1. Stand tall (shoulders back), with your feet shoulder width apart. Lift your left foot behind you and grab your ankle (or foot) with your left hand.

2. Gently push your left hip forward, while keeping a straight line with your body and maintaining your balance on your right heel. Hold for 3 seconds, then release your left ankle.

Repeat the same sequence with your right leg. Perform 5 repetitions on each leg.

DYNAMIC SUMO SQUATS

1. Stand tall (shoulders back), with your feet close together. Take a large lateral step to the right and drop into a deep squat (think of a sumo wrestler). Pause, then return to the starting standing position.

2. Now take a large lateral step to the left and drop into a deep squat. Pause, then return to the starting position.

Perform 5 repetitions on each side.

HITZ CARDIO #1

All warmed up? Got some water nearby? Then let's do this.

Here's how the chart works. It's designed for use on a treadmill, but you can adapt it to your chosen activity. The key is to pay close attention to the time blocks and the PES. So, you'll start by doing a 5 minute–warmup at a PES of 4. If you're on a treadmill, that should put you at about 4 miles per hour at an incline of 1%. Then—without a break—do one minute at a PES of 5, then one minute at a PES of between 5 and 7, then one minute at a PES of 5 or 6, and so on until you hit the bottom of the grid.

Time	Description	Perceived Exertion Scale (PES)	Speed (mph)	Incline
1 min.	You should be working at a brisk pace. Stride it out.	Level 5	4.5–5.5	2–5%
1 min.	Okay, now push the pace a little more—you can reach that 7, I know you can.	Level 5–7	5–6	3–6%
1 min.	Back off a little, recoup and refresh. You're probably a little shiny now.	Level 5–6	4.5–5.5	2%
1 min.	Work hard for this minute. Here's your chance to find your second wind.	Level 5–7	5–6	3–6%
3 min.	Grab some H$_2$O, keep on moving, let that heart rate drop a little. I want you working at 50% intensity. If you're dizzy or light-headed, take another minute.	Level 5	4–5	0%

Time	Description	Perceived Exertion Scale (PES)	Speed (mph)	Incline
1 min.	Ease into this one—come on, go with it.	Level 6	4.5–5.5	5%
1 min.	Time to let it go. You're more than halfway through—PUSH IT!	Level 7–8	5–7	7%
1 min.	Catch your breath; we're gonna hit it again in the next sprint.	Level 5–6	4.5–5.5	2%
1 min.	Go! I want you working at 80% of your maximum speed.	Level 7–8	5–7	7%
3 min.	Stride this one out. You should be regaining your composure. Flush those legs out.	Level 5	5	0%
5 min.	Kool Moe Dee! This is the start of your cool-down. If you're on foot or wheels, get back to home base and finish your cool-down.	Level 4–5	4	0%

COOL-DOWN

Congratulations! You've just completed your first cardio day.

Mind you, it was the easiest one you're going to do over the course of the 10PS. That's right—it's only going to get harder from here on in. But it's going to start to *seem* easier as your body starts to believe that you mean business.

That may be hard to believe right now, but for now, just trust me and focus on cooling down and stretching.

Almost done now. You can stay on the same piece of equipment at a low intensity for 10 minutes, try something else out or go for a relaxing walk or jog. The important thing is that you should be at an intensity of Level 3 on the PES. You should be relatively comfortable. This is designed to slowly bring your heart rate down, so go easy with it.

STATIC STRETCHES

Once you have finished your 10-minute cool-down, it's time for you to do your static stretches. Perform the following three stretches and hold each one for 30 seconds per side. And hey, if you want to add in a few more of your own, please do.

SPINAL TWISTS

1. Lie on the floor, with your arms extending outward in a T position. Put your right foot on your left knee.

2. Using your left hand, gently pull your right knee toward the floor, twisting your spine and keeping your left arm straight out, hips and shoulders on the floor. Hold for 30 seconds.

Repeat, using the right hand and left knee.

QUADRICEPS/HIP FLEXOR STRETCHES

1. Starting in a standing position, take a big step forward with your left leg, then place your right knee on the ground.

2. Maintaining this posture, shift the entire body slightly forward from the hip. You should feel this stretch down the front of your quad and hip flexor. Exhale and hold the stretch. Don't arch your back.

Hold for 30 seconds, then gently release and switch legs.

HAMSTRING STRETCHES

1. Lie down on your back, with a slight bend in both legs.

2. Lift your right leg straight up and grab it behind your calf. If you are flexible enough, grab your ankle (or even your toe). Gently pull your right leg toward you, keeping your back straight.

Hold the stretch for 30 seconds. Repeat with the left leg.

OKAY, YOU'RE DONE FOR THE DAY. NICE WORK. TOMORROW IS YOUR SECOND RESISTANCE-TRAINING DAY, SO MAKE SURE YOU FUEL YOURSELF PROPERLY. IF YOU DON'T TAKE CARE OF THE MACHINE, IT WON'T TAKE CARE OF YOU.

SEE YOU TOMORROW.

DAY 3 MEAL PLAN

Remember, stick to the assigned portions; it's all about creating healthy habits, every day! Regardless of what time you plan to do your cardio, please do not work out on an empty stomach. If you're on the run, then plan ahead and pack your meals accordingly.

BREAKFAST Oatmeal (1/2 cup raw, cooked with water); 1/4 cup low-fat cottage cheese; 1/2 cup strawberries; 1-1/2 cup skim or soy milk.

SNACK 1 cup grapes; 10 walnut halves.

LUNCH Chicken pita: 1 whole-wheat pita, filled with 2 oz. sliced chicken breast, 1 cup spinach and tomato, 1 oz. grated light havarti cheese and 1 tsp. of mustard.

SNACK 1/4 cup granola; 3/4 cup low-fat yogurt.

DINNER Honey-lemon salmon: 4 oz. salmon, grilled with 1/2 tsp. honey and lemon and 1/2 tsp. olive oil; 1/2 cup brown rice; 2 cups salad of mixed greens, cucumber, grape tomato and light salad dressing.

DAY 4
HITZ Resistance #2

TOMMY RULE #4: REPEAT OUT LOUD, "TODAY I WILL BE BETTER. TODAY I WILL BE BETTER. TODAY I WILL BE BETTER!"

Feeling a little sore today? Maybe a little stiff?

As long as we're talking about a "good" sore, then we're on the right track. That soreness is your body breaking down and building itself back up. And that's exactly what we want to do.

We will continue to push the pace today and have you ready for whatever the world has to throw at you. The trick is to focus on today—and today *only*. There's only one time to do it right, and that's today. As long as you're doing it right today, there is absolutely no reason to worry about tomorrow.

The goal is to create healthy habits while strengthening your mind, body and soul. You've already done the hard part by getting started, so now we will continue to lay the foundation for your healthy future! Before we get to the workout, make sure that you warm up to get your body ready. And, as always, you should familiarize yourself with the exercises before you begin each workout.

Why are you still sitting there? It's go time!

TODAY'S WORKOUT

FOCUS	EQUIPMENT	REPETITIONS	SETS
Core and upper body.	Skipping rope, stability ball (SB) and 15- to 20-pound dumbbells (DBs).	Beginners, you're up for 20 seconds; intermediates, you've got 40.	Three—they do say that 3 times is the charm! Again, that means you're doing all 8 exercises 3 times.

HERE'S WHAT'S COMING AT YOU:
Warmup
Dynamic Stretches
HITZ Resistance #2

• SKIPPING • STABILITY BALL SUPERMANS
Take a 45-second rest. Your juices should be flowing now. Very nice start, but keep up the pace!

• PRISONER SQUATS • SPIDERMAN PUSH-UPS
45-second rest. Get some water!

• SKATERS • DUMBBELL DEAD LIFTS
45-second rest. One more batch to go before you're on to the second set.

• CORE AB POPPERS • STABILITY BALL HAMSTRING CURLS
Great job! Take a 1-minute water break before the next set. You've earned it.

Cool-Down
Static Stretches

WARMUP

Jump on a spin bike or a road bike for your 10-minute warmup.

For the first five minutes, work at an intensity Level of 4 on the PES. You should be sweating a little, but feeling good and able to carry on a conversation effortlessly.

For the last five minutes, work at an intensity of Level 5. You should be just above comfortable, sweating more and still able to talk easily.

DYNAMIC STRETCHES

After your warmup, perform the following three dynamic stretches:

DYNAMIC GLUTE AND HAMSTRING STRETCHES

1. Stand tall (shoulders back), with your feet shoulder width apart. Lift your left foot and grab just below your left knee with both hands.

2. With both hands, gently pull your left knee up, while maintaining your balance on your right heel. This will activate your butt and the backs of your legs. Hold for 3 seconds, then release your left leg.

**Repeat this sequence with your right leg.
Perform 5 repetitions with each leg.**

DYNAMIC QUAD STRETCHES

1. Stand tall (shoulders back), with your feet shoulder width apart. Lift your left foot behind you and grab your ankle (or foot) with your left hand.

2. Gently push your left hip forward, while keeping a straight line with your body and maintaining your balance on your right heel. Hold for 3 seconds, then release your left ankle.

Repeat the same sequence with your right leg. Perform 5 repetitions on each leg.

DYNAMIC SUMO SQUATS

1. Stand tall (shoulders back), with your feet close together. Take a large lateral step to the right and drop into a deep squat (think of a sumo wrestler). Pause, then return to the starting standing position.

2. Now take a large lateral step to the left and drop into a deep squat. Pause, then return to the starting position.

Perform 5 repetitions on each side.

SWEET. LET'S GET READY TO ROLL WITH HITZ RESISTANCE #2.

SKIPPING

Skipping will work your core hard, since your abs need to contract to stabilize your entire body. You will also get a great calf and shoulder burn. We're going for a little longer today; try and make it through the entire minute (beginner) or two (intermediate).

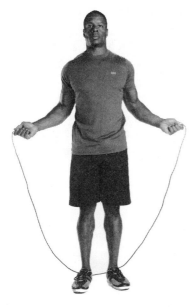 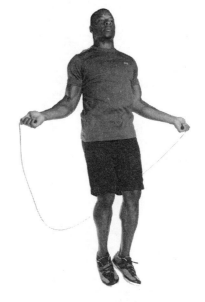

1. Place your skipping rope on the ground and stand in the middle of it. Grab the handles, which should reach about 6 inches below your collarbone when you pull the handles straight up.

2. Start to rotate the rope. The rotation should come from your wrists. To increase the speed of the rotations, increase the tightness of the circles that your wrists are making.

Skip for 1 minute if you're a beginner, 2 minutes if you're an intermediate.

TOMMY TIP

Beginners can use a double jump (your feet can touch the ground twice in the time it takes you to bring the rope through a full rotation); intermediates should use a single jump between rotations. Your arms shouldn't move much at all. Just think Rocky.

STABILITY BALL SUPERMANS

It's time to work your lower back. This is a great exercise that will help prevent lower-back pain. If you want to create a strong core, the Superman must be part of your routine. We are building your foundation, and it starts with a strong core.

1. Grab an SB and position it in front of you. Then get down on your knees, with your stomach on the SB.

2. Roll forward so that your hands and your toes are grazing the ground. Your knees should be hovering about 4 inches above the ground. (If you are sliding, brace your feet against a wall or bench.)

3. Engage your core, butt, hamstrings and shoulder, and raise your right hand and left leg simultaneously. Do not rotate your pelvis. Keep your right arm and your left leg straight. Hold for 2 seconds, then slowly lower your hand and foot and alternate to the left arm and right leg.

Repeat the sequence for 20 seconds if you're a beginner, 40 seconds if you're an intermediate.

 **45-SECOND REST**

TOMMY TIP

Imagine someone placing a baseball bat on your spine; now imagine staying flat enough that it wouldn't roll off even in the midst of your Superman. Go slow.

PRISONER SQUATS

You remember these bad boys from your fitness test, don't you?

Don't forget: shoulder blades back, head up and core engaged. Go!

1. Stand tall, with your feet slightly wider than shoulder width. Place your hands on your ears and pull your elbows back. Engage your core and pull your shoulder blades together.

2. Bend at your knees and hips, then push your hips backward as if trying to sit on a chair that's behind you. Drop until your knees are at 90 degrees, while keeping your back straight and your weight on your heels.

3. Now return to your upright standing position.

That's one—now you just have to last for 20 seconds if you're a beginner, 40 if you're an intermediate.

SPIDERMAN PUSH-UPS

Today I'm going to throw another type of push-up at you. It worked for Peter Parker, and it will work for you, too! It's more challenging than a regular push-up, but that means it'll shred you that much faster.

1. Start in a push-up position, with your hands directly under your shoulders. Your head and hips should be neutral and in line with your toes (if you're still struggling a bit, try these from your knees until you get stronger; if you're an intermediate, you can challenge yourself by holding two DBs, as I am here).

2. Engage your core, and lift your right hand and place it 6 to 10 inches ahead of your left hand (while bending your elbows and lowering yourself to within a couple of inches of the ground). At the same time, drive your left knee to the outside of your left arm. (Your hands should be staggered.)

3. Pause, then push your body up and return your right hand and left leg to the starting position. Repeat the same action with your left hand and right knee.

Repeat this sequence for your allotted time: beginners, 20 seconds; intermediates, 40 seconds.

 **45-SECOND REST**

TOMMY TIP

Your back should never sag throughout the movement. The closer your elbows are to your sides, the more you will work your triceps muscles; the wider you have them, the more you will work your chest.

Keep your head neutral (flat) and focus on lowering your chest, not your chin. If you cannot do a push-up from your knees, then stand up and use a wall.

SKATERS

You are going to love or hate this one, because it will hit those areas in your butt that you always want to target—but it will burn! Your gluteus medius will be working overtime, so hang in there; just think of a speed skater skating with long and powerful strides.

1. Stand tall on your (slightly bent) right leg, with your foot hovering above the ground. Keep your head and chest up.

2. Push off your right foot and jump laterally (sideways) as far as you can to your left foot. Avoid letting the other foot touch as you jump across.

3. Pause, then jump back across to your right foot.

This is a continuous-movement exercise that you must maintain for your allotted time: beginners, 20 seconds; intermediates, 40 seconds. Keep going!

TOMMY TIP

Keep a constant, controlled speed. The harder you push off jumping laterally, the more effective the exercise. You should feel this one in the side of your butt (glute meds). Make sure that you bend your knees at all times.

DUMBBELL DEAD LIFTS

The dead lift is a great exercise that should always be part of your overall routine. Using the proper technique is key to making this exercise effective, so always pay close attention to what you are doing by trying to think of squeezing a penny between your butt cheeks.

1. Stand tall, with your feet slightly wider than shoulder width apart and your weight balanced on your heels. Keep your legs as straight as possible, engage your core and keep your back flat. Hold a 15- to 20-pound DB in each hand, keeping them by your sides.

2. Lean forward and slowly lower your body until your back is parallel to the floor, while letting the DBs hang.

 **45-SECOND REST**

3. Pause for 1 second and then return to your original standing position.

Repeat this sequence for your allotted time: beginners, 20 seconds; intermediates, 40 seconds.

TOMMY TIP

Your core must be engaged and your back flat at all times throughout the exercise. You can put a slight bend in your knees to take some of the pressure off your back.

CORE AB POPPERS

Do you want to get those lower abdominals *really* flat? Of course you do, and core poppers are the exercise to really target your lower abs. This is a very small movement, and it should be done with as little momentum as possible. Get ready to say goodbye to your beer belly once and for all.

1. Lie on your back on a mat (or the floor), with your arms flat on the mat beside you. Then raise both your legs straight up in the air. Lift your head off the ground while looking up at the ceiling; do not tuck your chin.

2. Engage your core and lift your butt off the mat. If you're on the right track, your heels should be moving directly above you.

3. Pause, then return your butt to the mat in a controlled motion, keeping your head lifted.

Repeat this sequence for 20 seconds if you're a beginner and 40 seconds if you're an intermediate.

TOMMY TIP

Minimize any momentum and keep your legs as straight as you can.

STABILITY BALL HAMSTRING CURLS

This exercise will tighten and strengthen your bottom line, literally. Go at a smooth steady speed to feel the burn.

1. Lie on your back on a mat (or the floor), with your arms flat beside you. Place both your legs on an SB—your calves and heels must be in contact with the SB at all times.

2. Lift your hips up so that your butt is off the ground. Contract your core and squeeze your glutes.

3. While keeping your hips high, pull the SB toward your butt with your heels, pause, then return to your starting position (hips up at all times).

Repeat this sequence for 20 seconds if you're a beginner and 40 seconds if you're an intermediate.

THAT'S THE SET. TAKE A WELL-EARNED 1-MINUTE BREAK TO REST AND HYDRATE BEFORE THE NEXT ONE.

TOMMY TIP

If you are feeling this movement primarily in your calves, it means your hips are not high enough. The first time you do this, it's possible that your hamstring will cramp. If that happens, you should stretch it until it feels normal again, then continue with the exercise.

COOL-DOWN

Time to slow things down after a hard day of work. Take these next few minutes to clear your head (and perhaps an ache or two). You can stay on the same piece of equipment at a low intensity for 10 minutes, or try something else. The important thing is that you should be at an intensity of Level 3 on the PES. You should be relatively comfortable. Again, this is designed to slowly bring your heart rate down, so go easy with it.

STATIC STRETCHES

Once you have finished your 10-minute cool-down, it's time for you to do your static stretches. Perform the following three stretches and hold each one for 30 seconds per side. And hey, if you want to add a few more of your own, please do.

SPINAL TWISTS

1. Lie on the floor, with your arms extending outward in a T position. Put your right foot on your left knee.

2. Using your left hand, gently pull your right knee toward the floor, twisting your spine and keeping your left arm straight out, hips and shoulders on the floor. Hold for 30 seconds.

Repeat, using the right hand and left knee.

QUADRICEPS/HIP FLEXOR STRETCHES

1. Starting in a standing position, take a big step forward with your left leg, then place your right knee on the ground.

2. Maintaining this posture, shift the entire body slightly forward from the hip. You should feel this stretch down the front of your quad and hip flexor. Exhale and hold the stretch. Don't arch your back.

Hold for 30 seconds, then gently release and switch legs.

HAMSTRING STRETCHES

1. Lie down on your back, with a slight bend in both legs.

2. Lift your right leg straight up and grab it behind your calf. If you are flexible enough, grab your ankle (or even your toe). Gently pull your right leg toward you, keeping your back straight.

Hold the stretch for 30 seconds. Repeat with the left leg.

THAT'S IT—YOU'VE OFFICIALLY BATTLED THROUGH FOUR DAYS OF WORKOUTS. KEEP IT UP!

DAY 4 MEAL PLAN

I know that the 10PS can feel like a big time commitment—but Maria's really helped you out by planning many dinners that make a second appearance as a satisfying lunch. Just make sure to follow her portion sizes exactly, no matter how hungry your workouts make you. You are probably noticing fewer cravings throughout the day, so stay with the plan. It works. Seriously.

BREAKFAST 1 whole-wheat English muffin; 1 scrambled egg; 1 oz. part-skim mozzarella cheese; apple; 1-1/2 cups skim or soy milk.

SNACK 1 banana; 3/4 cup low-fat yogurt.

LUNCH 1 cup butternut squash soup (stock-based, not cream-based); 2 oz. canned light tuna mixed with 1 tbsp. light mayonnaise, onion and celery, spread on 3 light rye crackers; 1/2 cup baby carrots.

SNACK 1/3 cup hummus; 1 cup grape tomatoes; sliced red pepper.

DINNER Turkey Pasta: 4 oz. lean ground turkey, 1/2 cup whole-wheat spaghettini, 1/2 cup pasta sauce, 1 cup mushrooms, red pepper. Brown the turkey and then drain the fat. Add mushrooms and red pepper and let cook for a few minutes, then add the pasta sauce. Cook the spaghettini to your taste, drain, then toss with 1 cup raw spinach and 2 tsp. olive oil. Mix in the pasta sauce and top with 1 tbsp. grated Parmesan. **Cook-ahead option:** Double the sauce recipe and cook an extra cup of pasta, then set aside for tomorrow's lunch.

DAY 5
HITZ Cardio #2

TOMMY RULE #5: THERE ARE NOT A LOT OF PEOPLE I KNOW WHO ACTUALLY LIKE TO DO CARDIO, INCLUDING ME. BUT IT'S SOMETHING THAT MUST BE DONE, SO YOU MIGHT AS WELL STOP COMPLAINING ABOUT IT AND DO IT RIGHT. IF YOU'RE GOING TO DO IT (AND YOU ARE), YOU'D BETTER MAKE IT WORTH YOUR WHILE.

How did you enjoy your first cardio day? It's one thing to say you believe there is no gain without some pain, but it's a different matter when you're in the middle of a lung-burning workout you know is going to leave you staggering, isn't it? But you've done it once. Time to lace up your shoes for Cardio Day #2.

As before, don't worry too much about speed or incline—I want you focused on the PES, instead. (And, as before, if you cannot run or you have any health conditions, just get moving and stay within your limits.)

Make sure that today—and every day—you get six to eight glasses of water. Hydration is incredibly important during the 10PS.

TODAY'S WORKOUT

FOCUS	EQUIPMENT	TOTAL TIME
Burning that flab.	A treadmill is ideal, but any cardio equipment will do—even just a pair of running shoes.	About 45 minutes.

HERE'S WHAT'S ON DECK:
Warmup
Dynamic Stretches
HITZ Cardio #2
Cool-Down
Static Stretches

WARMUP

All right, then, time to warm up.

For five minutes, work at an intensity of Level 4 on the PES. You should be sweating a little, but should be able to carry on a conversation effortlessly.

DYNAMIC STRETCHES

After your warmup, perform the following two dynamic stretches:

DYNAMIC GLUTE AND HAMSTRING STRETCHES

1. Stand tall (shoulders back), with your feet shoulder width apart. Lift your left foot and grab just below your left knee with both hands.

2. With both hands, gently pull your left knee up, while maintaining your balance on your right heel. This will activate your butt and the backs of your legs. Hold for 3 seconds, then release your left leg.

Repeat the same sequence with your right leg. Perform 5 repetitions with each leg.

DYNAMIC QUAD STRETCHES

1. Stand tall (shoulders back), with your feet shoulder width apart. Lift your left foot behind you and grab your ankle (or foot) with your left hand.

2. Gently push your left hip forward, while keeping a straight line with your body and maintaining your balance on your right heel. Hold for 3 seconds, then release your left ankle.

Repeat the same sequence with your right leg. Perform 5 repetitions on each leg.

HITZ CARDIO #2

Right, then. All warmed up? Now it's time for HITZ Cardio #2. Good luck! I'll be right here with you. Remember to have some water close by.

Time	Description	Perceived Exertion Scale (PES)	Speed (mph)	Incline
5 min.	Time to get the juices flowing. You should be at 50% of your maximum ability.	Level 5	4–4.5 (walk/slow jog)	5%
1 min.	Gradually open it up a little bit.	Level 6	4.5–5.5 (speed-walk/run)	2%
2 min.	Use these two minutes to really go after it. Breathe slowly.	Level 5	4–5 (walk/slow jog)	5%
1 min.	Here's your first sprint—70 to 80% of your maximum ability.	Level 6–7	5–7 (speed-walk/run)	2%
2 min.	Back to 50%.	Level 5	4–5 (walk/slow jog)	8%
1 min.	Push the pace back to 70 to 80%.	Level 7	5.5–7 (speed-walk/run)	1–2%

Time	Description	Perceived Exertion Scale (PES)	Speed (mph)	Incline
2 min.	Grab a blast of water as you cruise.	Level 5	4–5 (walk/slow jog)	6%
1 min.	"Give 'er"—80% is the pace you should be at.	Level 7–8	Walk or run as fast as you can	1–2%
2 min.	Breathe in . . . breathe out—50% pace.	Level 5	4–5 (walk/slow jog)	5%
1 min.	This is your last burst. I want you at 80% of your maximum ability for the entire minute.	Level 7–8	Walk or run as fast as you can	1–2%
2 min.	Time to get that heart rate back down again—40 to 50% pace.	Level 5	4–5 (walk/slow jog)	5%

Feeling a little winded? If you gave it your all, you'd better be!

HITZ Cardio #1 and #2 are the two least challenging in the series, so if you found them a pretty tough slog, keep on working. If there are any HITZ Cardio sessions that you just can't complete, you can substitute the program from the previous HITZ Cardio day. I want you to keep up, though, so it may mean you just have to work a little harder.

On the other hand, if you aren't feeling winded, you're going to have to pick up the pace. Saddle up, my friend, because next week HITZ Cardio #3 and #4 are going to test your mettle.

For now, take a quick water break, then let's get to the cool-down.

COOL-DOWN

Nice work today. Tomorrow, you will be doing your third resistance-training workout, but before that happens I want you to cool down. You can stay on the same piece of equipment at a low intensity for 10 minutes. You should be at an intensity of Level 3 on the PES—that is, you should be relatively comfortable, so go easy with it.

STATIC STRETCHES

When you're done, settle in for three static stretches:

QUADRICEPS/HIP FLEXOR STRETCHES

1. Starting in a standing position, take a big step forward with your left leg, then place your right knee on the ground.

2. Maintaining this posture, shift the entire body slightly forward from the hip. You should feel this stretch down the front of your quad and hip flexor. Exhale and hold the stretch. Don't arch your back.

Hold for 30 seconds, then gently release and switch legs.

HAMSTRING STRETCHES

1. Lie down on your back, with a slight bend in both legs.

2. Lift your right leg straight up and grab it behind your calf. If you are flexible enough, grab your ankle (or even your toe). Gently pull your right leg toward you, keeping your back straight.

Hold the stretch for 30 seconds. Repeat with the left leg.

HIP STRETCHES

1. Lie down and cross your left foot over your right knee.

2. Clasp your hands behind your right knee.

3. Gently pull your right knee toward you, while keeping your upper body relaxed. Hold for 30 seconds, then untangle slowly.

Switch legs and repeat the sequence.

AMAZING WORK. IF YOU'RE HAVING ANY NEGATIVE THOUGHTS DANCING THROUGH YOUR HEAD, FIGHT THROUGH THEM. YOU ARE ALMOST DONE YOUR FIRST WEEK. STAY ON THE PATH AND GREAT THINGS WILL HAPPEN. NOW GO AND EAT!

DAY 5 MEAL PLAN

You are what you eat, so keep up the great eating habits! You are paving the way toward a healthy lifestyle. Your meal plan is stacked with fibre to brush your insides, and protein, fats and carbs to sustain you through the day.

BREAKFAST 3/4 cup low-fat yogurt; 1/4 cup granola; 1/4 cup All-Bran cereal; 1/2 apple or mango; 1-1/2 cups skim or soy milk.

SNACK 1 apple; 1/4 cup low-fat cottage cheese.

LUNCH Leftover turkey pasta: Half of last night's turkey pasta sauce with 1 cup cooked whole-wheat spaghettini, served with 1 cup spinach and cooked vegetables.

SNACK Granola bar; 10 walnut halves.

DINNER Chicken quesadilla: In a non-stick pan, cook 2 oz. diced chicken breast. Once completely cooked, place the chicken, 1 oz. part-skim mozzarella cheese, red and green peppers, onion and salsa on one half of a large whole-wheat wrap, then fold it over to form a half-moon. Place the quesadilla back into your pan and cook until the cheese is melted, turning once. Serve with 2 cups mixed-green salad with 1 tbsp. light Italian dressing. **Cook-ahead option:** Cook an extra 2 oz. of chicken tonight so that you're ready for tomorrow's lunch.

DAY 6
HITZ Resistance #3

TOMMY RULE #6: I'VE ADAPTED THIS ONE FROM ONE OF MY FIRST TRAINERS, STEVE RAMS. WHENEVER SOMEONE WOULD COMPLAIN, HE ALWAYS HAD THE SAME QUIP READY: "PAIN IS JUST WEAKNESS LEAVING THE BODY!" SO WHAT'S YOUR EXCUSE? INSTEAD OF GRIPING ABOUT THE PAIN, FOCUS ON THE MUSCLES THAT YOU ARE USING, AND YOU WILL FEEL A MUCH DEEPER, MORE SATISFYING BURN.

This is your last resistance workout of the week. You should be feeling aches and strength in muscles that may seem foreign to you. Let those aches be a reminder of all the muscles you weren't using while you were sitting on the couch or hunched over your computer. You're going to keep those muscles active for the rest of your life.

Are you beginning to notice some changes in your body? You're starting to recover from the first aches and have taken on a few more. You may feel a little sluggish, or you may have a bit more energy than you did before you started the 10PS. Regardless of where you stand, keep it up. This is just the tip of the iceberg.

For now, keep on challenging yourself. If you have to work a little bit longer than your prescribed times, then do it. If you have to rest a little bit longer as you progress through the program, so be it. It takes 21 days to build a habit, and you are well on your way. Replace all of those "I can't" thoughts with a whole bunch of "Yes, I can!" thoughts.

Sound good? I thought so. All right, get going!

TODAY'S WORKOUT

FOCUS	EQUIPMENT	REPETITIONS	SETS
Whole body.	Skipping rope, stability ball (SB) and 10-, 15- and 20-pound dumbbells (DBs).	Beginners, go for 20 seconds; intermediates, for 40.	Three sets once again!

HERE'S WHAT I'VE GOT UP MY SLEEVE—MAKE IT COUNT!
Warmup
Dynamic Stretches
HITZ Resistance #3

• HIGH-KNEE RUNNING • STATIC LUNGES
Take a 45-second rest.

• STABILITY BALL ONE-ARM ROWING • DUMBBELL PLIÉ SQUATS
45-second rest . . . Grab some water.

• HIGH-KNEE RUNNING • CORE DOWN2, UP2
45-second rest.

• AB CRUNCHES WITH DUMBBELLS • STABILITY BALL REVERSE HYPEREXTENSIONS
Get some water—you have a 1-minute break before you repeat the exact same circuit two more times. Don't hold back! The harder you work, the better your results.

   And as a special treat, let's throw in a **CORE PLANK** as the last exercise of the third set. Hey, the good news is, you're doing this only once!

Cool-Down
Static Stretches

WARMUP

Today, you are going to warm up by skipping. Set your watch or look at the clock, because you will be skipping for five minutes.

For the first minute, you can skip any style. If you do not have a skipping rope, use an imaginary one—jump in place, mimicking a skipping motion.

For the second minute, you will skip with a double hop between rotations.

For the third minute, go back to any style.

For the last two minutes, it's double leg hops again.

DYNAMIC STRETCHES

After your skipping, perform the following three dynamic stretches:

DYNAMIC QUAD STRETCHES

1. Stand tall (shoulders back), with your feet shoulder width apart. Lift your left foot behind you and grab your ankle (or foot) with your left hand.

2. Gently push your left hip forward, while keeping a straight line with your body and maintaining your balance on your right heel. Hold for 3 seconds, then release your left ankle.

Repeat this sequence with your right leg. Perform 5 repetitions on each leg.

DYNAMIC CHEST AND BICEP STRETCHES

1. Stand tall (shoulders back), with your feet shoulder width apart. Slowly move your arms out to the sides, slightly behind you, with your thumbs up (just like The Fonz).

2. As your arms go back, rotate your thumbs down and back until they are pointing to the wall behind you. Pause, then return to the starting position. You should feel this one in your chest and biceps.

Perform 10 repetitions.

DYNAMIC SUMO SQUATS

1. Stand tall (shoulders back), with your feet close together. Take a large lateral step to the right and drop into a deep squat (think of a sumo wrestler). Pause, then return to the starting standing position.

2. Now take a large lateral step to the left and drop into a deep squat. Pause, then return to the starting position.

Perform 5 repetitions on each side.

**OKAY, THE WARMUP IS COMPLETE, AND IT'S TIME FOR SOME ACTION—
AND THAT MEANS HITZ RESISTANCE #3.**

HIGH-KNEE RUNNING

1. Stand tall, with your feet shoulder width apart. Run on the spot, lifting your knees as high as possible and pumping your arms vigorously. Ideally, your knees will be coming up to waist height.

2. You must remain tall at all times. Do not slump.

Keep going for 40 seconds (beginner and intermediate).

STATIC LUNGES

The static lunge is the most basic lunge; when done right, it will target your entire lower body. We are all about building strong foundations, right? Well, the "tight buns express" starts with lunges.

1. Stand tall, with your feet shoulder width apart.

2. Take a large lunge step forward with your left leg, while at the same time bending both knees until your left thigh is parallel to the ground and your right knee is pointing down at the ground. Avoid pushing your body forward as you descend. Keep 70% of your weight on your left (front) heel, and stay balanced with 30% of your weight on your right toe.

3. Push off your left heel/right toe to an upright position, pause and then return to your "lower lunge" position.

Repeat this sequence for 20 seconds per leg if you're a beginner (aim for at least 10 reps per leg), or 40 seconds per leg if you're an intermediate exerciser (aim for at least 15 reps per leg). Once you have completed the repetitions with the left leg in front, switch legs and repeat the sequence, stepping with the right foot.

 **45-SECOND REST**

STABILITY BALL ONE-ARM ROWING

This is a compound exercise, so get ready to feel it everywhere. The primary muscles being used are your lats, but your core, glutes and arms will get a workout, as well. Focus on your lats with each pull.

1. Place your left hand on a medium-sized SB and hold a 15- or 20-pound dumbbell in your right hand.

2. Brace your abdominals and lift your right leg so that it is straight (parallel with your back).

3. Pull (row) the dumbbell up toward your right hip, pause and return to the starting position.

Keep going for 20 seconds per arm if you're a beginner (aim for a minimum of 10 reps on each arm), 40 seconds per arm if an intermediate (aim for 15 to 20 reps on each arm).

TOMMY TIP

Keep your back flat and your core engaged throughout the entire exercise. The straighter you keep your supporting leg, the more you will activate your hamstring and glute muscles—yes, you get to work your butt, too!

DUMBBELL PLIÉ SQUATS

Plié squats have been used by dancers for years; now it's your turn. This is a great exercise for your butt and your lower body in general. When done right, you will also feel the burn from your inner thighs, so get ready for it—you're going to love it!

1. Stand tall, with your feet wider than shoulder width and your toes turned out. Engage your core and pull your shoulder blades together. Cup your hands and hold a 20-pound (beginners) to 40-pound (intermediate) dumbbell between your legs.

2. Begin the movement by bending at your knees and hips, then push your hips backward as if trying to sit in a deep imaginary basket behind you.

3. Bend your knees to 90 degrees while keeping your back straight and your weight on your heels. Pause for 1 second, then return to your upright, standing position.

Repeat this sequence for 20 seconds if you're a beginner, 40 seconds if you're an intermediate.

REST UP FOR 45 SECONDS. AND GRAB SOME WATER!

HIGH-KNEE RUNNING

Keep those knees high for max results!

1. Stand tall, with your feet shoulder width apart. Run on the spot, lifting your knees as high as possible and pumping your arms vigorously. Ideally, your knees will be coming up to waist height.

2. You must remain tall at all times. Do not slump.

Keep going for 40 seconds (beginner and intermediate).

CORE DOWN2, UP2

I really love this one—the D2/U2 is a core shredder! Your entire core and upper body will be engaged and worked to the max. As a beginner, you will be on the floor, but as you improve, you will move to the stability ball. Have fun with this one!

1. Place your hands on a mat, shoulder width apart, and extend your feet straight back so that you are in an upright push-up position (arms fully locked). Keep your elbows as close to your sides as possible and spread your legs a little wider than normal to minimize body tilting.

2. Shift your weight to your left arm, then drop your right arm so that your forearm is on the mat, then repeat the same sequence with your left arm. Pause in a plank position (on both fore-arms).

3. Return your right arm to push-up position and then your left.

Repeat this sequence for 20 seconds if you're a beginner, 40 seconds if you're an inter-mediate. Make sure to switch up the order in which you lower yourself to your forearms—so lead with the right arm as above, then switch and lead with your left arm halfway through.

 45-SECOND REST

TOMMY TIP

Keep your body in a straight line at all times by engaging your core, and keep your head neutral.

AB CRUNCHES WITH DUMBBELLS

Let's tighten up your midsection . . . deal? Getting a flat stomach requires a variety of core and abdominal movements.

The ab crunch is just one of many that you will encounter as the weeks go by.

Don't save anything for tomorrow if you can push through it today.

1. Start by lying down on your back with your legs out in front of you, knees bent and feet shoulder width apart. Hold a 5- or 10-pound dumbbell above your belly button, while your palms cup each end of the dumbbell.

2. Curl your shoulder blades while pressing the DB with arms extended straight up toward the ceiling.

3. Pause, then return to the starting position (DB on your belly button).

Repeat the sequence 30 times if you're a beginner, 40 times if you're an intermediate.

STABILITY BALL REVERSE HYPEREXTENSIONS

If you want to avoid comments like "Do fries come with that shake?" then reverse hyperextensions are the exercise for you! This one is great for the butt and lower back, and the core in general.

1. Begin on your knees and place a stability ball under your pelvis. Roll forward on the SB so that both your hands are on the ground with a slight bend in your elbows.

2. Let both feet hover above the ground (once you start, they never touch the ground).

3. Contract your glutes and hamstrings to raise both legs, while keeping them straight.

Repeat this sequence for 20 seconds if you're a beginner, 40 seconds if you're an intermediate.

TOMMY TIP

Your legs will start in an extremely wide base, but once they are raised, your heels will be together at the top. Do not swing your legs—no momentum is allowed. As your legs are being raised, do not let your chin dip toward the ground.

THAT'S A WRAP FOR THE SET. TAKE A MINUTE BEFORE STARTING THE CIRCUIT AGAIN. AFTER THE FINAL SET, THERE'S ONE LAST THING I WANT YOU TO DO . . .

CORE PLANK

The core plank is a workout staple and should be a part of your daily exercise routine because it is extremely effective in strengthening your core. You will feel this one through your lower back, as well. You can perform the plank on the floor, or on a stability ball or bench.

1. Begin on all fours (hands and knees) on a mat.

2. Extend your legs so that your entire body is flat, in a straight-arm plank position, then go down to your forearms.

3. Raise your hips so that your body is in a straight line and your weight is on your elbows and toes. Beginners, you may need to be on your knees. That's fine for now—just ensure that your hips are down, with your core engaged and back flat. This should be hard work.

Hold the plank position for up to 1 minute. You have only a single set of this, so challenge yourself.

COOL-DOWN

Get a really good cool-down today. We are through three resistance training workouts now, and I'm sure your muscles are really tight. Today, cool down for 15 minutes on a bike to really flush your muscles.

STATIC STRETCHES

Once you have finished your 15-minute cool-down, it is time for you to do the following four static stretches:

HAMSTRING STRETCHES

1. Lie down on your back, with a slight bend in both legs.

2. Lift your right leg straight up and grab it behind your calf. If you are flexible enough, grab your ankle (or even your toe). Gently pull your right leg toward you, keeping your back straight.

Hold the stretch for 30 seconds. Repeat with the left leg.

SPINAL TWISTS

1. Lie on the floor, with your arms extending outward in a T position. Put your right foot on your left knee.

2. Using your left hand, gently pull your right knee toward the floor, twisting your spine and keeping your left arm straight out, hips and shoulders on the floor. Hold for 30 seconds.

Repeat, using the right hand and left knee.

QUADRICEPS/HIP FLEXOR STRETCHES

1. Starting in a standing position, take a big step forward with your left leg, then place your right knee on the ground.

2. Maintaining this posture, shift the entire body slightly forward from the hip. You should feel this stretch down the front of your quad and hip flexor. Exhale and hold the stretch. Don't arch your back.

Hold for 30 seconds, then gently release and switch legs.

CHEST COMPLEX TRIPLE STRETCHES

1. For the first stretch, stand next to a wall or door frame. Extend one arm and bend at the elbow, so that your arm forms a right angle, with your upper arm parallel to the ground and your forearm sticking straight up. Place your forearm against the wall or door frame. Now, twist your whole body away from the wall, with a special emphasis on pushing your chest through the turn, so that you feel a gentle stretch in your chest. Hold this for 10 seconds.

2. For the next stretch, step away from the wall so that, instead of your forearm, only your hand is on the wall. The arm still forms a right angle from your body, but this time your hand and shoulder are at the same level. Make the same twist, pushing your chest into the turn, to stretch the chest in the new position. Hold this for 10 seconds.

3. For the third and final variation, step further from the wall and extend your arm straight, so that the entire arm is parallel to the ground. Place your hand on the wall, then twist again into the stretch. You should feel the tension in your chest. Hold this for 10 seconds.

Switch arms and repeat this same sequence.

SIX DAYS IN—ARE YOU STARTING TO FEEL THE MOMENTUM? IS YOUR MORNING MUFFIN A LITTLE EASIER TO PASS UP? THE SMELL OF FRENCH FRIES AS YOU PASS A RESTAURANT NOT QUITE SO TEMPTING? KEEP IT UP—THE CRAVINGS WILL ONLY GET EASIER TO RESIST, AND YOUR RESULTS WILL ONLY GET BETTER.

DAY 6 MEAL PLAN

Remember, you need to eat everything on the menu—or sub it out for an equivalent. As strange as it feels initially, you need all of this food to get stronger—and to replace fat with muscle. Chow down!

BREAKFAST 2 slices whole-grain toast with 2 tbsp. natural peanut butter; 1 banana; 1-1/2 cups skim or soy milk.

SNACK 1 orange; 1/4 cup low-fat cottage cheese.

LUNCH Chicken-salsa wrap: 2 oz. chicken, with peppers and onion and 2 tbsp. salsa in a whole-wheat wrap.

SNACK 1/4 cup granola; 3/4 cup low-fat yogurt.

DINNER Beef and broccoli spaghettini: Stir-fry 4 oz. sliced beef tenderloin with 1-1/2 cups broccoli, 1 tbsp. hoisin sauce and 1 tsp. olive oil. Serve with 1/2 cup whole-wheat spaghettini. **Cook-ahead option:** Cook an extra 2 oz. beef, 1 cup broccoli and 1 cup spaghettini to set aside for tomorrow's lunch.

DAY 7
Nutrition Advice

TOMMY RULE #7: KEEP GOING STRONG.
DON'T USE SHORT-TERM THINKING ON LONG-TERM GOALS!

Finally, a break!

Today is a day of active rest, meaning you don't have anything structured to do today. But that doesn't mean you can just lie on the couch, licking your wounds from the week's workouts. I can give you 12 reasons not to follow your instincts on this one. The first 10 are the pounds you're going to lose over the course of the 10PS. Number 11 is the fact that *you're not like that anymore*. You are no longer the kind of person who sits around getting fatter and slacker. That's someone else.

And here's number 12: The best thing you can do if you are feeling sore and worn out is to get out and do anything active. You can take a fitness class or yoga class, or you can get outside and take a walk, light jog or ride, and then do some static stretches. It may seem like the last thing you want to do, but trust me, you'll feel a million times better by doing it.

The fact that you've made it through the week and are on Day 7 of the 10PS means that you have jump-started your system, and, consequently, your body is going through some drastic changes. You've had three HITZ Resistance sessions, along with two HITZ Cardio sessions, which have delivered quite a jolt to your poor old system. However, it doesn't stop there.

Those are just two out of the three important elements necessary in order to be successful with your healthy lifestyle makeover. Nutrition is an equally important part that many overlook. If you have not been following the meal plan, you are short-changing yourself.

I know this is a lot to digest—literally—but you have to stay with it, because if you don't, I can promise that your results will be average at best.

Okay, I know: It's not easy to follow the plan. It's easier to eat whatever you happen to stumble upon or scarf down whatever junk the delivery man is willing to bring. But trust me on this one. Maria has invested time, effort and science in creating your meal plan. I chose Maria because I have seen her results. As they say, the proof of the pudding is in the eating, but since you're not eating much pudding these days, I've asked Maria to share some insight, so here are her thoughts:

You have been on the menu for one week now. At this point, many of my clients tell me they feel as though they are eating more food than usual, and are not used to it. As long as you are feeling satisfied and energized, that is perfect—you shouldn't be starving! If you are, it means you are leaving too much of a gap between your meals. Your meal plan will see you take in approximately 1,500 to 1,600 calories per day. If your current weight is over 180 pounds and you are still hungry while sticking to the plan, then you can add another snack to bring your caloric intake up to around 1,800 calories.

The menu has been put together to allow you to have a snack in the morning and a snack in the afternoon. However, if you are not hungry between breakfast and lunch, but are starving by dinnertime, you can shift the morning snack to the afternoon.

I often hear from clients that the menu is great, but that they would like to switch meals around so it works better with their schedule. Generally, this works, as long as you exchange breakfast for breakfast, lunch for lunch and dinner for dinner. You can't have breakfast for dinner!

Some participants on the show have asked me what they can cut from the meal plan to lose weight faster. I always say the menu is balanced to help you lose weight and keep you energized, but also to make sure you can keep the weight off over the long term. Losing weight is tough, but keeping it off is the bigger challenge, and that is what the menu is designed to do. To help you lose weight, to get you in better shape and ultimately to keep the weight off without feeling deprived. So no skipping meals!

So there you have it from my R&D department. I'll add to Maria's wisdom by giving you some take-home information to think about. What you're eating these days is called a balanced meal plan, which is quite different from a diet. Some diets that you see popularized on TV, or used by celebrities, actually deprive you of the nutrients that you need to survive. Should I repeat that? Some diets are bad for you.

Some popular diets restrict your carbohydrates. Since carbs are your body's fuel, you can see right away why this is going to be a problem sooner or later. You wouldn't get into your car and try to drive it with no gas, would you? Well, that is how you have to think of your body. Keep it fuelled at all times and it will be reliable. Take away its fuel and you better expect it to run like a lemon!

Think about it another way. If your diet is temporary, that's what your weight loss is going to be, as well. And when weight comes back, you usually end up with more than you started with. That's why Maria and I are putting you on a balanced meal plan—because balance is something you can sustain. If you have a history of dieting, or flipping from one diet-of-the-month to another, it may take a little longer for your body to adjust to eating real food with proper portions. But that's okay—this is a long-term change, with long-term results, so stick with it!

See y'all tomorrow. I've got a great story to share with you to keep you going strong into the next week of the 10PS.

DAY 7 MEAL PLAN

All this talk about food is making me hungry, so I'm about to go and chow down. Hey, so should you . . . with your meal plan, of course!

BREAKFAST 2-egg omelette with mushrooms and red pepper; 1 slice whole-grain toast; 1 tsp. non-hydrogenated margarine; 1/2 cup watermelon; 1-1/2 cups skim or soy milk.

SNACK Plum or orange; 3/4 cup yogurt.

LUNCH Leftover beef and broccoli spaghettini.

SNACK Granola bar; 20 almonds.

DINNER 4 oz. grilled turkey breast; 3 nugget potatoes, each cut in half; 2 cups spinach salad with mushrooms and red onion and 1 tsp. olive oil, mixed with 1 tbsp. balsamic vinegar for dressing.

DAY 8
Motivation Day!

TOMMY RULE #8: IT'S THIRD AND GOAL WITH NO TIME ON THE CLOCK. STAY IN THE GAME, BECAUSE YOU'RE GETTING THE BALL . . . AND YOU'RE GOING TO SCORE! ONE WEEK IN ALREADY . . . THAT WASN'T TOO HARD, WAS IT?

You probably can't see the end from here, but that's all right. You have your goals written down, so you *know* where you're going to end up when the dust has settled. But a little bit of reassurance won't hurt on a quiet day like today, and it might even help you get through the workouts I have in store for the days ahead.

So as you continue with your lifestyle change, I thought it would be a great idea to share one of my success stories with you.

When I meet someone for the first time, I always hear the same thing: "Tommy, I'll do whatever I have to in order to lose weight and get in shape. Really . . . I'll do anything you say!"

Well, not everybody manages to keep their word, and not everyone puts in the work. And when they are doing it for me, that's the problem—they should be doing it for themselves. If you're doing this for someone else, today is the day you should give your head a bit of a shake, because anyone who works hard only when someone is watching is sure to cheat as soon as they're on their own.

Now, don't get me wrong. I love hearing how committed people are. I hope I can inspire you from time to time, and I am inspired by the people I work with. Words are important, but actions speak much louder than words. That's something I kept thinking about during my time working with Candice, who really kicked butt each and every day, and who inspired me so immensely that she's now become a lifelong friend.

If you are questioning your drive and motivation at this point, just read her story, which is in her own words. Once you do, I guarantee you will be back at it tomorrow, full of enthusiasm. I told you from the outset that this mission would not be easy, but it will forever change your life. Here's Candice's story:

As someone who once weighed 247 pounds, I am quite familiar with the struggles and difficulties of weight loss. My first 90 pounds came off at home—through exercise, change in diet and some crazy amount of willpower that gave me the ability to drive past fast-food restaurants and their deliciously horrible meals.

When I met Tommy, I had hit a major plateau. It seemed that no matter what I did, my weight would not fluctuate from the 160-pound mark. I was completely frustrated with myself and the workouts that had taken me this far in my weight-loss journey.

People always talked about how the last 10 pounds would be the hardest to lose, but I think a better description would be to call them "the most rewarding to lose." You can feel how close you are to success, so when someone gives you the key to getting there and guides you through the last obstacles, you begin to feel unstoppable.

Once I began Tommy's workouts, I noticed a difference within the first few days. The sessions took only 30 to 60 minutes, and they incorporated all different areas of exercise—strength, cardio, resistance—which resulted in an overall body toning and weight loss that I couldn't have imagined. My body felt so strong, and my endurance level was increasing with each passing day.

The biggest difference I noticed from the workouts was that I didn't need to be spending six hours a day in order to make a huge difference. I could confidently walk into the gym, or any park outside, and spend half an hour sweating continuously. When Tommy said "Pain is weakness leaving the body," I started to realize that the pain is subconscious. I had hit the plateau because I did not know how to push my body past that pain, and couldn't see what my true potential was.

The meal plan was a real eye-opener, as well, because it showed me that I did not need to skip meals, starve myself or eat only lettuce to shed the pounds. In the past, I would eat less to try and lose more, and with Maria's and Tommy's guidance, I quickly learned that there really is a science behind weight loss. Once I understood why the foods I chose to eat affected me in certain ways, it made sticking to the menu plan a lot easier. There are certain foods that are way more beneficial to my body, mind and energy levels. The menu plan was designed to make sure I had enough energy to withstand the workouts so that I wasn't hungry throughout the day, and my metabolism was ready to step into high gear so that I could lose that many more inches. Forget rabbit food! The meal plan was delicious, and three years later, I continue to adapt my daily meals around that same plan.

I want to be able to share one piece of insight with anyone who is trying to lose the last 10 pounds, or more: It is possible. Not only is it possible, but if you can focus and commit to the plan, it will come off quicker than you ever could have imagined. Give yourself 31 days to be completely focused on yourself, and remember that the only person you cheat when you hit up that drive-thru window is you.

It has been almost three years since Tommy helped me lose 17 pounds in four weeks. I am very proud to say that I have been able to keep the weight off, and I am happier and more confident than I have ever been. Use the book to learn and understand the tools you need to be successful, and believe me when I say that it will change your entire outlook on life!

How about that for a story? Does it make you feel like going for a walk, jumping on your bike or getting out there in some other way? Then do it! Swim, Rollerblade, hike, sail, whatever. In other words, enjoy the remainder of your day! Rest up and get ready to chip away at your goal tomorrow. I'll be waiting!

DAY 8 MEAL PLAN

Don't be tempted on your off-days to make them days off from your meal plan—every bite counts. Remember, I'm watching!

BREAKFAST Oatmeal (1/2 cup raw, cooked with water) with 1/4 cup slivered almonds and 2 tbsp. dried cranberries; 1-1/2 cups skim or soy milk.

SNACK 1 cup watermelon; 1/4 cup low-fat cottage cheese.

LUNCH Grilled cheese sandwich: Place 1 oz. light havarti cheese slices between 2 slices of whole-grain bread, then spread 2 tsp. non-hydrogenated margarine on the outside of the sandwich. Grill until the cheese is melted. Serve with 1/2 cup baby carrots.

SNACK 1/3 cup hummus; 2 rye crackers.

DINNER Chicken teriyaki stir-fry: Stir-fry 4 oz. chicken breast with 1 tsp. olive oil, then add 2 cups Asian vegetables (peppers, mushrooms, bok choy, etc.) and 2 tbsp. light teriyaki sauce. Serve with 1/2 cup brown rice.

And here are your meals for next week.

Use a bit of the extra time you have today to hit the grocery store so you don't find yourself starving in front of an empty fridge later in the week—or worse, starving in front of a fast-food cashier! Make sure you plan ahead to stay ahead.

MEAL PLAN #2

	DAY 9	DAY 10	DAY 11	DAY 12	DAY 13	DAY 14	DAY 15
Breakfast	Yogurt with granola and All-Bran cereal, grapes and a glass of milk	Toast with almond butter, orange and a glass of milk	English muffin, scrambled egg, strawberries and a glass of milk	Oatmeal with dried cranberries, cottage cheese and a glass of milk	Toast with natural peanut butter, banana and a glass of milk	Pancakes with maple syrup and back bacon, orange and a glass of milk	Toast with boiled or poached egg, grapes and a glass of milk
Snack	Blueberries and almonds	Mango with yogurt	Banana with yogurt	Grapes and almonds	Orange and yogurt	Strawberries and almonds	Blueberries with yogurt
Lunch	Salmon sandwich with baby carrots	Leftover pork tenderloin wrap	Leftover BBQ chicken breast with mashed sweet potato and broccoli	Grilled ham and cheese sandwich	Split pea or minestrone soup with tuna salad on rye crackers	Chicken Caesar salad	Leftover turkey pita
Snack	Granola bar	Hummus with rye crackers and grape tomatoes	Granola bar and almonds	Hummus with rye crackers and red pepper	Edamame	Granola bar	Edamame
Dinner	Pork tenderloin with fresh corn and mixed-green salad	BBQ chicken breast with sweet potato and broccoli	Salad with mixed-greens and veggies	Honey-lemon salmon	Chicken fajita	Turkey sandwich with baby carrots	Baked ziti with spinach salad

DAY 9
HITZ Resistance #4

TOMMY RULE #9: WE DO NOT STOP, WE DO NOT GIVE UP AND WE NEVER, EVER SETTLE FOR AVERAGE!

Here we are already: Week 2.

Notice any changes? You may not look like a supermodel yet, but pay attention to how you feel before, during and after your workouts. Your recovery rate (how long it takes you to get your breath back after a big effort) should be starting to improve, and you should be getting used to your healthy meal plan. In other words, you're well on your way to where you want to be. And that's just after one week. Imagine what permanent change is going to feel like. In the meantime (since you can't do a month's worth of work in one day), just keep on fighting through your comfort zone and the results will be that much sweeter: believe, achieve and succeed!

Good luck with today's workout. We will be pushing the pace, and your repetition time will be increased. Please keep yourself hydrated: Remember to drink six to eight glasses of water per day. Play safe and have fun.

TODAY'S WORKOUT

FOCUS	EQUIPMENT	REPETITIONS	SETS
A full-body HITZ blast.	Skipping rope, resistance band (RB), stability ball (SB), two pairs of 10- to 20-pound dumbbells (DBs), and a bench, step or dip bar.	Beginners, you're kicking it up to 30 seconds; intermediates, you're in for 50 seconds.	Crank it up to three sets today—get ready for a challenge.

HERE'S WHAT'S ON DECK:
Warmup
Dynamic Stretches
HITZ Resistance #4

· SKIPPING · RESISTANCE BAND SQUAT PRESSES
30-second rest.

· STABILITY BALL JACKNIFES · DUMBBELL CORE ROWING
30-second rest.

· SKIPPING · CORE WALKOUTS
45-second rest. One more batch to go before you're on to the second set.

· DUMBBELL ONE-LEG DEAD LIFTS · DIPS
Take 1-minute to rest and have some water. Then repeat!

Cool-Down
Static Stretches

WARMUP

Jump on a bike or treadmill for your 10-minute warmup. If you are training outdoors, then jog or bike.

For the first five minutes, work at an intensity of Level 4 on the PES. You should be sweating a little, but feeling good and able to carry on a conversation effortlessly.

For the last five minutes, work at an intensity of Level 5. You should be just above comfortable, sweating more but still able to talk easily.

DYNAMIC STRETCHES

After your warmup, get loose with the following three dynamic stretches:

DYNAMIC CHEST AND BICEP STRETCHES

1. Stand tall (shoulders back), with your feet shoulder width apart. Slowly move your arms out to the sides, slightly behind you, with your thumbs up (just like The Fonz).

2. As your arms go back, rotate your thumbs down and back until they are pointing to the wall behind you. Pause, then return to the starting position. You should feel this one in your chest and biceps.

Perform 5 repetitions.

DYNAMIC QUAD STRETCHES

1. Stand tall (shoulders back), with your feet shoulder width apart. Lift your left foot behind you and grab your ankle (or foot) with your left hand.

2. Gently push your left hip forward, while keeping a straight line with your body and maintaining your balance on your right heel. Hold for 3 seconds, then release your left ankle.

Repeat this sequence with your right leg. Perform 5 repetitions on each leg.

DYNAMIC SUMO SQUATS

1. Stand tall (shoulders back), with your feet close together. Take a large lateral step to the right and drop into a deep squat (think of a sumo wrestler). Pause, then return to the starting standing position.

2. Now take a large lateral step to the left and drop into a deep squat. Pause, then return to the starting position.

Perform 5 repetitions on each side.

OKAY, IT'S TIME TO GET AFTER IT AND GET YOU ONE DAY CLOSER TO YOUR ULTIMATE GOALS. GRAB SOME WATER AND GET GOING!

SKIPPING

"Adrian! . . . Adrian! . . ."

Okay, that was my *Rocky* bit. Is it possible to watch that movie and not want to skip? Well, there's a reason boxers work with the ropes: Skipping is a killer workout.

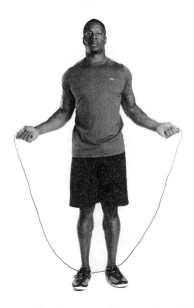 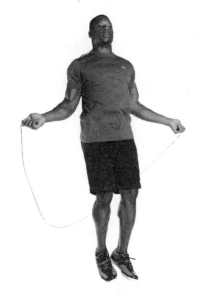

1. Place your skipping rope on the ground and stand in the middle of it. Grab the handles, which should reach about 6 inches below your collarbone when you pull the handles straight up.

2. Start to rotate the rope. The rotation should come from your wrists. To increase the speed of the rotations, increase the tightness of the circles that your wrists are making.

Skip for 1 minute if you're a beginner, 2 minutes if you're an intermediate.

RESISTANCE BAND SQUAT PRESSES

This is a full-body exercise; let your legs help you with the press. If you can't fully extend your arms, then go with a lighter or longer band.

1. Step in the middle of a medium-tension resistance band and straddle the RB with your feet. Stand tall and make sure that your feet are slightly wider than shoulder width.

2. Squat down (shoulders straight, butt pushing back as though you're aiming for a chair you can't see) and lift both handles of the RB to your shoulders, your palms facing forward.

 **30-SECOND REST**

3. Slowly stand up tall, while at the same time pressing both handles of the RB over your head. Pause, then return to a squat position.

Repeat this sequence for 30 seconds if you're a beginner, 50 seconds if you're an intermediate.

TOMMY TIP

In the bottom of your squat position, your thighs should be parallel to the floor (that is, your knees should be at a 90-degree angle). Keep 80% of your weight on your heels.

STABILITY BALL JACKKNIFES

Core, core, core! You want to lose that "Buddha belly"? Then the jackknife is for you. If you can't perform this one with perfect form, place your forearms on a bench.

1. Place your hands on the floor in push-up position.

2. Place one shin on a medium-sized SB. Now the other.

3. Engage your core and pull your knees up toward your chest. Pause, then return to the starting position.

Repeat this sequence for 30 seconds if you're a beginner, 50 seconds if you're an intermediate.

TOMMY TIP

Do not arch your back or let it sag. The tops of your feet should be in contact with the SB throughout the entire exercise.

DUMBBELL CORE ROWING

Now we get to have some fun . . . maybe me a little more than you. You will feel this one through your entire body. This exercise will make you think you really are in boot camp . . . well, guess what? You are!

1. Place two 10- to 20-pound dumbbells on a mat, shoulder width apart. Position yourself so that you are lying horizontal and face down.

2. Grab the handles of the DBs directly under your shoulders, and extend your arms so that they are straight and you are in the plank position. Keep your elbows as close to your sides as possible.

3. Engage your core, maintain a flat back (neutral spine) and row (pull) one dumbbell up toward your hip; you will be stabilizing your body with the other arm. Pause and repeat with your other arm.

Repeat this sequence for 30 seconds if you're a beginner, 50 seconds if you're an intermediate.

 **30-SECOND REST**

TOMMY TIP

To avoid tilting, form a wide base with your legs.

SKIPPING

You know the routine: Go get 'em!

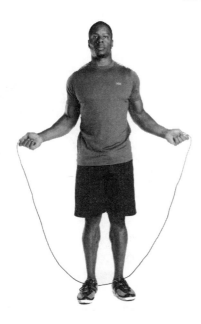 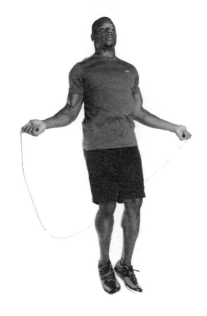

1. Place your skipping rope on the ground and stand in the middle of it. Grab the handles, which should reach about 6 inches below your collarbone when you pull the handles straight up.

2. Start to rotate the rope. The rotation should come from your wrists. To increase the speed of the rotations, increase the tightness of the circles that your wrists are making.

Skip for 1 minute if you're a beginner, 2 minutes if you're an intermediate.

CORE WALKOUTS

This is another compound exercise. The further you walk your hands, the more effective the exercise will be.
This is great for the upper body and core.

1. From a standing position, bend at your waist and knees while placing your hands on the floor in front of you. You should be on your toes with your butt high in the air. Beginners, you can start on your knees.

2. Without moving your feet, walk your hands out in front of you as far as you can while straightening your legs. Pause, making sure you keep your abs engaged.

3. Slowly walk your hands back to a push-up position and pause.

Repeat this sequence for 30 seconds if you're a beginner, 50 seconds if you're an intermediate.

NOW, REST FOR 30 SECONDS BEFORE MOVING ON TO . . .

TOMMY TIP

Do not arch your back or let it sag. Keep your body weight equally on your hands and your toes at all times.

DUMBBELL ONE-LEG DEAD LIFTS

You've conquered the dead lift already, so now we are going to challenge your balance a bit more—I know you're ready for it. Focus on your hamstrings and glutes on this one.

1. Stand tall, with your shoulders back, and hold a 10- to 15- pound DB in your left hand. Let your left leg hover above the ground, with your weight balanced on your right heel. Keep your leg as straight as possible, engage your core and keep your back flat.

2. Slowly bend at your hips to lower your body toward the ground, while letting the DB hang above your right foot.

3. Pause for 1 second, then return to your original standing position.

Repeat with the DB in your left hand for 30 seconds if you're a beginner, 50 seconds if you're an intermediate. Switch the DB into your right hand, standing on your left leg, with your right leg hovering above the ground, and repeat.

TOMMY TIP

Your core must be engaged and your back flat at all times throughout the exercise. The straighter you keep your supporting leg, the more you will work your hamstrings and glutes.

DIPS

Everyone I know wants nice, toned arms—how about you? The dip will give you exactly that. Concentrate on your triceps throughout the entire exercise, and don't try to speed through it. Savour the burn.
'Cause that's what it feels like to get nice arms.

1. Grab a dip bar, a bench or a chair and stand facing away from it. Lower yourself so that your hands are gripping the edge on either side of your hips. If you're on a chair or bench, let your butt hang off the edge, but don't let it get too far away from your equipment. If you're on a dip machine at the gym, this won't be something to worry about—just grab the handles and get ready.

2. Bend your elbows and slowly lower your body until your arms are at 90-degree angles.

3. Pause, then return to the starting position, ensuring that you move in a slow, controlled way.

Repeat this sequence for your allotted time: beginners, 30 seconds; intermediates, 50 seconds.

BOO-YAH! ONCE YOU'VE WORKED THROUGH ALL THAT, YOU'LL BE ONE SET DOWN. GET SOME WATER AND CHILL FOR 1 MINUTE. AFTER THE FIRST SET, MAKE SURE TO ASK YOURSELF (AND ANSWER HONESTLY): DID YOU PUSH YOURSELF THROUGH SET ONE? IF NOT, YOU HAVE TWO MORE CHANCES. AFTER THAT, THE DAY IS OVER. DO YOU UNDERSTAND WHAT I'M GETTING AT?

COOL-DOWN

It's time to cool down and reflect on the day. Are you happy with your performance? Are you sore? Winded? Good!

Time for a solid cool-down, though. Ten minutes will do . . . unless you want to get in a little bit of extra cardio!

STATIC STRETCHES

Once you've finished, it's time for you to do your four static stretches:

SPINAL TWISTS

1. Lie on the floor, with your arms extending outward in a T position. Put your right foot on your left knee.

2. Using your left hand, gently pull your right knee toward the floor, twisting your spine and keeping your left arm straight out, hips and shoulders on the floor. Hold for 30 seconds.

Repeat, using the right hand and left knee.

CHEST COMPLEX TRIPLE STRETCHES

1. For the first stretch, stand next to a wall or door frame. Extend one arm and bend at the elbow, so that your arm forms a right angle, with your upper arm parallel to the ground and your forearm sticking straight up. Place your forearm against the wall or door frame. Now, twist your whole body away from the wall, with a special emphasis on pushing your chest through the turn, so that you feel a gentle stretch in your chest. Hold this for 10 seconds.

2. For the next stretch, step away from the wall so that, instead of your forearm, only your hand is on the wall. The arm still forms a right angle from your body, but this time your hand and shoulder are at the same level. Make the same twist, pushing your chest into the turn, to stretch the chest in the new position. Hold this for 10 seconds.

3. For the third and final variation, step further from the wall and extend your arm straight, so that the entire arm is parallel to the ground. Place your hand on the wall, then twist again into the stretch. You should feel the tension in your chest. Hold this for 10 seconds.

Switch arms and repeat the sequence.

QUADRICEPS/HIP FLEXOR STRETCHES

1. Starting in a standing position, take a big step forward with your left leg, then place your right knee on the ground.

2. Maintaining this posture, shift the entire body slightly forward from the hip. You should feel this stretch down the front of your quad and hip flexor. Exhale and hold the stretch. Don't arch your back.

Hold for 30 seconds, then gently release and switch legs.

HAMSTRING STRETCHES

1. Lie down on your back, with a slight bend in both legs.

2. Lift your right leg straight up and grab it behind your calf. If you are flexible enough, grab your ankle (or even your toe). Gently pull your right leg toward you, keeping your back straight.

Hold the stretch for 30 seconds. Repeat with the left leg.

GREAT WORK TODAY. YOU'LL FIND THERE ARE ALWAYS HILLS TO CLIMB IN THE 10PS (JUST WAIT FOR TOMORROW), BUT YOUR BODY SHOULD BE ADJUSTING A BIT TO THE EFFORT. KEEP IT UP!

DAY 9 MEAL PLAN

How is the meal plan working for you? If you need to make any minor changes, such as substituting a food in the same group, then go for it. Here's your grub for the day:

BREAKFAST 3/4 cup low-fat yogurt; 1/4 cup granola; 1/4 cup All-Bran cereal; 1/2 cup grapes; 1-1/2 cups skim or soy milk.

SNACK 1 cup blueberries; 20 almonds.

LUNCH Salmon sandwich: Mix 2 oz. canned salmon with 1 tbsp. light mayonnaise, celery and onion; spread on 2 slices whole-wheat bread and garnish with lettuce and tomato. Serve with 1/2 cup baby carrots.

SNACK Granola bar.

DINNER Pork tenderloin: Marinate 4 oz. pork for 2 hours in 2 tbsp. each of lime juice, stir-fry sauce and reduced-sodium soy sauce, plus 1/2 tsp. fresh ginger (1/4 tsp. powdered). Serve with 1/2 cup corn or 1/2 cob (no butter!) and 2 cups mixed-green salad with 1 tbsp. light dressing. **Cook-ahead option:** Cook an extra 2 oz. of pork and set aside for tomorrow's lunch.

DAY 10
HITZ Cardio #3

TOMMY RULE #10: YOU WERE BLESSED WITH THE ABILITY TO BE PHYSICALLY ACTIVE—DON'T TAKE IT FOR GRANTED.

HITZ Cardio #3 is really gonna push you to the wall. You'll be on the treadmill today if you're indoors. If you're outdoors, you should also be running. I like to think of today's workout as the "ass kicker"—you will find out why very shortly. There are four separate challenges in today's session, so complete all the reps of each challenge and then move on to the next. The workout should take you about 30 minutes to complete. You are into your second week now, so you should be getting used to judging where you are on the Perceived Exertion Scale and working up accordingly—don't focus on speed or incline; just work strictly with the PES. And don't forget to get all of your water in (six to eight glasses per day), especially for these HITZ Cardio days.

TODAY'S WORKOUT

FOCUS	EQUIPMENT	TOTAL TIME
Pushing your boundaries.	Treadmill or good route to run.	About 30 minutes.

HERE'S YOUR NEW CHALLENGE:
Warmup · Dynamic Stretches · HITZ Cardio #3 · Cool-Down · Static Stretches

WARMUP

This is important, so let's focus. Get on a bike, rowing machine or whatever gets you going, and go for it. For 5 to 10 minutes, work at an intensity of Level 4 on the PES. You should be sweating a little, but feeling good and able to carry on a conversation effortlessly.

DYNAMIC STRETCHES

After your warmup, perform the following three dynamic stretches:

DYNAMIC GLUTE AND HAMSTRING STRETCHES

1. Stand tall (shoulders back), with your feet shoulder width apart. Lift up your left foot and grab just below your left knee with both hands.

2. With both hands, gently pull your left knee up, while maintaining your balance on your right heel. This will activate your butt and the backs of your legs. Hold for 3 seconds, then release your left leg.

Repeat this sequence with your right leg.
Perform 5 repetitions with each leg.

DYNAMIC QUAD STRETCHES

1. Stand tall (shoulders back), with your feet shoulder width apart. Lift your left foot behind you and grab your ankle (or foot) with your left hand.

2. Gently push your left hip forward, while keeping a straight line with your body and maintaining your balance on your right heel. Hold for 3 seconds, then release your left ankle.

**Repeat this sequence with your right leg.
Perform 5 repetitions on each leg.**

DYNAMIC SUMO SQUATS

1. Stand tall (shoulders back), with your feet close together. Take a large lateral step to the right and drop into a deep squat (think of a sumo wrestler). Pause, then return to the starting standing position.

2. Now take a large lateral step to the left and drop into a deep squat. Pause, then return to the starting position.

Perform 5 repetitions on each side.

HITZ CARDIO #3

Now it's time for HITZ Cardio #3. If for any reason you feel light-headed, please stop, collect yourself and then get back at it. Keep a towel and water close by. Have a drink between each of the four stages.

Here's how this works. The instructions are the same as your last two cardio workouts, but this time they're organized into sets. So you'll sprint for one minute, then walk for one minute, then repeat four more times before moving on to your next set—sprinting for 30 seconds then jogging for 30 seconds. Then onward like that, all the way through to your final minute at a PES of 7. Grab some water and take a one-minute break between sets. See you at the top!

Reps	Time	Description	Perceived Exertion Scale (PES)	Speed (mph)	Incline
		Set 1			
5	1 min. sprint	Gradually increase your speed (outdoors) or resistance (on a bike or elliptical) until you're working at an intense pace (70 to 80% of your maximum ability).	Level 7	5–7	0%
	1 min. walk	Gradually decrease your speed (outdoors) or resistance (on a bike or elliptical) until you're at a cruising pace (50% of your maximum ability). This is a level that you can do all day.	Level 4	3	0%
		Set 2			
5	30 sec. sprint	I want you to open it up on this one, going at about 80 to 85% of your maximum. Hang in there for 30 seconds.	Level 8	6–8	0%

Reps	Time	Description	Perceived Exertion Scale (PES)	Speed (mph)	Incline
	30 sec. jog/ walk	Gear down slowly and catch your breath, 'cause you're going again shortly.	Level 5	4	0%
	1 min. jog	Okay, this one starts off at about 60%, so pace yourself.	Level 6	3.5	10%
Set 3					
1	2 min. sprint	Giddyup! Time to move that thing. Maintain at 75-to-80% for two minutes. You should get winded.	Level 7–8	4.5	12%
	1 min. jog	Drop the intensity down just a little bit. You should be rolling at about 70%.	Level 7	5.5	5%
Set 4					
1	2 min. run	You're in the tail stretch, so if you're outdoors, running, biking, hiking or rowing, work at 70%, and use a hill if one is around.	Level 7	4	10%
	1 min. jog	Cruise for one minute—great set.	Level 6	5	0%

COOL-DOWN

Remember, you should be relatively comfortable. This cool-down is designed to slowly bring your heart rate back to normal, so go easy with it. Just 10 minutes.

STATIC STRETCHES

Now that you're cooled down, it's time for the following four stretches:

SPINAL TWISTS

1. Lie on the floor, with your arms extending outward in a T position. Put your right foot on your left knee.

2. Using your left hand, gently pull your right knee toward the floor, twisting your spine and keeping your left arm straight out, hips and shoulders on the floor. Hold for 30 seconds.

Repeat, using the right hand and left knee.

QUADRICEPS/HIP FLEXOR STRETCHES

1. Starting in a standing position, take a big step forward with your left leg, then place your right knee on the ground.

2. Maintaining this posture, shift the entire body slightly forward from the hip. You should feel this stretch down the front of your quad and hip flexor. Exhale and hold the stretch. Don't arch your back.

Hold for 30 seconds, then gently release and switch legs.

HAMSTRING STRETCHES

1. Lie down on your back, with a slight bend in both legs.

2. Lift your right leg straight up and grab it behind your calf. If you are flexible enough, grab your ankle (or even your toe). Gently pull your right leg toward you, keeping your back straight.

Hold the stretch for 30 seconds. Repeat with the left leg.

HIP STRETCHES

1. Lie down and cross your left foot over your right knee.

2. Clasp your hands behind your right knee. Gently pull your right leg toward you, keeping your back straight.

Hold the stretch for 30 seconds.
Repeat with the left leg.

THE EASIEST WAY TO RECOVER FROM A WORKOUT LIKE THAT IS TO REST AND REFUEL, SO IF YOU NEED TO TAKE A LITTLE BIT LONGER TO COOL DOWN, THEN SO BE IT. ONE THING ABOUT WORKING OUT IS THAT IT MAKES JUST RESTING AND BREATHING CALMLY THAT MUCH MORE ENJOYABLE . . . AM I RIGHT? TWO WEEKS AGO YOU COULDN'T HAVE HAD THIS PLEASURE.

IN ANY CASE, ONCE YOU'VE COOLED DOWN, IT'S TIME TO CHOW DOWN!

DAY 10 MEAL PLAN

You are what you eat, so keep up the great eating habits! You are paving the way to a healthy lifestyle. Your meal plan is stacked with fibre to brush your insides, and protein, fats and carbs to sustain you through the day. You may miss cheesies and soft drinks, but I promise you don't need them.

BREAKFAST 2 slices whole-grain toast with 2 tbsp. natural almond butter; 1 orange; 1-1/2 cups skim or soy milk.

SNACK 1 mango; 3/4 cup of low-fat yogurt.

LUNCH 2 oz. leftover pork tenderloin (sliced), fresh spinach, sliced red pepper and 2 tbsp. salsa, in 1 large whole-wheat wrap.

SNACK 1/3 cup hummus; 2 rye crackers; 1 cup grape tomatoes.

DINNER **BBQ chicken breast:** Grill 4 oz. chicken breast with BBQ sauce; 1/2 cup sweet potato (microwave or boil, then mash with 1 tsp. non-hydrogenated margarine or butter); 1-1/2 cups steamed broccoli and 1 tsp. olive oil. **Cook-ahead option:** Cook an extra chicken breast, an extra cup of sweet potato and an extra cup of steamed broccoli and put them aside for tomorrow's lunch.

DAY 11
HITZ Resistance #5

TOMMY RULE #11: PROPER EXECUTION OF THE PLAN WILL PROVIDE YOU WITH LIFELONG RESULTS!

I hope you enjoyed your HITZ Cardio yesterday. Even if you didn't, one thing I learned from sports is that, good or bad, you put your last performance behind you and move on. So now it's time to battle today's workout.

Have you been able to keep up with the pace? You are now starting to create healthy habits, so stay on course. You should be paying attention to how you are feeling, as well as to the time of day you do your workout. If you're feeling tired, try changing your routine a little. Some people are more energized in the morning, and some in the evening. With a bit of experimentation you should be able to figure out when you have the most energy and how your workout affects the rest of your day. Sleep is also an important element, so don't burn the candle at both ends. Your body needs to recharge in order for your workouts to be efficient and effective.

All right. No time like the present. Let's do this. By the end of it, you're going to feel like you climbed a mountain—you're going to be hurting all over, and feeling great. Now it's time for some work, so let's get to it!

TODAY'S WORKOUT

FOCUS	EQUIPMENT	REPETITIONS	SETS
You're gonna get a little bit of everything today, so put on your game face.	Stability ball (SB) and a pair of 5-, 10- and 15-pound dumbbells (DBs).	Beginners, you're staying strong at 30 seconds; intermediates, you're still in for 50 seconds.	Three sets today—but I know you're up for it.

HERE'S TODAY'S SWEATFEST:
Warmup
Dynamic Stretches
HITZ Resistance #5

• **HIGH-KNEE RUNNING** • **DUMBBELL SCAP SQUATS**
30-second rest.

• **SPIDERMAN PUSH-UPS** • **DUMBBELL CORE TWIST TAPS**
30-second rest . . . grab some water!

• **DUMBBELL LATERAL SIDE LUNGES** • **STABILITY BALL MOUNTAIN CLIMBERS**
30-second rest.

• **DUMBBELL STATIC ONE-ARM CURLS** • **STABILITY BALL ROLLOUTS**
Take 1 minute to rest and have some water. Then repeat!

Cool-Down
Static Stretches

WARMUP

Tomorrow's HITZ Cardio workout will involve skipping, so let's get you hooked on it by doing a five minute skipping warmup today! Do you have your watch ready? Go!

For the first minute, you can skip any style—if you don't have a skipping rope, use an imaginary rope.

For the second minute, you will skip with a double hop between rotations.

For the third minute, go back to any style.

For the last two minutes, it's double leg hops again.

DYNAMIC STRETCHES

After your five minute warmup, perform the following three dynamic stretches:

DYNAMIC QUAD STRETCHES

1. Stand tall (shoulders back), with your feet shoulder width apart. Lift your left foot behind you and grab your ankle (or foot) with your left hand.

2. Gently push your left hip forward, while keeping a straight line with your body and maintaining your balance on your right heel. Hold for 3 seconds, then release your left ankle.

**Repeat this sequence with your right leg.
Perform 5 repetitions on each leg.**

DYNAMIC CHEST AND BICEP STRETCHES

1. Stand tall (shoulders back), with your feet shoulder width apart. Slowly move your arms out to the sides, slightly behind you, with your thumbs up (just like The Fonz).

2. As your arms go back, rotate your thumbs down and back until they are pointing to the wall behind you. Pause, then return to the starting position. You should feel this one in your chest and biceps.

Perform 5 repetitions.

DYNAMIC SUMO SQUATS

1. Stand tall (shoulders back), with your feet close together. Take a large lateral step to the right and drop into a deep squat (think of a sumo wrestler). Pause, then return to the starting standing position.

2. Now take a large lateral step to the left and drop into a deep squat. Pause, then return to the starting position.

Perform 5 repetitions on each side.

HIGH-KNEE RUNNING

Are you getting tired of this one yet? Each time you do it, lift your knees as high as you can to maximize the core benefit as well.

1. Stand tall, with your feet shoulder width apart. Run on the spot, lifting your knees as high as possible and pumping your arms vigorously. Ideally, your knees will be coming up to waist height.

2. You must remain tall at all times. Do not slump.

Keep going for 30 seconds if you're a beginner, 50 seconds if you're an intermediate.

DUMBBELL SCAP SQUATS

The scap (scapula) squat is an exercise that will force you to engage your entire body. Along with the benefits from the squat, you will also experience an upper-body burn.

1. Stand tall, with your feet shoulder width apart, and hold a 5- to 10-pound DB in each hand, letting the DBs hang at your sides. Get into a half-squat position, keeping your weight balanced on your heels.

2. Tilt forward so that your upper body is at a 45-degree angle.

TAKE A 30-SECOND REST. THEN . . .

3. Extend and lift both arms behind you (holding the DBs) as high as you can. Then return to the starting position.

Keep your arms and core braced and squat continuously, all the way up, and then down, for your allotted time: beginners, 30 seconds; intermediates, 50 seconds.

TOMMY TIP

Do not use heavy dumbbells; 5 to 10 pounds will be plenty. Speed is not your friend on this one; think of taking 3 seconds to move down, then 2 seconds to move back to your standing position.

SPIDERMAN PUSH-UPS

This is your second crack at this exercise, so push yourself—you should notice a difference
compared with the first time that you did it.

1. Start in a push-up position, with your hands directly under your shoulders. Your head and hips should be neutral and in line with your toes (if you're still struggling a bit, try the push-ups from your knees until you get stronger).

2. Engage your core, and lift your right hand and place it 6 to 10 inches ahead of your left hand (while bending your elbows and lowering yourself to within a couple of inches of the ground), at the same time driving your left knee to the outside of your left arm. (Your hands should be staggered.)

3. Pause, then push your body up and return your right hand and left leg to the starting position. Repeat with your left hand and right knee.

Repeat this sequence for your allotted time: beginners, 30 seconds; intermediates, 50 seconds.

DUMBBELL CORE TWIST TAPS

It's time to reshape your midsection from saggy to toned, and to do it we are going to attack the oblique muscles.

This twisting motion will help give you the definition that your abdominals have been clamouring for!

1. Sit on a mat, with your feet out in front of you. Hold a 10- to 20-pound DB with both hands.

2. Bend your knees and lift both feet off the ground (beginners can start with both feet on the ground).

3. Twist your arms to the left and tap the DB on the ground (beside your left hip). Pause, then repeat on the right side.

Repeat this sequence for your allotted time: beginners, 30 seconds; intermediates, 50 seconds.

TIME FOR ANOTHER 30-SECOND BREAK FOR REST AND WATER.

TOMMY TIP

Your core must be engaged throughout the entire movement. Avoid swinging your legs from side to side.

DUMBBELL LATERAL SIDE LUNGES

This is a great exercise for your legs, butt and hips. It will make you stronger and help define your lower half.

1. Standing tall, with your feet shoulder width apart, cup your hands and hold a 15- to 30-pound DB between your legs.

2. With your left leg, take a large lateral (sideways) step as far as you can to the left—you need to bend your left knee while keeping your right leg straight.

3. Pause, then push off from your left foot to your original standing position. Repeat the same action to the right.

Alternate from side to side for your allotted time: beginners, 30 seconds; intermediates, 50 seconds.

TOMMY TIP

Keep your head up and your back straight at all times. Your shoulders should remain squared at all times. To make the exercise a little harder, power up as hard and fast as you can once your foot hits the ground.

STABILITY BALL MOUNTAIN CLIMBERS

See, I told you we were going to climb a mountain today. This exercise is a great one for really challenging your core while shredding your abdominals. Sound like fun?

1. Place both hands on an SB, with your thumbs facing forward (your hands must be directly under your shoulders).

2. Walk both feet back so that you are in a prone (push-up) position. Keep your body in a straight line at all times, with your head neutral.

3. Brace your abs and drive your right knee toward your chest. Pause, then return your right foot toward the ground and repeat with your left leg.

Alternate sides for your allotted time: beginners, 30 seconds; intermediates, 50 seconds.

 **30-SECOND REST**

TOMMY TIP

Do not let your hips sag or rotate. You must make sure that your body weight is directly over the ball; otherwise, the SB will fly out from under you. If you can't do it on an SB, then place your hands on a bench.

DUMBBELL STATIC ONE-ARM CURLS

It's time to work the pipes and get those arms in tip-top shape. You will be going double duty with this exercise, so you will not need too much weight.

1. Hold two 15- to 20-pound DBs at your side while standing tall, with your feet shoulder width apart.

2. Lift the DB in your left hand, bending your arm until it's at a 90-degree angle (hold that position). Then lift your left leg up with your knee bent (also at a 90-degree angle).

3. Curl the DB in your right hand up toward your shoulder and then slowly lower it back down.

Repeat for 30 seconds if you're a beginner, 50 seconds if you're an intermediate. Then switch sides. (That is, hold your right hand and right leg at a 90-degree angle, then curl the DB with your left hand.)

TOMMY TIP

This is a burner, but if you could not continue to curl for your required time, use a lighter dumbbell on your next set. If it was easy for you, step up to the challenge and use a heavier dumbbell.

STABILITY BALL ROLLOUTS

You're gonna love this one . . . well, at least you'll love the results. It will get you ready for bathing-suit season by making your stomach rock-hard.

1. Grab an SB and place your forearms on top of it, with your hands clasped. Extend your legs back, so that you are on your toes. Keep your body in a straight line at all times.

2. Push your elbows forward so that the SB is rolled away from your body.

3. Pause, then return to the starting position. The only things that should be moving are your arms; do not rock your body.

Repeat for your allotted time: beginners, 30 seconds; intermediates, 50 seconds.

CONGRATULATIONS, THAT'S ONE SET DOWN. ARE YOU FEELING UNSTOPPABLE YET? WELL, HOPEFULLY BY THE END OF TODAY YOU WILL. GET SOME WATER. YOU HAVE A 1-MINUTE BREAK BEFORE YOU REPEAT THE CIRCUIT TWO MORE TIMES. HANG IN THERE—YOU CAN DO IT!

TOMMY TIP

Beginners can kneel on a mat and perform the same movement. Keep your body rigid.

COOL-DOWN

I hope you didn't make too much of a mess. Breathe in . . . breathe out . . . time for your cool-down! Pick the cardio of your choice—it can be a walk, ride or whatever your heart desires.

STATIC STRETCHES

Once you have finished your 10-minute cool-down, perform the following four static stretches:

HAMSTRING STRETCHES

1. Lie down on your back, with a slight bend in both legs.

2. Lift your right leg straight up and grab it behind your calf. If you are flexible enough, grab your ankle (or even your toe). Gently pull your right leg toward you, keeping your back straight.

Hold the stretch for 30 seconds. Repeat with the left leg.

SPINAL TWISTS

1. Lie on the floor, with your arms extending outward in a T position. Put your right foot on your left knee.

2. Using your left hand, gently pull your right knee toward the floor, twisting your spine and keeping your left arm straight out, hips and shoulders on the floor. Hold for 30 seconds.

Repeat, using the right hand and left knee.

QUADRICEPS/HIP FLEXOR STRETCHES

1. Starting in a standing position, take a big step forward with your left leg, then place your right knee on the ground.

2. Maintaining this posture, shift the entire body slightly forward from the hip. You should feel this stretch down the front of your quad and hip flexor. Exhale and hold the stretch. Don't arch your back.

Hold for 30 seconds, then gently release and switch legs.

REMEMBER WHAT I SAID AT THE BEGINNING OF TODAY'S CHAPTER: YOU NEED YOUR SLEEP TO REALLY PERFORM. SO REST UP, BECAUSE I'VE GOT A BIG DAY PLANNED FOR YOU TOMORROW.

CHEST COMPLEX TRIPLE STRETCHES

1. For the first stretch, stand next to a wall or door frame. Extend one arm and bend at the elbow, so that your arm forms a right angle, with your upper arm parallel to the ground and your forearm sticking straight up. Place your forearm against the wall or door frame. Now, twist your whole body away from the wall, with a special emphasis on pushing your chest through the turn, so that you feel a gentle stretch in your chest. Hold this for 10 seconds.

2. For the next stretch, step away from the wall so that, instead of your forearm, only your hand is on the wall. The arm still forms a right angle from your body, but this time your hand and shoulder are at the same level. Make the same twist, pushing your chest into the turn, to stretch the chest in the new position. Hold this for 10 seconds.

3. For the third and final variation, step further from the wall and extend your arm straight, so that the entire arm is parallel to the ground. Place your hand on the wall, then twist again into the stretch. You should feel the tension in your chest. Hold this for 10 seconds.

Switch arms and repeat this sequence.

DAY 11 MEAL PLAN

You've been battling for days now. How are you doing? Don't forget that, along with your daily meals, you should be consuming six to eight glasses of water every day. You need that water!

BREAKFAST 1 whole-wheat English muffin with 1 scrambled egg (cooked with 1 tsp. non-hydrogenated margarine); 1/2 cup strawberries, 1-1/2 cups skim or soy milk.

SNACK 1 banana; 3/4 cup low-fat yogurt.

LUNCH 4 oz. BBQ chicken breast leftovers; 1 cup mashed sweet potato; 1 cup broccoli.

SNACK Granola bar; 20 almonds.

DINNER Large salad: 2 cups mixed greens with cucumber, tomato, red onion, mushrooms and whatever other veggies you'd like, tossed with 1/2 cup croutons, 1 oz. feta cheese, 2 tbsp. dried cranberries, 1/3 cup chick peas (canned ones are just fine, but try to buy a brand with no added salt—if you can't find those, just make sure to rinse well) and 2 tbsp. light dressing.

DAY 12
HITZ Cardio #4

TOMMY RULE #12: YOU CAN, YOU BETTER, YOU WILL!

And on the 12th day, you skip!

You got a little taste of the rope yesterday, but today we are going to get those feet moving and that heart pumping. Skipping is one of the best forms of cardio, yet not many people do it. I suppose there is a reason for that: It's hard. But we don't shy away from challenges, do we? We are not afraid of a little rope . . . we embrace the challenge to bring out the inner athlete in all of us.

I have heard it countless times from clients: "I haven't skipped since I was a kid." Well, today school is in session and we are going to burn a gang of calories. With today's workout, you will burn somewhere between 400 and 700 calories, plus you'll get a great cardio workout and tone your shoulders, arms and calves. I didn't say you were gonna love it, but I will promise you that you will love the results.

The best athletes in the world all follow some sort of skipping program because it promotes coordination between your hands and feet, increases your stamina and endurance, improves your reflexes and foot speed, and aids in achieving a flat stomach. Do you need any more convincing? I didn't think so, so let's get on with it. Eye of the tiger!

TODAY'S WORKOUT

FOCUS	EQUIPMENT	TOTAL TIME
Harness your inner Rocky—and push yourself harder than you thought you could.	Skipping rope—or just a spot where you can jump.	About 35 (crazy intense) minutes.

HERE'S WHAT'S ON DECK:
Warmup
Dynamic Stretches
HITZ Cardio #4
Cool-Down
Static Stretches

WARMUP

For 15 minutes, I want you to either jog or bike, working at a PES intensity of Level 5—just above comfortable, sweating, but still able to talk easily.

DYNAMIC STRETCHES

Once you're ready to go, perform the following four dynamic stretches:

DYNAMIC GLUTE AND HAMSTRING STRETCHES

1. Stand tall (shoulders back), with your feet shoulder width apart. Lift your left foot and grab just below your left knee with both hands.

2. With both hands, gently pull your left knee up, while maintaining your balance on your right heel. This will activate your butt and the backs of your legs. Hold for 3 seconds, then release your left leg.

Repeat this sequence with your right leg. Perform 5 repetitions with each leg.

DYNAMIC QUAD STRETCHES

1. Stand tall (shoulders back), with your feet shoulder width apart. Lift your left foot behind you and grab your ankle (or foot) with your left hand.

2. Gently push your left hip forward, while keeping a straight line with your body and maintaining your balance on your right heel. Hold for 3 seconds, then release your left ankle.

Repeat this sequence with your right leg. Perform 5 repetitions on each leg.

DYNAMIC SUMO SQUATS

1. Stand tall (shoulders back), with your feet close together. Take a large lateral step to the right and drop into a deep squat (think of a sumo wrestler). Pause, then return to the starting standing position.

2. Now take a large lateral step to the left and drop into a deep squat. Pause, then return to the starting position.

Perform 5 repetitions on each side.

DYNAMIC CHEST AND BICEP STRETCHES

1. Stand tall (shoulders back), with your feet shoulder width apart. Slowly move your arms out to the sides, slightly behind you, with your thumbs up (just like The Fonz).

2. As your arms go back, rotate your thumbs down and back until they are pointing to the wall behind you. Pause, then return to the starting position. You should feel this one in your chest and biceps.

Perform 10 repetitions.

HITZ CARDIO #4

Warm? Ready? Get some water and get ready to have some fun. Remember, a rep is a full turn (rotation) of the rope. We're going to do two full repetitions of the set below. Go all the way through, then take a 2-minute break after the first set of 11 moves. Then do it all over again! *GO!*

Double Bounce	20 Reps
Single Bounce	20 Reps
Speed Single Bounce	20 Reps
One-Foot Single Bounce	20 Right, 20 Left
Straddle	20 Reps
Front and Back	20 Reps
Side to Side	20 Reps
Heel–Toe	20 Reps
Crossover	20 Reps
Double Jump	20 Reps
Speed Single Bounce	100 Reps

Double Bounce: Bounce twice per turn of the rope, feet together.

Single Bounce: Bounce once per rope turn, feet together.

Speed Single Bounce: Perform single bounce at a rapid pace.

One-Foot Single Bounce: Perform a single bounce on one foot, alternating feet at each turn.

Straddle: Place feet together on first turn, spread legs on second—almost like you're doing jumping jacks inside the rope.

Front and Back: Bounce once at each rope turn, hopping forward with both feet on the first turn, then backward on the next turn.

Side to Side: Bounce once at each rope turn, hopping left with both feet on the first turn, then right with both feet on the next turn.

Heel–Toe: Bounce once at each rope turn, alternating heels so that the toe of the opposite foot makes contact with the ground at the same time. You land with your right heel and left toe touching the ground, then with your left heel and right toe.

Crossover: Start with a single bounce, then cross elbows on the second turn. This causes the rope to crisscross, so jump through the loop.

Double Jump: Turn the rope twice on a single bounce—you're going to have to bend at the hips.

All done? How was it? Did it bring back any fond memories, or was it more like a nightmare? You've probably whipped yourself a few times, but don't despair, the next time we do this you will be better!

COOL-DOWN

Now cool down, rest up and get ready to do HITZ Resistance #6 tomorrow. Oh yeah, baby! Do a nice, easy 10-minute cool-down, then grab some water.

STATIC STRETCHES

Better? Good, but you're not off the hook yet. Now perform the following four stretches:

HAMSTRING STRETCHES

1. Lie down on your back, with a slight bend in both legs.

2. Lift your right leg straight up and grab it behind your calf. If you are flexible enough, grab your ankle (or even your toe). Gently pull your right leg toward you, keeping your back straight.

Hold the stretch for 30 seconds. Repeat with the left leg.

SPINAL TWISTS

1. Lie on the floor, with your arms extending outward in a T position. Put your right foot on your left knee.

2. Using your left hand, gently pull your right knee toward the floor, twisting your spine and keeping your left arm straight out, hips and shoulders on the floor. Hold for 30 seconds.

Repeat, using the right hand and left knee.

QUADRICEPS/HIP FLEXOR STRETCHES

1. Starting in a standing position, take a big step forward with your left leg, then place your right knee on the ground.

2. Maintaining this posture, shift the entire body slightly forward from the hip. You should feel this stretch down the front of your quad and hip flexor. Exhale and hold the stretch. Don't arch your back.

Hold for 30 seconds, then gently release and switch legs.

IF YOU FOLLOW THE MEAL PLAN AND WORK HARD AT THE FITNESS PLAN, YOU *WILL* GET POSITIVE RESULTS. IF YOU'VE SOMEHOW FALLEN OFF THE WAGON, GET BACK UP ON IT AND STAY WITH IT. TOMORROW IS A NEW DAY—SEE YOU THEN!

CHEST COMPLEX TRIPLE STRETCHES

1. For the first stretch, stand next to a wall or door frame. Extend one arm and bend at the elbow, so that your arm forms a right angle, with your upper arm parallel to the ground and your forearm sticking straight up. Place your forearm against the wall or door frame. Now, twist your whole body away from the wall, with a special emphasis on pushing your chest through the turn, so that you feel a gentle stretch in your chest. Hold this for 10 seconds.

2. For the next stretch, step away from the wall so that, instead of your forearm, only your hand is on the wall. The arm still forms a right angle from your body, but this time your hand and shoulder are at the same level. Make the same twist, pushing your chest into the turn, to stretch the chest in the new position. Hold this for 10 seconds.

3. For the third and final variation, step further from the wall and extend your arm straight, so that the entire arm is parallel to the ground. Place your hand on the wall, then twist again into the stretch. You should feel the tension in your chest. Hold this for 10 seconds.

Switch arms and repeat this sequence.

DAY 12 MEAL PLAN

And now . . . your food.

BREAKFAST Oatmeal (1/2 cup raw, cooked with water) and 1/4 cup dried cranberries; 1/4 cup low-fat cottage cheese; 1-1/2 cups skim or soy milk.

SNACK 1 cup grapes; 10 almonds.

LUNCH Grilled ham and cheese sandwich: 2 slices whole-grain bread, 1 oz. part-skim mozzarella cheese, 2 slices lean ham, 2 tsp. margarine. Assemble the sandwich with the ham and cheese in the middle, then spread the margarine on the outside faces of the sandwich. Grill on each side until toasty brown.

SNACK 1/3 cup hummus, 2 rye crackers, and 1 cup of sliced red peppers.

DINNER Honey-lemon salmon: Broil 4 oz. salmon with lemon juice, 1/2 tsp. honey and 1 tsp. olive oil. Serve with 1/2 cup brown rice and 1-1/2 cups steamed green beans.

DAY 13
HITZ Resistance #6

TOMMY RULE #13: DON'T TALK ABOUT IT . . . *BE* ABOUT IT.

How are we feeling today? You are well on your way to building a better, stronger and healthier body, so you should be feeling great . . . maybe a little sore, but still great!

At this point, you should be in the groove of things and starting to notice concrete changes in your body—maybe your jeans are a little loose, maybe the buttons on your shirts sit a little flatter—provided that you are putting in the work, of course. Each and every day, you should be pushing the pace more and more. Your recovery rate should also be improving, which will make the next day that much easier to conquer. Next week, the workouts will continue to progress, repetition times will increase, and you'll be two weeks closer to your goal. Now it's workout time, so let's buckle down and get after it!

TODAY'S WORKOUT

FOCUS	EQUIPMENT	REPETITIONS	SETS
A core-intensive upper-body overhaul.	A pair of 10-, 12- and 15-pound dumbbells (DBs) and a bar for pull-ups.	Beginners, you've got 30 seconds; intermediates, 50.	Today you'll do three sets again—with a special bonus exercise at the end of your third set. Lucky you!

HERE'S WHAT'S ON THE MENU:
Warmup
Dynamic Stretches
HITZ Resistance #6

• BURPEE PUSH-UPS • DUMBBELL HEEL-TO-TOE CHOPS
30-second rest.

• PULL-UPS OR DUMBBELL ROWING • SKATERS
30-second rest . . . grab some water!

• DUMBBELL LUNGE SHOULDER PRESSES • CORE SLIDERS
30-second rest.

• CORE SCISSORS • FLOOR TRICEPS EXTENSIONS
Hydrate, mentally refresh and get ready to roll in 1 minute. And as another special treat, let's throw in a **CORE PLANK** as the last exercise of the third set.

Cool-Down
Static Stretches

WARMUP

Jump on a bike or treadmill for your 10-minute warmup. If you are training outdoors, you should be jogging or riding a bike.

For the first five minutes, work at an intensity of Level 4 on the PES. You should be sweating a little, but feeling good and able to carry on a conversation effortlessly.

For the last five minutes, work at an intensity of Level 5. You should be just above comfortable, sweating more but still able to talk easily.

DYNAMIC STRETCHES

After your 10-minute warmup, perform the following four dynamic stretches:

DYNAMIC QUAD STRETCHES

1. Stand tall (shoulders back), with your feet shoulder width apart. Lift your left foot behind you and grab your ankle (or foot) with your left hand.

2. Gently push your left hip forward, while keeping a straight line with your body and maintaining your balance on your right heel. Hold for 3 seconds, then release your left ankle.

Repeat the same sequence with your right leg. Perform 5 repetitions on each leg.

DYNAMIC CHEST AND BICEP STRETCHES

1. Stand tall (shoulders back), with your feet shoulder width apart. Slowly move your arms out to the sides, slightly behind you, with your thumbs up (just like The Fonz).

2. As your arms go back, rotate your thumbs down and back until they are pointing to the wall behind you. Pause, then return to the starting position. You should feel this one in your chest and biceps.

Perform 10 repetitions.

DYNAMIC SUMO SQUATS

1. Stand tall (shoulders back), with your feet close together. Take a large lateral step to the right and drop into a deep squat (think of a sumo wrestler). Pause, then return to the starting standing position.

2. Now take a large lateral step to the left and drop into a deep squat. Pause, then return to the starting position.

Perform 5 repetitions on each side.

DYNAMIC BACK SWINGS

1. Stand tall (shoulders back), with your feet shoulder width apart. Lift and hold both arms up to the side at shoulder height. Twist as far as you can to the right, so that you can feel a good stretch in your mid- to lower back.

2. Pause, then twist to the left (you should resemble a propeller as you twist).

Repeat for 10 revolutions.

ALL RIGHT, NOW. READY TO SHRED? ALL WARMED UP? YOUR MUSCLES BEGGING FOR SOME HARD WORK? WELL, I'M SERVING UP EXACTLY WHAT THEY WANT.

BURPEE PUSH-UPS

We are stepping up the burpee today and adding a push-up to it. Go as fast as you can on this one, but maintain proper form.

1. Stand tall, with your feet shoulder width apart. Bend at your knees and waist, while placing both hands on the floor.

2. Step (beginner) or thrust (intermediate) both feet back so you are in a push-up position.

3. Perform 1 push-up, then kick both feet back in with tucked knees, stand up (beginner) or jump (intermediate).

Repeat this sequence for your allotted time. Beginners, you're going for 30 seconds; intermediates, you're going for 50.

TOMMY TIP

When you kick your feet back and perform a push-up, do not let your back sag! And remember that breathing is essential.

DUMBBELL HEEL-TO-TOE CHOPS

Operation "core"! This is a ballistic movement that will require some coordination. It is literally a heel-to-toe movement. Perfect practice makes perfect!

1. Stand tall, with your feet shoulder width apart. Cup your hands and hold a 15- to 20-pound DB between your legs. Keep your arms straight and bend your knees into a squat position.

2. Now "explode" to a standing position, while at the same time bringing your arms directly over your head. As the DB comes over your head, your arms should be straight and you should be on your toes. Drop your arms and return to the squat position, with your weight on your heels.

Repeat this sequence for your allotted time: beginners, you're going for 30 seconds; intermediates, 50.

 **30-SECOND REST**

TOMMY TIP

Start with a lighter weight and engage your core. The DB should be directly overhead, not behind you.

PULL-UPS

When they say you have to pull your weight, you'd better hope they're not talking about pull-ups, because I can guarantee you won't be able to do many of these . . . at least at first. This is one of the tougher exercises you will ever have to do. But it will also pay big dividends by working your entire upper back and arms. If you don't have a bar, do the dumbbell rows on the next page, instead.

1. Set a bar at about hip height. If you're in the gym, you can use a Smith machine, squat rack or other bar. If you're not in a gym, you can use a bar stretched between two chairs, like I did! Lie down on your back so that the bar is directly above your chest.

2. Extend your legs (bent knees for beginners, straight legs for intermediates). Grab the bar using an overhand grip that is slightly wider than shoulder width.

3. Focus on your upper back/lats and row (pull) your body up to the top position (the bar should graze your chest). Pause, then return to the starting position.

Repeat this sequence for your allotted time. Beginners, you're going for 30 seconds; intermediates, you're going for 50.

TOMMY TIP

Do not to use any momentum to get your body up—focus on your lats!

DUMBBELL ROWING

If you don't have a bar, you don't get a free pass on pull-ups—dumbbell rowing for you, instead!

This is how you get a sexy V-shaped back.

1. Stand up straight, holding a pair of 10- to 20-pound dumbbells in your hands. Brace your abdominals and slightly bend your knees (20 degrees). In your half-squat position, bend at the waist to a 45-degree angle. Now you're leaning forward, with your legs slightly bent.

2. Keep your elbows tight to your body and, with a rowing motion, lift both DBs up to your hips. As you pull, think of pulling with your back (lats) instead of your biceps.

3. As the DBs reach slightly above your hips (your elbows should be at a 90-degree angle), pause for 1 second, then return to the starting position. Maintain a constant speed (2 seconds pulling the weight up, pause, 2 seconds bringing the weight down) thoughout your repetition time. No jerking or heaving.

Beginners, you're up for 30 seconds; intermediates, you've got 50 on tap.

TOMMY TIP

Always keep your back flat. You will have the urge to round it as you fatigue, but be strong and stay strong! This is not a race—focus on your upper back and keep your core engaged throughout the exercise. It's not just about your muscles; you're using your mind too.

SKATERS

This is your second time doing this exercise, so try and push yourself. Increase the distance travelled with each jump, and you will make the exercise more effective.

1. Stand tall on your (slightly bent) right leg, with your left foot hovering above the ground. Keep your head and chest up.

2. Push off your right foot and jump laterally (sideways) as far as you can to your left foot. Avoid letting the other foot touch as you jump across.

3. Pause, then jump back across to your right foot.

This is a continuous-movement exercise that you must maintain for your allotted time: beginners, 30 seconds; intermediates, 50 seconds. Keep going!

PHEW! TAKE A 30-SECOND REST, GRAB SOME WATER AND GET READY TO GO AGAIN!

DUMBBELL LUNGE SHOULDER PRESSES

The way to make your workouts more effective is to work as many muscle groups as possible. Well, this one definitely fits the bill! You will be working your quads, hamstrings, lower back, core, shoulders and stabilizing muscles. Just talking about it is making me tired. But we're not here to talk, so let's get to work now.

1. Stand tall, with your feet shoulder width apart, holding a 10- to 20-pound DB in each hand at shoulder height.

2. Take a large lunge step forward with your right leg until your right thigh is parallel to the ground, while at the same time pressing both DBs over your head.

3. Push off your right heel, return to the standing position and bring the weights back down to your shoulders.

Repeat the action with your left leg. Continue to alternate legs for your allotted time. Beginners, you're going for 30 seconds; intermediates, you're going for 50.

TOMMY TIP

Ensure that your weight is supported on the heel of your front foot. Keep your spine in a neutral position. Do not let the DBs drop below shoulder height.

CORE SLIDERS

Time to hit the "muffin top" or "spare tire," you know what I mean? You should feel your sides cringe with each crunch.

1. Lie on your back, with your feet on the ground and your knees bent. Put your hands flat by your sides and raise your head 3 inches or so off the ground, while looking up toward the ceiling.

2. Keep both hands in contact with the mat at all times, and reach and slide your left hand forward toward a spot between your feet. Make sure you slide far enough to challenge yourself.

3. Pause and repeat the slide with your right hand.

Follow the same action for 30 seconds if you're a beginner, 50 if you're an intermediate.

 **30-SECOND REST**

CORE SCISSORS

This is a two-part action, and it is *not* easy. You will really feel this one in your obliques, hips and lower back.

Keep it up, and you'll be "skinny in the waist."

1. Lie down on your right side, with your weight balanced on your right hip and elbow. Keep your legs straight and push your butt back so that you make a V with your body.

2. Lift your left leg up as high as you can and hold it there. Then lift your right leg so that your right thigh hovers above the ground, and hold it there.

3. Now mimic the movement of a pair of scissors and bring both your legs together.

Repeat for 15 seconds if you're a beginner, 30 if you're an intermediate, then switch sides and repeat the sequence, lying on your left hip.

TOMMY TIP

Keep your weight focused on your elbow and hip! This movement should be performed at a slow and controlled pace.

FLOOR TRICEPS EXTENSIONS

Time to make those arms earn their keep. Your triceps will be burning after this one, for sure.

1. Lie down on your left side, with your knees bent. Place your right hand flat on the ground, in front of your belly button, and your left hand on top of your right triceps.

2. Push through your right hand and extend your body until your right arm is straight.

3. Pause, then lower your body back toward the ground—but don't touch the ground!

Beginners, repeat for 30 seconds; intermediates, it's 50 seconds for you. Then switch sides, working on your left triceps.

THAT COMPLETES THE SET. TAKE 1 MINUTE TO HYDRATE AND TO GET MENTALLY REFRESHED AND READY FOR THE NEXT ONE. AFTER YOUR THIRD SET, DON'T FORGET THERE'S ONE MORE ITEM ON YOUR "TO DO" LIST . . .

TOMMY TIP

Keep your knees pinned together and do not let your body touch the ground.

CORE PLANK

Challenge yourself and notice the difference the second time around.

1. Begin on all fours (hands and knees) on a mat.

2. Extend your legs so that your entire body is flat, in a straight-arm plank position, then go down to your forearms.

3. Raise your hips so that your body is in a straight line and your weight is on your elbows and toes. Beginners, you may need to be on your knees. That's fine for now—just ensure that your hips are down, with your core engaged and back flat. This should be hard work.

Hold the plank position for up to 1 minute. You have only a single set of this one, so challenge yourself.

TOMMY TIP

Do not let your lower back become rounded. As you continue to contract your core, you must remember to breathe. If you are an intermediate exerciser, use an SB.

COOL-DOWN

Woo-hoo! You've completed your second week of HITZ Resistance. Over the next two days, think about how far you've come and the benefits that are going to follow. Take your time now to cool down and reflect on the workout. Your cool-down today can be done on a treadmill, bike or elliptical machine or something similar outdoors. Let's go! Just 10 minutes.

STATIC STRETCHES

Once you're done, perform the following four stretches:

SPINAL TWISTS

1. Lie on the floor, with your arms extending outward in a T position. Put your right foot on your left knee.

2. Using your left hand, gently pull your right knee toward the floor, twisting your spine and keeping your left arm straight out, hips and shoulders on the floor. Hold for 30 seconds.

Repeat, using the right hand and left knee.

QUADRICEPS/HIP FLEXOR STRETCHES

1. Starting in a standing position, take a big step forward with your left leg, then place your right knee on the ground.

2. Maintaining this posture, shift the entire body slightly forward from the hip. You should feel this stretch down the front of your quad and hip flexor. Exhale and hold the stretch. Don't arch your back.

Hold for 30 seconds, then gently release and switch legs.

HAMSTRING STRETCHES

1. Lie down on your back, with a slight bend in both legs.

2. Lift your right leg straight up and grab it behind your calf. If you are flexible enough, grab your ankle (or even a toe). Gently pull your right leg toward you, keeping your back straight.

Hold the stretch for 30 seconds. Repeat with the left leg.

HIP STRETCHES

1. Lie down and cross your left foot over your right knee.

2. Clasp your hands behind your right knee. Gently pull your right leg toward you, keeping your back straight.

**Hold the stretch for 30 seconds.
Repeat with the left leg.**

DON'T FORGET TO GIVE YOURSELF THE CREDIT YOU'RE DUE FOR ALL OF THE HARD WORK YOU'VE PUT IN SO FAR. TWELVE DAYS OF WORKOUTS IS NOTHING TO SNIFF AT, SO BE AS PROUD OF YOURSELF AS I AM OF YOU—BUT DON'T LET THAT BE AN EXCUSE TO SLACK. ONWARD WE GO! I HOPE YOU ENJOY THE VARIETY OF EXERCISES. JUST WAIT—IT'S GONNA GET EVEN BETTER.

DAY 13 MEAL PLAN

Feel like a big, greasy pork sandwich with a side of fries dripping with liquefied lard? I didn't think so. Your cravings should be changing as the 10PS progresses. So stick with the plan—it works. And don't forget your six to eight glasses of water per day, either.

BREAKFAST 2 slices whole-grain toast with 2 tbsp. natural peanut butter; 1 banana; 1-1/2 cups skim or soy milk.

SNACK 1 orange; 3/4 cup low-fat yogurt.

LUNCH 1 cup split pea or minestrone soup; 3 rye crackers spread with 2 oz. light canned tuna (mixed with 1 tbsp. light mayonnaise, celery and onion).

SNACK 1/2 cup edamame.

DINNER Chicken fajita: Stir-fry 4 oz. chicken breast in 1 tsp. olive oil. Once it's cooked, add 1 cup sliced peppers and onion and cook until tender. Serve in 1 large whole-wheat fajita with 3 tbsp. salsa. **Cook-ahead option:** Cook an extra 3 oz. of chicken breast and remove from the pan before you add the peppers and onion. Set aside for tomorrow's lunch.

DAY 14
Motivation Day!

TOMMY RULE #14: THE ONLY THING THAT YOU CAN CHANGE IS WHAT YOU'RE ABOUT TO DO, SO MAKE THE CHOICE THAT BEST ALIGNS WITH YOUR GOAL.

You've made it to Day 14—and that means you're two-thirds of the way to a whole new way of living your life. It takes 21 days to build a habit that sticks. Aren't three weeks a small price to pay for creating a healthy lifestyle change? Well, you're nearly there already.

Maybe this process doesn't seem as though it's going fast enough. If that's the case, I'd say hey, let's not get impatient—yet. Four weeks is barely even a moment compared with the time it took you to put on the weight. And 14 days? That's nothing. In any case, we'll get to the bottom of this tomorrow.

Today, though, I want to share another success story with you. It comes from a guy who underestimated what the 10PS was going to require of him when he signed up. At the beginning, my man thought everything was going to be a cakewalk—he found out rather quickly that he was going to have to sweat his way back to a healthy lifestyle. To his credit, he manned up and got down to business!

His name was Ari, and I had a lot of fun with him along the way. Over the past year, I've bumped into him a few times, and he still looks great, having lost even more weight by keeping active and eating right. (Sounds so simple, doesn't it?) Still, it took him some real effort and willpower to get there. Like Ari, you're probably finding that this process has its peaks and valleys. So, like him, you have to keep the momentum going, because if you do, it will work. Each day, you have the opportunity to hit the Reset button and tackle the challenges in front of you. Because guess what: There are always going to be challenges in front of you, so you might as well figure out how to overcome them.

You must continue to maintain a positive attitude and build on your healthy habits, using the tools in the 10PS. But you don't have to take it from me. Just listen to Ari:

It's my pleasure to write about my success story. It's been just over two years, and I don't stop thinking about the experience that literally changed my life.

To give you a quick background, I'd always been a slim, fit person growing up, but after high school I stopped sports and didn't care anymore. I was drinking heavily and smoking about a pack a day. Between 2001 and 2008, I gained almost 60 pounds. One day, I stepped on a scale and weighed in at almost 235 pounds! I was fat.

I quit smoking, started eating right and lost around 20 pounds on my own with help from Maria Thomas. Just eating right goes a long way. But when I started training with Tommy, I was still tipping the scales at about 215 pounds.

Working with Tommy for four weeks changed my life! I knew that I wanted to change, and just knowing I was ready was only part of the battle. When I finally got into the training, I knew it was going to be tough, but I wanted to lose the weight. I figured it was worth the sweat and effort. Every workout we did taught me to push myself and work much harder. Through the whole process, Tommy made me realize that this was about not just getting in shape, but that exercise and eating right are a lifestyle. Knowing that made the changes I needed to make that much easier. I don't think there was a single workout where I came away not feeling like I'd got my ass kicked. I think if not for the ass-kicking, I would not have had the foundation or the drive to continue on the way I did after the four weeks.

When all was said and done, I lost 19 pounds in a month, putting me below 200 pounds, the lightest I've been in seven years. This was also in large part thanks to Maria's meals. She made them so I didn't get bored with what I was eating and she showed me how to make the proper choices when I snack. Two years later, I still have Maria's seven-day eating plan up on my fridge. I still follow the plan, and use it as a guide of proper portions.

Even after I finished working with Tommy, my training never stopped; the techniques that Tommy taught me have stuck with me. I use a variety of exercises, continue to push myself past my comfort zones, and as Tommy used to always tell me, I "never settle for average." Tommy and

Maria helped me transform my body and adopt healthy lifestyle habits.

I will never go back to the way that I was, and I have used what I learned from Tommy and lost another 20 pounds over the past year. I am now down to around 180 pounds and I feel so good. People that I have not seen in a while don't even recognize me anymore. Thank you, Tommy and Maria, for giving me my "swagger" back. It is something that I will always be grateful for. I'm proud of myself for sticking with it, because I did it for me!

Now, time for you to do it for you, too. Get out there and hit the pavement with your running shoes, your bike, your Rollerblades, whatever. Take your boyfriend or girlfriend, take your kids, take your dog. You may be doing it for yourself, but you don't have to do it alone.

DAY 14 MEAL PLAN

All right . . . today we're having fried chicken, onion rings, milkshakes, and cake and ice cream for dessert. No? You don't feel like polluting yourself with those empty calories? Fine, then. How about a little something stacked with fibre to brush your insides, and protein, fats and carbs to sustain you through the day? Does that sound about right? Good.

BREAKFAST 2 pancakes (the size of the palm of your hand, and whole-wheat if possible); 1 tbsp. maple syrup; 2 slices back bacon; 1 large orange; 1-1/2 cups skim or soy milk.

SNACK 1 cup strawberries; 20 almonds.

LUNCH Chicken Caesar salad: 3 oz. chicken breast, 2 cups romaine lettuce with 1/2 cup croutons and 1 tbsp. light Caesar dressing.

SNACK Granola bar.

DINNER Turkey sandwich: 3 oz. turkey breast, tomato, mustard, lettuce and 1 oz. part-skim mozzarella cheese on 2 (very thin) slices sourdough bread. Serve with 1 cup baby carrots.

DAY 15
Midpoint Weigh-In

TOMMY RULE #15: NORMALLY, I'M NOT A STATS MAN, BUT THE NUMBERS DON'T LIE!

Wakey, wakey! The early bird gets a midterm!

I want you to grab your measuring tape and your scale. We're gonna see if you've been walking the walk or just talking a good game.

Ready?

Record the following measurements:

Chest/Bust. Stretch the tape around your back and your nipples. Make sure it's straight.	
Waist. Use your belly button as the centre point, just like on Day 1. And don't suck it in—I know that trick!	
Hips. Measure around the widest part of your hips, all the way around, just like you did on Day 1.	
Weight. Take your shoes off and use the same scale that you did on Day 1.	

So, how did you do?

If your numbers are amazing, give yourself a quick pat on the shoulder . . . I'm waiting . . . done yet?

Good. Way to go.

If your numbers aren't spectacular, this is not the time to jump off a cliff. (Actually, it never is.) This just gives us an idea of what needs to be done in the *second* half of the 10PS. That's right, it's a 10-Pound Shred no matter how many inches or pounds you've lost so far, so if you're not yet where you want to be, now you know how far to go in the next two weeks. Trust me, some people start to lose weight right away, while others take a bit longer to get their metabolisms going. I mean, it's only been two weeks!

In any case, I don't want you getting too high or too low, no matter what your measurements have to say. It's what you do over the next 16 days that will make the biggest difference in your overall results.

Today's results are just a reality check to get you ready to turn up the heat. Tomorrow, your rep time will increase and the exercises will be a little more demanding, so I need you to put your game face back on and challenge yourself to be the best you can be!

"It's not how you start—it's how you finish." That's what athletes tell themselves so they can keep pushing. A strong start is great, but it's nothing without a strong finish. And that's true in spades when it comes to the 10PS. Although this is only a 31-day process, I want you to be a champion with goals that will continue well into your life. To win a war, you may not have to win *all* the little battles along the way, but you have to show up ready to fight and bounce back from any defeats that come your way. Well, this is both mental and physical warfare—do you get where I'm coming from?

I'm saying let's lock and load.

And you don't have to wait until tomorrow to do it, either. Your body is getting used to all the action you've been throwing at it these past two weeks. It's probably telling you it's time to get at it. Well? Why aren't you listening to it?

It used to tell you to sit on the couch, and you were happy to comply then. Now that it's prodding you to get busy, it's time to listen up.

Keep it interesting. Think of an activity you haven't done in a long time and do it. I don't care what it is—canoeing, ultimate Frisbee, soccer, tennis, road hockey . . . whatever! I just need you to work and be unstoppable, and I already know you can do that.

Now I just need *you* to know it, too.

DAY 15 MEAL PLAN

Hey, fighting those battles is going to take some serious energy. Your meal plan for today will consist of the following:

BREAKFAST 2 slices whole-grain toast with 2 tsp. non-hydrogenated margarine or butter; 1 boiled or poached egg; 1/2 cup grapes; 1-1/2 cups skim or soy milk.

SNACK 1 cup blueberries; 3/4 cup of low-fat yogurt.

LUNCH Turkey pita: Stuff 1 whole-wheat pita bread with 3 oz. turkey, 1 cup lettuce, tomato, onion, and mustard mixed with 1/4 tsp. honey.

SNACK 1/2 cup edamame.

DINNER Baked ziti: Tonight, cooking ahead isn't an option! Here's a recipe for tonight's dinner and tomorrow's lunch. Preheat your oven to 350°F. Cook 6 oz. extra-lean ground beef with onion, garlic and whichever spices you'd like, then drain the fat. Mix with 1-1/2 cups cooked penne, 1 to 1-1/2 cups pasta sauce and 1-1/2 oz. grated part-skim mozzarella. Put the entire mixture in a baking dish and sprinkle 1 oz. cheese on top. Bake for about 30 minutes. Once cooked, put 2/3 of the ziti into a container for tomorrow's lunch, and serve the rest with 2 cups spinach salad with a dressing of balsamic vinegar and 1 tsp. olive oil.

Can you believe you've already made it to the end of another week? Time for next week's meal plan. Remember, if you fail to prepare, you should be prepared to fail, so get on this week's grocery run.

MEAL PLAN #3

DAY 16	DAY 17	DAY 18	DAY 19	DAY 20	DAY 21	DAY 22
Breakfast	**Breakfast**	**Breakfast**	**Breakfast**	**Breakfast**	**Breakfast**	**Breakfast**
Fruit smoothie, English muffin with natural peanut butter and a glass of milk	Whole-grain toast, poached egg and a glass of milk	Yogurt with granola, All-Bran cereal, blueberries and a glass of milk	Bagel with natural almond butter, apple and a glass of milk	Yogurt with granola, All-Bran cereal, strawberries and a glass of milk	Omelette, toast, orange and a glass of milk	Fruit smoothie with protein powder, English muffin with natural peanut butter and a glass of milk
Snack	**Snack**	**Snack**	**Snack**	**Snack**	**Snack**	**Snack**
Bran muffin and light cheese	Watermelon and yogurt	Apple and cottage cheese	Watermelon and yogurt	Mango and almonds	Grapes and almonds	Bran muffin and light cheese
Lunch	**Lunch**	**Lunch**	**Lunch**	**Lunch**	**Lunch**	**Lunch**
Baked ziti leftovers with spinach salad	Chicken leftovers with brown rice and spinach salad	Vegetarian wrap and baby carrots	Leftover pork with roast vegetables and sweet potato	Chicken pita	Beef wrap	Turkey sandwich
Snack	**Snack**	**Snack**	**Snack**	**Snack**	**Snack**	**Snack**
Hummus with rye crackers and grape tomatoes	Edamame	Salmon salad on rye crackers	Hummus with rye crackers and sliced red peppers	Edamame	Granola bar	Edamame
Dinner	**Dinner**	**Dinner**	**Dinner**	**Dinner**	**Dinner**	**Dinner**
Rosemary chicken thighs with brown rice and mixed-green salad	Baked cod with potatoes and steamed green beans	BBQ pork with roasted vegetables	Chicken Greek salad with brown rice	Beef fajita	Soup and salad	Grilled salmon with brown rice and asparagus

DAY 16
HITZ Resistance #7

TOMMY RULE #16: DON'T ASK WHY. THE QUESTION IS, WHY NOT?

We just passed the midpoint of the 10PS, so I've got a few questions for you. Are you happy with your measurements from yesterday? Have you put in the work during the last 15 days? Have you stuck to the meal plan? Do your clothes feel more comfortable than they did 15 days ago? Are you stronger and more toned? Is your recovery getting better?

There should be only one answer for all these questions, and that is yes! If a no managed to sneak in, you have been holding back somewhere over the past two weeks. Remember, you're not just doing a workout here or there, or eating a healthier meal from time to time—you are changing your whole lifestyle.

I'm not a magician, and you don't need to rely on miracles. This is all pretty simple: You just put in the work, and leave it to your body to take care of the details. Should I put that another way? If you give everything you have and follow each day's program as it appears here, you will improve your fitness level and measurements, complete your weight-loss quest and guarantee a feeling of accomplishment. It's that easy. Well, maybe not easy. Before you can enjoy the fruits, you must put in the labour. But it's simple.

Those are my words for today. Now, you can't do anything more about the past 15 days. If you didn't give it your all, that's too bad. But it's not the end of the world, and it's no reason to lose hope in the 10PS. No matter what the tape had to say, there is only one thing to do: Charge full steam ahead for the next 16 days. So let's get to it!

TODAY'S WORKOUT

FOCUS	EQUIPMENT	REPETITIONS	SETS
Top-to-bottom shred.	Skipping rope, a pair of 5- and 10-pound dumbbells (DBs), plus a 20-pound (for beginners) or 40-pound (intermediate) DB, a stability ball (SB) and a bench or bars for dips.	If you're a beginner, your repetitions are going up to 45 seconds. That's right: You're past the point where the intermediates were when this all started. If you're an intermediate, take a deep breath: Your repetitions are going to be one minute long.	Today you have three sets; each set will have two quad-set circuits (four exercises in a row without a break). It sounds more complicated than it is, trust me. We up the tempo to once again shock the system! You ready?

HERE'S THE GAME PLAN:
Warmup
Dynamic Stretches
HITZ Resistance #7

• SKIPPING • DUMBBELL PLIÉ SQUATS • DUMBBELL PUSH-UP SIDE PLANKS • CORE HEEL SCRAPERS
1-minute rest . . . grab some water.

• SKIPPING • STABILITY BALL WITH DUMBBELL REVERSE FLIES • DIPS • STABILITY BALL CORE REACH CRUNCHES
How do you like those quad sets? Grab some H_2O and saddle up for the next set.

I know you loved this last time, so we're going to do it again. That's right: Do a **CORE PLANK** until failure.

Cool-Down
Static Stretches

WARMUP

Jump on a bike or treadmill for your 10-minute warmup. If you are training outdoors, you should be jogging or riding a bike.

For the first five minutes, work at an intensity of Level 4 on the PES. You should be sweating a little, but feeling good and able to carry on a conversation effortlessly.

For the last five minutes, work at an intensity of Level 5. You should be just above comfortable, sweating more and still able to talk easily.

DYNAMIC STRETCHES

After your warmup, perform the following three dynamic stretches:

DYNAMIC QUAD STRETCHES

1. Stand tall (shoulders back), with your feet shoulder width apart. Lift your left foot behind you and grab your ankle (or foot) with your left hand.

2. Gently push your left hip forward, while keeping a straight line with your body and maintaining your balance on your right heel. Hold for 3 seconds, then release your left ankle.

**Repeat this sequence with your right leg.
Perform 5 repetitions on each leg.**

DYNAMIC CHEST AND BICEP STRETCHES

1. Stand tall (shoulders back), with your feet shoulder width apart. Slowly move your arms out to the sides, slightly behind you, with your thumbs up (just like The Fonz).

2. As your arms go back, rotate your thumbs down and back until they are pointing to the wall behind you. Pause, then return to the starting position. You should feel this one in your chest and biceps.

Perform 10 repetitions.

DYNAMIC BACK SWINGS

1. Stand tall (shoulders back), with your feet shoulder width apart. Lift and hold both arms to the side at shoulder height. Twist as far as you can to the right, so that you can feel a good stretch in your mid- to lower back.

2. Pause, then twist to the left (you should resemble a propeller as you twist).

Repeat for 10 revolutions.

NOW YOU'RE READY TO COMPETE AND CONTINUE THE GOOD FIGHT. TODAY'S WORKOUT WILL FORCE YOU TO GREATER LEVELS OF INTENSITY. REMEMBER TO USE PERFECT FORM—IF YOU NEED TO GO LIGHTER IN WEIGHT TO KEEP IT RIGHT, DO IT. GOOD LUCK, AND HAVE FUN!

SKIPPING

Now you're getting into the groove. Every time you skip, you should be stopping less and less, while rotating the rope faster and faster!

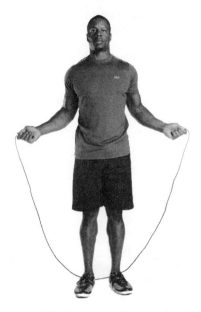 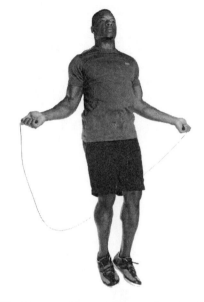

1. Place your skipping rope on the ground and stand in the middle of it. Grab the handles, which should reach about 6 inches below your collarbone when you pull the handles straight up.

2. Start to rotate the rope. The rotation should come from your wrists. To increase the speed of the rotations, increase the tightness of the circles that your wrists are making.

Skip for 1 minute if you're a beginner, 2 minutes if you're an intermediate.

DUMBBELL PLIÉ SQUATS

This is your second time around with this one, so make sure you do the squats with proper form.

1. Stand tall, with your feet wider than shoulder width and your toes turned out. Engage your core and pull your shoulder blades together. Cup your hands and hold a 20-pound (beginners) to 40-pound (intermediate) dumbbell between your legs.

2. Begin the movement by bending at your knees and hips, then push your hips backward as if trying to sit in a deep imaginary basket behind you.

3. Bend your knees to 90 degrees while keeping your back straight and your weight on your heels. Pause for 1 second, then return to your upright, standing position.

Repeat the sequence for 45 seconds if you're a beginner, 1 minute if you're an intermediate.

DUMBBELL PUSH-UP SIDE PLANKS

This is another variation of a push-up, but it is going to be supertaxing on your core. You must do this one slowly—if you are a beginner, you can be on your knees. You will work every muscle in your body, so stay "strong and long."

1. Place a pair of 5- or 10-pound DBs on a mat, shoulder width apart, then move into a push-up position, with your hands on the DBs directly under your shoulders and your elbows as close to your sides as possible.

2. Bend your elbows and lower your body so that it is 2 inches above the DBs. Pause.

3. Now push your body up, rotating through your torso and lifting your right arm (still holding the DB) so that your arms are straight. Turn your head so that you're looking straight up at your right arm. Return to the push-up starting position and repeat the action on the left arm.

Alternate sides for 45 seconds if you're a beginner, 1 minute if you're an intermediate.

TOMMY TIP

Engage your core and do not let your back sag. Ensure that the hand on top of the DB (on the ground) is directly under your shoulder at all times.

CORE HEEL SCRAPERS

Time to blast your lower abdominals again, so that you are well on your way to having abs of steel!

1. Lie flat on your back (use your mat if you have one). Without tucking your chin, raise your head off the ground and look up at the ceiling. Then lift your heels off the ground while bending your knees, so that your thighs are at a 90-degree angle to the mat.

2. Lower both legs from the hip until your heels graze the ground.

3. Now push your heels out until both legs are straight. As you extend your legs, push your lower back into the ground for support. Beginners, you can have a slight bend in the knees—for now. Pause, then return your legs to the starting position.

Keep going for 45 seconds if you're a beginner, 1 minute if you're an intermediate.

TIME FOR A WELL-EARNED 1-MINUTE REST. GRAB SOME WATER, THEN GRAB THAT ROPE FOR SOME MORE . . .

SKIPPING

I know you're getting good at this now. Wipe that brow and get to work!

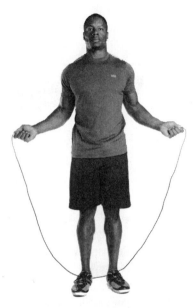 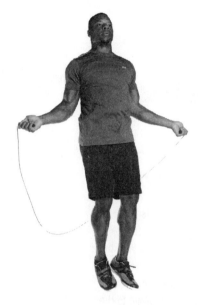

1. Place your skipping rope on the ground and stand in the middle of it. Grab the handles, which should reach about 6 inches below your collarbone when you pull the handles straight up.

2. Start to rotate the rope. The rotation should come from your wrists. To increase the speed of the rotations, increase the tightness of the circles that your wrists are making.

Skip for 1 minute if you're a beginner, 2 minutes if you're an intermediate.

STABILITY BALL WITH DUMBBELL REVERSE FLY

Are you tired of having a flabby back? You better have said yes! This is a great exercise to tighten, tone and strengthen your upper back and core. There is no momentum or swinging on this one, just a steady burn.

1. Begin on your knees and place an SB under your gut. Hold a 10- to 15-pound DB in each hand in front of the ball and elevate your chest. Bend your knees and brace your feet (use a wall or bench if you are sliding).

2. Maintain a flat back and lift both DBs to the side as if you're trying to fly (you can have a slight bend in your elbows). As you elevate your arms, focus on squeezing your shoulder blades together as if you are trying to grip a penny between them. Pause, then return to the starting position.

Repeat the sequence for 45 seconds if you're a beginner, 1 minute if you're an intermediate.

TOMMY TIP

Your core must be engaged at all times, and your head must remain neutral. Imagine that you are a bird with a wide wingspan . . . holding on to a pair of dumbbells.

DIPS

Remember when your third-grade teacher waved at you and her arm jiggled more than a bowl of Jell-O?
Well, by doing these dips we're gonna get rid of that fat for good and target your triceps muscles!

1. Grab a dip bar, a bench or a chair and stand facing away from it. Lower yourself so that your hands are gripping the edge on either side of your hips. If you're on a chair or bench, let your butt hang off the edge, but don't let it get too far away from your equipment. If you're on a dip machine at the gym, this won't be something to worry about—just grab the handles and get ready.

2. Bend your elbows and slowly lower your body until your arms are at 90-degree angles.

3. Pause, then return to the starting position, ensuring that you move in a slow, controlled way.

Repeat this sequence for your allotted time: beginners, 45 seconds each side; intermediates, 1 minute.

STABILITY BALL CORE REACH CRUNCHES

There are many ways to work your abdominals, but this one in particular will force you to reach for the burn. To get the most out of this crunch, squeeze the SB as hard as you can so that you work your inner thighs, as well.

1. Lie on your back and squeeze the SB between your legs (just below your knees). Lift your feet straight up so they're pointing at the ceiling. Engage your core and do not tuck your chin.

2. Raise your arms, reach and crunch so that you touch the top of the SB. Pause, then return till your shoulder blades are on the floor. Your arms must remain up at all times.

Repeat the sequence for 45 seconds if you're a beginner, 1 minute if you're an intermediate.

PHEW! FEELING LIKE YOUR SYSTEM'S BEEN SHOCKED YET? TAKE A MINUTE, GRAB SOME WATER AND REPEAT THE CIRCUIT. AFTER YOUR THIRD SET, REMEMBER TO DO ONE LAST THING . . .

CORE PLANK

Do this at the end of your third and final set, and hold it in perfect form until failure.

1. Begin on all fours (hands and knees) on a mat.

2. Extend your legs so that your entire body is flat, in a straight-arm plank position, then go down to your forearms.

3. Raise your hips so that your body is in a straight line and your weight is on your elbows and toes. Beginners, you may need to be on your knees. That's fine for now—just ensure that your hips are down, with your core engaged. This should be hard work.

Hold the plank position for as long as you can. You have only a single set of this one, so challenge yourself.

COOL-DOWN

How did that one feel? Grab some water, and after you've done your third set, including the plank, it's time to cool down.

The first workout of the week is now done, and we're off to a good start. I hope you gave it everything you had. Follow the cool-down and get ready for a tough one tomorrow. I'll meet you then!

STATIC STRETCHES

Once you have finished your 10-minute cool-down, do your static stretches.

SPINAL TWISTS

1. Lie on the floor, with your arms extending outward in a T position. Put your right foot on your left knee.

2. Using your left hand, gently pull your right knee toward the floor, twisting your spine and keeping your left arm straight out, hips and shoulders on the floor. Hold for 30 seconds.

Repeat, using the right hand and left knee.

QUADRICEPS/HIP FLEXOR STRETCHES

1. Starting in a standing position, take a big step forward with your left leg, then place your right knee on the ground.

2. Maintaining this posture, shift the entire body slightly forward from the hip. You should feel this stretch down the front of your quad and hip flexor. Exhale and hold the stretch. Don't arch your back.

Hold for 30 seconds, then gently release and switch legs.

HAMSTRING STRETCHES

1. Lie down on your back, with a slight bend in both legs.

2. Lift your right leg straight up and grab it behind your calf. If you are flexible enough, grab your ankle (or even your toe). Gently pull your right leg toward you, keeping your back straight.

Hold the stretch for 30 seconds. Repeat with the left leg.

GREAT WORK! ARE YOU FEELING UNSTOPPABLE? I THOUGHT SO. KEEP AT IT!

DAY 16 MEAL PLAN

I don't know about you, but I'm getting hungry. If you're having cravings not quite in keeping with what's on the day's menu, that fine. If you need to swap out foods, go right ahead, but keep them in the same food groups.

BREAKFAST Fruit smoothie: Blend 3/4 cup low-fat yogurt, 1 cup mixed frozen berries, 1/4 cup orange juice (optional) and 1/2 scoop protein powder; serve with 1/2 English muffin and 1 tbsp. natural peanut butter; 1-1/2 cups skim or soy milk.

SNACK 1/2 bran muffin; 1 oz. light cheese.

LUNCH 2/3 of the leftover baked ziti from last night's dinner served with 1 cup spinach salad with 1 tbsp. light dressing.

SNACK 1/3 cup hummus; 2 rye crackers; 1/2 cup grape tomatoes.

DINNER Rosemary chicken thighs: Rub 2 small chicken thighs (4 oz.) with a mix of 1 tsp. olive oil, 1/4 tsp. garlic powder, 1/4 tsp. oregano and 1/2 tsp. rosemary, then cook. Serve with 1/2 cup brown rice and 2 cups mixed-green salad with 1 tbsp. light dressing. **Cook-ahead option:** Cook an extra chicken thigh (2 oz.) for tomorrow's lunch.

DAY 17
HITZ Cardio #5

TOMMY RULE #17: THIS IS THE DAY THE CREAM RISES TO THE TOP (ALONG WITH YOUR LUNCH IF YOU WORK OUT TOO SOON AFTER EATING)!

Today you will conquer your fifth cardio challenge. Your cardio choices are a treadmill or heading outside to "run to the hills"! Here's the disclaimer again: If you are a beginner, extremely deconditioned or obese, I recommend that you do not focus on speed or incline—instead, work to appropriate levels on the PES. This workout should take you about 30 minutes to complete. You're going to get out of it what you put into it.

TODAY'S WORKOUT

FOCUS	EQUIPMENT	TOTAL TIME
PES challenge.	Treadmill or the sweet sound of your treads on asphalt—up to you.	About 45 minutes.

RIGHT THEN, LET'S GET TO THE NITTY-GRITTY:
Warmup
Dynamic Stretches
HITZ Cardio #5
Cool-Down
Static Stretches

WARMUP

For five minutes, work at an intensity of Level 4 on the PES. You should be sweating a little, but feeling good and still able to carry on a conversation effortlessly.

DYNAMIC STRETCHES

After your warmup, it's time for the following three dynamic stretches:

DYNAMIC GLUTE AND HAMSTRING STRETCHES

1. Stand tall (shoulders back), with your feet shoulder width apart. Lift up your left foot and grab just below your left knee with both hands.

2. With both hands, gently pull your left knee up, while maintaining your balance on your right heel. This will activate your butt and the backs of your legs. Hold for 3 seconds, then release your left leg.

Repeat this sequence with your right leg.
Perform 5 repetitions with each leg.

DYNAMIC QUAD STRETCHES

1. Stand tall (shoulders back), with your feet shoulder width apart. Lift your left foot behind you and grab your ankle (or foot) with your left hand.

2. Gently push your left hip forward, while keeping a straight line with your body and maintaining your balance on your right heel. Hold for 3 seconds, then release your left ankle.

Repeat this sequence with your right leg.
Perform 5 repetitions on each leg.

DYNAMIC SUMO SQUATS

1. Stand tall (shoulders back), with your feet close together. Take a large lateral step to the right and drop into a deep squat (think of a sumo wrestler). Pause, then return to the starting standing position.

2. Now take a large lateral step to the left and drop into a deep squat. Pause, then return to the starting position.

Perform 5 repetitions on each side.

HITZ CARDIO #5

Now it's time for HITZ Cardio #5. Good luck—I'll be right here with you. Remember to have some water close by!

Time	Description	Perceived Exertion Scale (PES)	Speed (mph)	Incline
2 min.	You should be cruising at 50% of your maximum ability.	Level 5–6	4–4.5	5%
2 min.	Gradually start to increase your speed (every 15 seconds) until you are rolling at 80% of your maximum ability.	Level 7–8	5–6.5	Increase incline by 1% every 15 seconds.
2 min.	Gradually bring it down to 65% and take a quick H_2O blast.	Level 6–7	5–5.5 (walk/slow jog)	Decrease incline by 1% every 15 seconds.
1 min.	Hit 80% and hold it for 1 minute.	Level 7–8	6–7	5%
2 min.	This is your recoup phase; you should be at 50%.	Level 5–6	5	3%
2 min.	Gradually start to increase your pace or resistance (every 15 seconds) until you are working at 80% of your maximum ability.	Level 7–8	5–6.5	3%, then increase incline by 1% every 15 seconds.

2 min.	Gradually bring your resistance down—hold your speed, though.	Level 6–7	5–5.5	Decrease incline by 1% every 15 seconds.
1 min.	Full blast: You should be at 80 to 85% of your maximum ability.	Level 8	6–7	8%
2 min.	Recoup: you should be at 50%.	Level 5–6	5	3%
2 min.	Gradually start to increase your pace or resistance (every 15 seconds) until you are working at 80% of your max.	Level 7–8	5–6	3%, then increase incline by 1% every 15 seconds.
2 min.	Gradually bring your resistance down—hold your speed, though.	Level 5–6	4–5.5	Decrease incline by 1% every 15 seconds.
1 min.	Full blast: You should be at 80 to 85% of your maximum ability.	Level 8-ish	8	10%
5 min.	This is the start of your cool-down. Work your way back to home base.	Level 3–4	3–4	0%

Never thought it would end, did you? Well, you're done now. Here's the good news for those of you on the treadmill: By raising the incline over the course of the workout, you were actually really working your abs in addition to feeling the wicked cardio effect. No wonder you're ready for a break. Grab your water, and let's get to the cool-down.

COOL-DOWN

You can stay on the treadmill or simply go for a nice slow walk, head up and eyes open. Stay at a low intensity for a minimum of 10 minutes. You should be at an intensity of Level 3 on the PES. You should be relatively comfortable; this cool-down is designed to slowly bring your heart rate down, so go easy with it.

STATIC STRETCHES

Once you're cool, you're ready for the following four stretches:

SPINAL TWISTS

1. Lie on the floor, with your arms extending outward in a T position. Put your right foot on your left knee.

2. Using your left hand, gently pull your right knee toward the floor, twisting your spine and keeping your left arm straight out, hips and shoulders on the floor. Hold for 30 seconds.

Repeat, using the right hand and left knee.

QUADRICEPS/HIP FLEXOR STRETCHES

1. Starting in a standing position, take a big step forward with your left leg, then place your right knee on the ground.

2. Maintaining this posture, shift the entire body slightly forward from the hip. You should feel this stretch down the front of your quad and hip flexor. Exhale and hold the stretch. Don't arch your back.

Hold for 30 seconds, then gently release and switch legs.

HAMSTRING STRETCHES

1. Lie down on your back, with a slight bend in both legs.

2. Lift your right leg straight up and grab it behind your calf. If you are flexible enough, grab your ankle (or even your toe). Gently pull your right leg toward you, keeping your back straight.

Hold the stretch for 30 seconds.
Repeat with the left leg.

HIP STRETCHES

1. Lie down and cross your left foot over your right knee.

2. Clasp your hands behind your right knee. Gently pull your right leg toward you, keeping your back straight.

Switch legs and repeat the sequence.

THAT'S IT! NOW, GET OFF OF YOUR FEET AND GO AND EAT! AT THIS POINT IN THE 10PS, YOU'RE STARTING TO GET A BIT COMFORTABLE, SO TAKE SOME TIME TO ASK YOURSELF WHETHER YOU'RE JUST SURVIVING YOUR WORKOUTS OR STARTING TO THRIVE IN THEM. IF YOU'RE THRIVING, AMAZING WORK! IF YOU'RE JUST SURVIVING, ASK YOURSELF WHERE YOU CAN FIND THAT LAST 10% YOU NEED TO PUSH HARDER.

DAY 17 MEAL PLAN

Be careful not to eat too close to your workout today, or you will throw up . . . I can pretty much guarantee that one.

BREAKFAST 2 slices whole-grain toast; 2 tsp. margarine or butter; 1 poached egg; 1 orange; 1-1/2 cups skim or soy milk.

SNACK 1 cup watermelon; 3/4 cup low-fat yogurt.

LUNCH 1 chicken thigh (2 to 3 oz.); 1 cup brown rice; 1 cup spinach salad with 1 tbsp. light dressing.

SNACK 1/2 cup edamame.

DINNER Baked cod: Coat 4 oz. cod with 1 tbsp. light salad dressing. Dip in 1/4 cup crushed croutons, then bake in a 350°F oven alongside 3 to 4 small (1 in.) potatoes drizzled with 1 tsp. olive oil. Serve with 1-1/2 cups steamed green beans.

DAY 18
HITZ Resistance #8

TOMMY RULE #18: WWTD? (WHAT WOULD TOMMY DO?) HE WOULDN'T SIT AROUND TELLING HIMSELF HE DIDN'T FEEL LIKE WORKING OUT, THAT'S FOR SURE!

Welcome to Day 18. You're on such a great roll that it would be a shame to fall back on old habits. Looking beyond the horizon won't really help you—just keep your eye on the prize and what's in front of you now. Attack today with zest and zeal, and the rest will take care of itself. Your friends and family are jealous of where you are now, I know it—and I hope they are supporting you and have decided to join you, as well. Healthy habits are contagious, so continue to be the leader of the pack. Remember, you are only three days away from making it a permanent habit.

Now, what are you going to do today to make yourself better?

TODAY'S WORKOUT

FOCUS	EQUIPMENT	REPETITIONS	SETS
Today your upper body and core are gonna get a beatdown . . . Tommy-style!	A pair of 10- to 20-pound dumbbells (DBs), a stability ball (SB) and resistance band (RB).	Beginners, you're still on 45 seconds; intermediates, sit tight at a minute—I know you can handle it.	Three complete sets again today, so better get moving!

ARE YOU STARTING TO WONDER WHAT'S COOKING IN TOMMY'S KITCHEN TODAY? WELL, WONDER NO LONGER, BECAUSE BELOW IS A RECIPE FOR A FULL-BODY WORKOUT THAT'S NOT GOING TO LEAVE ANY ROOM FOR SECONDS.

Warmup
Dynamic Stretches
HITZ Resistance #8

• HIGH-KNEE RUNNING • DUMBBELL ONE-ARM SNATCHES • CORE LATERAL LEG DROPS • STABILITY BALL PUSH-UPS
1-minute rest . . . grab some water!

• HIGH-KNEE RUNNING • RESISTANCE BAND LAT PULL-DOWNS • STABILITY BALL ONE-LEG BRIDGES • CORE DOWN2, UP2
1-minute rest (don't forget to hydrate!) before your next set.

Cool-Down
Static Stretches

WARMUP

Today you are going to warm up by skipping. Set your watch or look at the clock, because you will be skipping for 5 minutes.

For the first minute, you can skip any style. If you don't have a skipping rope, use an imaginary rope.

For the second minute, you will skip with a double hop between rotations.

For the third minute, go back to any style.

For the last 2 minutes, it's double leg hops again.

DYNAMIC STRETCHES

After your warmup, perform the following three dynamic stretches:

DYNAMIC QUAD STRETCHES

1. Stand tall (shoulders back), with your feet shoulder width apart. Lift your left foot behind you and grab your ankle (or foot) with your left hand.

2. Gently push your left hip forward, while keeping a straight line with your body and maintaining your balance on your right heel. Hold for 3 seconds, then release your left ankle.

**Repeat this sequence with your right leg.
Perform 5 repetitions on each leg.**

DYNAMIC CHEST AND BICEP STRETCHES

1. Stand tall (shoulders back), with your feet shoulder width apart. Slowly move your arms out to the sides, slightly behind you, with your thumbs up (just like The Fonz).

2. As your arms go back, rotate your thumbs down and back until they are pointing to the wall behind you. Pause, then return to the starting position. You should feel this one in your chest and biceps.

Perform 10 repetitions.

DYNAMIC BACK SWINGS

1. Stand tall (shoulders back), with your feet shoulder width apart. Lift and hold both arms up to the side at shoulder height. Twist as far as you can to the right, so that you can feel a good stretch in your mid- to lower back.

2. Pause, then twist to the left (you should resemble a propeller as you twist).

Repeat for 10 revolutions.

HIGH-KNEE RUNNING

Just like *Flashdance*—get 'em up!

1. Stand tall, with your feet shoulder width apart. Run on the spot, lifting your knees as high as possible and pumping your arms vigorously. Ideally, your knees will be coming up to waist height.

2. You must remain tall at all times. Do not slump.

Keep going for 45 seconds if you're a beginner, 1 minute if you're an intermediate.

DUMBBELL ONE-ARM SNATCHES

This is a demanding exercise that will require your full attention to detail. The one-arm snatch is a ballistic (fast) move that needs some coordination. Watch your face as the DB comes up!

1. Stand tall, with your feet shoulder width apart. Hold a 10- to 20-pound DB in your right hand and let it hang between your legs. Keeping your arm straight, squat down.

2. Keep the DB close to your body as you "explode" to an upright position, pushing up strongly through your legs.

3. As you explode through your legs, lift the DB, leading with your elbows. Finish in a completely extended position over your head (think of the Statue of Liberty). Follow the same path on the way down.

Repeat with your right hand for 45 seconds if you're a beginner, 1 minute if you're an intermediate, then switch to your left hand.

TOMMY TIP

Do not round your lower back, but do keep the DB as close to your body as possible throughout the entire movement (no further than 3 inches away). Think of this sequence as you perform this move: shoulder up, elbow up, wrist up, DB up.

CORE LATERAL LEG DROPS

Let's get you that sleek midsection by working your obliques. The more slowly you perform this exercise,
the more you will engage your abdominal muscles . . . period!

1. Lie flat on your back on a mat, with your hands palms down and out to the side, making a wide base, then raise your legs so they're pointing straight up.

2. Pin your knees together, engage your core and let your legs drop to the right side without letting them touch the ground.

3. Pause, then repeat on the left side.

Repeat this action for 45 seconds if you're a beginner, 1 minute if you're an intermediate.

TOMMY TIP

Keep your shoulder blades on the ground at all times.

STABILITY BALL PUSH-UPS

I know you're ready for this one. The SB push-up is a complete chest, shoulders and triceps blast. You should not be bouncing, so slow down. You will learn to love this one, as it forces you to engage your entire body—have fun with it!

1. Place both hands on your SB, with your thumbs facing forward (your hands must be directly under your shoulders).

2. Walk both feet back so that you are in a push-up position. Brace your abs and keep your body in a straight line from your toes (intermediate) or knees (beginner).

3. Bend your elbows and slowly lower yourself until your chest is 2 inches from the SB. Pause, then push yourself up to the start position.

Repeat this action for 45 seconds if you're a beginner, 1 minute if you're an intermediate.

TAKE A 1-MINUTE BREATHER (AND GRAB A DRINK OF WATER), THEN CONTINUE.

TOMMY TIP

Keep your body in a straight line at all times, with your head neutral.

Ensure that you have your entire body weight directly over the SB.

HIGH-KNEE RUNNING

Up to it, down to it, we do it because we're used to it!

1. Stand tall, with your feet shoulder width apart. Run on the spot, lifting your knees as high as possible and pumping your arms vigorously. Ideally, your knees will be coming up to waist height.

2. You must remain tall at all times. Do not slump.

Keep going for 45 seconds if you're a beginner, 1 minute if you're an intermediate.

RESISTANCE BAND LAT PULL-DOWNS

"Back fat," "back ass," whatever you want to call it, doing lat pull-downs with a resistance band is going to get rid of it. Now, you've probably been in the gym and noticed the "no-necks" lifting the rack by using momentum and bracing their legs on a machine. We are not gonna do that here. Focus on your lat muscles, and your results will dwarf anything you've ever imagined. The same principles hold true whether you are on a lat pull-down cable machine or doing it my way, with the RB!

1. Attach your resistance band to an elevated bar or other solid structure and hold on to the handles with a wide overhand (thumbs-down) grip. Drop into a squat position—you should be leaning forward at a 45-degree angle.

2. Using your lats as the primary mover, shrug down and then pull your elbows down toward your hips.

3. Pause, then fully extend your arms.

Repeat this action for 45 seconds if you're a beginner, 1 minute if you're an intermediate.

STABILITY BALL ONE-LEG BRIDGES

It's time to work on your ass-ets. Doing the one-leg bridge will ensure that you never hear "Do fries come with that shake?" If this exercise is too difficult for you to do, just place both feet on the SB to take some of the pressure off.

1. Lie on your back, with your arms flat on the ground. Bend your right leg and place your right heel on an SB. Then raise your left leg high in the air.

2. Pushing through your right heel, lift your hips up so that your butt and mid-back are off the ground. The higher you lift your hips, the more effective the exercise will be. Pause, then drop your hips to within 2 inches of the ground.

Repeat this action for 45 seconds if you're a beginner, 1 minute if you're an intermediate. Then switch by putting your left heel on the SB and doing it all over again.

TOMMY TIP

Contract your core and glutes as if you are squeezing a dime between your butt cheeks.

CORE DOWN2, UP2

The first time you did this, you were on the ground. Now it's Day 18, so we're gonna up the ante by using an SB. Start with a wider base to your legs. You will tilt a bit, so you must make sure that the SB is directly under you. If you want to brace the SB against the wall, go ahead, but be warned: in a head-butt contest, the wall always wins.

1. Place your hands on a mat, shoulder width apart, and extend your feet straight back so that you are in an upright push-up position (arms fully locked). Keep your elbows as close to your sides as possible and spread your legs a little wider than normal to minimize body tilting.

2. Shift your weight to your left arm and drop your right arm so that your forearm is on the mat. Then repeat this sequence with your left arm. Pause.

3. Return your right arm to push-up position and then your left.

Repeat the sequence for 45 seconds if you're a beginner, 1 minute if you're an intermediate. Make sure to switch up the order in which you lower yourself to your forearms—so lead with the right arm as above, then switch and lead with your left arm halfway through.

COME ON, WHAT ARE YOU WAITING FOR? GET ONE SET COMPLETE, THEN ONLY THREE MORE TO GO. JUST KNOCK THEM OFF ONE AT A TIME, PAUSING FOR 1 MINUTE IN BETWEEN, AND I'LL BE WAITING AT THE END FOR YOU.

COOL-DOWN

You are really gonna need a solid cool-down today, so take your time and jump on an elliptical machine, using the handles to help that upper body relax. A minimum of 10 minutes here to bring your heart rate down.

STATIC STRETCHES

Cool now? Time to breathe in . . . breathe out . . . and chill a bit. You've earned the right to a proper cool-down today, so perform the following three stretches:

SPINAL TWISTS

1. Lie on the floor, with your arms extending outward in a T position. Put your right foot on your left knee.

2. Using your left hand, gently pull your right knee toward the floor, twisting your spine and keeping your left arm straight out, hips and shoulders on the floor. Hold for 30 seconds.

Repeat, using the right hand and left knee.

CHEST COMPLEX TRIPLE STRETCHES

1. For the first stretch, stand next to a wall or door frame. Extend one arm and bend at the elbow, so that your arm forms a right angle, with your upper arm parallel to the ground and your forearm sticking straight up. Place your forearm against the wall or door frame. Now, twist your whole body away from the wall, with a special emphasis on pushing your chest through the turn, so that you feel a gentle stretch in your chest. Hold this for 10 seconds.

2. For the next stretch, step away from the wall so that, instead of your forearm, only your hand is on the wall. The arm still forms a right angle from your body, but this time your hand and shoulder are at the same level. Make the same twist, pushing your chest into the turn, to stretch the chest in the new position. Hold this for 10 seconds.

3. For the third and final variation, step further from the wall and extend your arm straight, so that the entire arm is parallel to the ground. Place your hand on the wall, then twist again into the stretch. You should feel the tension in your chest. Hold this for 10 seconds.

Switch arms and repeat this sequence.

QUADRICEPS/HIP FLEXOR STRETCHES

1. Starting in a standing position, take a big step forward with your left leg, then place your right knee on the ground.

2. Maintaining this posture, shift the entire body slightly forward from the hip. You should feel this stretch down the front of your quad and hip flexor. Exhale and hold the stretch. Don't arch your back.

Hold for 30 seconds, then gently release and switch legs.

AFTER A BRUTAL WORKOUT LIKE TODAY'S, YOU MIGHT FIND YOU'RE ESPECIALLY SORE. A WARM (BUT NOT SUPERHOT) BATH WITH EPSOM SALTS CAN REALLY TAKE THE ACHE OUT OF SORE MUSCLES—GIVE IT A TRY. STAY IN THERE FOR AT LEAST 22 MINUTES, AND YOUR MUSCLES WILL GET A BIG RELEASE.

DAY 18 MEAL PLAN

We've got a great meal plan for you today. I hope you took the time to plan out your meals so that you don't sell yourself short!

BREAKFAST 3/4 cup low-fat yogurt; 1/4 cup granola; 1/4 cup All-Bran cereal; 1/2 cup blueberries; 1-1/2 cups skim or soy milk.

SNACK 1 large apple; 1/2 cup low-fat cottage cheese.

LUNCH **Vegetarian wrap:** Spread 1/2 cup hummus and 1 oz. light feta cheese on a large whole-wheat wrap, then top with 1/4 avocado, roasted red pepper and lettuce. Serve with 1/2 cup baby carrots.

SNACK Mix 1 oz. canned salmon with 1 tbsp. light mayo, celery and onion and spread over 2 rye crackers.

DINNER **BBQ pork:** Grill 4 oz. pork tenderloin with 1 tbsp. BBQ sauce. Serve with 2 cups roasted vegetables (red onion, peppers and asparagus) and sweet potato. **Cook-ahead option:** Grill an extra 2 to 3 oz. of pork and roast an extra cup of veggies for tomorrow's lunch.

DAY 19
HITZ Cardio #6

TOMMY RULE #19: FATIGUE MAKES FAILURES OF US ALL . . . IF WE LET IT!

This is your second "skip" at the can. For HITZ Cardio #6 the repetitions get a little bit longer, but I know you're ready. Let's get after them and burn some more calories. You should be getting better with your steps now, especially as you fatigue . . . and boy, will you ever fatigue. Fight through it and you will be shredded in no time at all. We are going to do three sets of this circuit, followed by your cool-down. Good luck and have fun.

TODAY'S WORKOUT

FOCUS	EQUIPMENT	TOTAL TIME
Building your high-intensity stamina.	Skipping rope.	About 40 minutes.

HERE'S THE PLAN FOR SKIPPING DOMINATION:
Warmup
Dynamic Stretches
HITZ Cardio #6
Cool-Down
Static Stretches

WARMUP

Before we get to the skipping, let's warm you up!

For 15 minutes, I want you to either jog or bike, working at a PES intensity of Level 5. You should be just above comfortable, but still able to speak easily.

DYNAMIC STRETCHES

After your warmup, I've got three dynamic stretches for you:

DYNAMIC GLUTE AND HAMSTRING STRETCHES

1. Stand tall (shoulders back), with your feet shoulder width apart. Lift your left foot and grab just below your left knee with both hands.

2. With both hands, gently pull your left knee up, while maintaining your balance on your right heel. This will activate your butt and the backs of your legs. Hold for 3 seconds, then release your left leg.

Repeat the same sequence with your right leg. Perform 5 repetitions with each leg.

DYNAMIC QUAD STRETCHES

1. Stand tall (shoulders back), with your feet shoulder width apart. Lift your left foot behind you and grab your ankle (or foot) with your left hand.

2. Gently push your left hip forward, while keeping a straight line with your body and maintaining your balance on your right heel. Hold for 3 seconds, then release your left ankle.

Repeat this sequence with your right leg. Perform 5 repetitions on each leg.

DYNAMIC CHEST AND BICEP STRETCHES

1. Stand tall (shoulders back), with your feet shoulder width apart. Slowly move your arms out to the sides, slightly behind you, with your thumbs up (just like The Fonz).

2. As your arms go back, rotate your thumbs down and back until they are pointing to the wall behind you. Pause, then return to the starting position. You should feel this one in your chest and biceps.

Perform 10 repetitions.

HITZ CARDIO #6

Get some water and get ready to burn some calories. Again, we are going to go through three sets. So take a 2-minute break after the first set and then power through. The full descriptions of the moves are below. Yeah, I know it's tough. But look at this way: Somewhere, right now, a bunch of school kids are doing these moves without even breaking a sweat. If they can do it, so can you.

Double Bounce	30 Reps
Single Bounce	30 Reps
Speed Single Bounce	30 Reps
One-Foot Single Bounce	30 Right, 30 Left
Straddle	30 Reps
Front and Back	30 Reps
Side to Side	30 Reps
Heel—Toe	30 Reps
Crossover	30 Reps
Double Jump	30 Reps
Speed Single Bounce	100 Reps

That's set one. Hope you didn't whip yourself too badly! Now, let's do it all over again . . . and again!

Double Bounce: Bounce twice per turn of the rope, feet together.

Single Bounce: Bounce only once per turn of the rope, feet together.

Single Speed Bounce: Perform single bounce at a rapid pace.

One-Foot Single Bounce: Perform a single bounce on one foot, alternating feet at each turn.

Straddle: Place feet together on first turn, spread legs on second—almost like you're doing jumping jacks inside the rope.

Front and Back: Bounce once at each rope turn, hopping forward with both feet on the first turn, then backward on the next turn.

Side to Side: Bounce once at each rope turn, hopping left with both feet on the first turn, then right with both feet on the next turn.

Heel—Toe: Bounce once at each rope turn, alternating right and left heels so that the toe of the opposite foot makes contact with the ground at the same time. So, you land with your right heel and left toe touching the ground, then with your left heel and right toe.

Crossover: Start with a single bounce, then cross elbows on the second turn. This causes the rope to crisscross, so jump through the loop.

Double Jump: Turn the rope twice on a single bounce—you're going to have to bend at the hips.

COOL-DOWN

Today should've gone more smoothly than Day 12, and the next time you skip, it will be even better. Go get your water and then finish up with your cool-down. Ten minutes will be plenty.

STATIC STRETCHES

As always, take the time to stretch it out. I've got four for you today:

HAMSTRING STRETCHES

1. Lie down on your back, with a slight bend in both legs.

2. Lift your right leg straight up and grab it behind your calf. If you are flexible enough, grab your ankle (or even your toe). Gently pull your right leg toward you, keeping your back straight.

Hold the stretch for 30 seconds.
Repeat with the left leg.

CHEST COMPLEX TRIPLE STRETCHES

1. For the first stretch, stand next to a wall or door frame. Extend one arm and bend at the elbow, so that your arm forms a right angle, with your upper arm parallel to the ground and your forearm sticking straight up. Place your forearm against the wall or door frame. Now, twist your whole body away from the wall, with a special emphasis on pushing your chest through the turn, so that you feel a gentle stretch in your chest. Hold this for 10 seconds.

2. For the next stretch, step away from the wall so that, instead of your forearm, only your hand is on the wall. The arm still forms a right angle from your body, but this time your hand and shoulder are at the same level. Make the same twist, pushing your chest into the turn, to stretch the chest in the new position. Hold this for 10 seconds.

3. For the third and final variation, step further from the wall and extend your arm straight, so that the entire arm is parallel to the ground. Place your hand on the wall, then twist again into the stretch. You should feel the tension in your chest. Hold this for 10 seconds.

Switch arms and repeat this sequence.

SPINAL TWISTS

1. Lie on the floor, with your arms extending outward in a T position. Put your right foot on your left knee.

2. Using your left hand, gently pull your right knee toward the floor, twisting your spine and keeping your left arm straight out, hips and shoulders on the floor. Hold for 30 seconds.

Repeat, using the right hand and left knee.

QUADRICEPS/HIP FLEXOR STRETCHES

1. Starting in a standing position, take a big step forward with your left leg, then place your right knee on the ground.

2. Maintaining this posture, shift the entire body slightly forward from the hip. You should feel this stretch down the front of your quad and hip flexor. Exhale and hold the stretch. Don't arch your back.

Hold for 30 seconds, then gently release and switch legs.

YOU REALLY EARNED TODAY'S CALORIES—GIVE YOURSELF A PAT ON THE BACK AND ENJOY IT, BECAUSE TOMORROW I'M GOING TO GIVE YOU A HITZ-RESISTANCE STYLE KICK IN THE PANTS!

DAY 19 MEAL PLAN

Your car can't run without gas, and your body will not perform optimally without fuel, so get with the program!

BREAKFAST 1 small whole-grain bagel (look for one that is about 180 to 220 calories) with 2 tbsp. natural almond butter; 1 apple; 1-1/2 cups skim or soy milk.

SNACK 1 cup watermelon; 3/4 cup low-fat yogurt.

LUNCH 2 to 3 oz. pork with 1 cup roasted vegetables.

SNACK 1/3 cup hummus; 2 rye crackers; 1 cup sliced red pepper.

DINNER Chicken Greek salad: Chop 3 oz. grilled chicken breast and arrange over 1 cup Greek salad (cucumber, tomato, green pepper) mixed with 1 oz. light feta and 1 tbsp. light Italian dressing. Serve alongside 1/2 cup brown rice. **Cook-ahead option:** Grill an extra 3 oz. of chicken tonight for tomorrow's lunch.

DAY 20
HITZ Resistance #9

TOMMY RULE #20: TRAIN AS IF EVERYONE IS WATCHING. THAT WAY, YOU WON'T CHEAT YOURSELF AND YOU'LL GIVE IT EVERYTHING YOU HAVE. AFTER ALL, YOU WOULD ONLY BE CHEATING YOURSELF, AND WE DON'T DO THAT HERE!

You're knocking the days off one by one, and you're already into the latter half of the 10PS. Are you as impressed as I am? You're probably feeling muscles that you never thought you had to begin with. Just think . . . this is the start of the rest of your life, a happier and healthier life.

But before you pat yourself on the shoulder, we've got to get through today. As you've noticed, each week the workouts have gotten a little more difficult, and today is no different. I want you to notice the differences in how you train. It's all about working smarter, not harder. Hours a day in the gym are not necessary to have an effective workout. Efficiency is the key to success, and you're blazing one hell of a trail. I don't want you resting on your laurels, so I'm not gonna waste any more of your time—have fun today!

TODAY'S WORKOUT

FOCUS	EQUIPMENT	REPETITIONS	SETS
Lower-body wonderland, so use the hand rails when you go down the stairs tonight!	10-, 12-, 15- and 20-pound dumbbells (DBs) and a stability ball (SB).	Beginners, most of your repetitions are going to be 45 seconds long. Intermediates? You're going for 1-minute reps.	Three sets today—easy compared with the last workout, right? Wrong! But you can do it!

ALL RIGHT, THEN. HERE'S TODAY'S WORKOUT:
Warmup
Dynamic Stretches
HITZ Resistance #9

• BURPEES • GLUTEUS MEDIUS HIP RAISES
• DUMBBELL PUSH-UPS • JUMP SQUATS
1-minute rest . . . grab some water

• BURPEES • STABILITY BALL AND DUMBBELL RUSSIAN TWISTS
• DUMBBELL LOW-TOE HI-FLIES • CORE LEG DROPS
There's your set. Take a minute for a quick drink, then do it two more times.

You got enough left for one more? You'd better. Do one STABILITY BALL ROLLOUT after your third set.

Cool-Down
Static Stretches

WARMUP

Jump on a bike or treadmill for your 10-minute warmup. If you are training outdoors, you should be jogging or riding a bike.

For the first five minutes, work at an intensity of Level 4 on the PES. You should be sweating a little, but feeling good and able to carry on a conversation effortlessly.

For the last five minutes, work at an intensity of Level 5. You should be just above comfortable, sweating more but still able to talk without any problem.

DYNAMIC STRETCHES

After your warmup, here are your three dynamic stretches:

DYNAMIC QUAD STRETCHES

1. Stand tall (shoulders back), with your feet shoulder width apart. Lift your left foot behind you and grab your ankle (or foot) with your left hand.

2. Gently push your left hip forward, while keeping a straight line with your body and maintaining your balance on your right heel. Hold for 3 seconds, then release your left ankle.

Repeat this sequence with your right leg. Perform 5 repetitions on each leg.

DYNAMIC SUMO SQUATS

1. Stand tall (shoulders back), with your feet close together. Take a large lateral step to the right and drop into a deep squat (think of a sumo wrestler). Pause, then return to the starting standing position.

2. Now take a large lateral step to the left and drop into a deep squat. Pause, then return to the starting position.

Perform 5 repetitions on each side.

DYNAMIC BACK SWINGS

1. Stand tall (shoulders back), with your feet shoulder width apart. Lift and hold both arms up to the side at shoulder height. Twist as far as you can to the right, so that you can feel a good stretch in your mid- to lower back.

2. Pause, then twist to the left (you should resemble a propeller as you twist).

Repeat for 10 revolutions.

READY NOW? I'M NOT GOING TO LIE TO YOU; THIS IS GOING TO MAKE YOUR LEGS FEEL LIKE THEY'RE MADE OF BRICKS. BUT THAT'S JUST THE FIRST STEP TOWARD LEGS OF STEEL. REMEMBER . . . THREE SETS, RIGHT? NO CHEATING!

BURPEES

I know you hate these, but the benefits far outweigh the way you feel at the moment.

Push, push, push . . . oh yeah, and breathe!

1. Stand tall, with your feet shoulder width apart.

2. Bend at your knees and hips, while placing both hands on the floor.

3. Step (beginner) or thrust (intermediate) both feet back so you are in a push-up position. Then reverse what you just did, kicking both feet back in, tucking your knees and standing up (beginner) or jumping (intermediate).

Repeat for your allotted time: beginners, 45 seconds; intermediates, 1 minute.

GLUTEUS MEDIUS HIP RAISES

Everybody wants to work on the one part of their bodies they never really see: their butts. Ever wondered which exercise is the best to keep your booty from shaking? Well, you're about to find out. This is a double whammy, as you will feel it in your glute meds (that muscle that gives your butt some boom, pow). Hate me now, thank me later.

1. Begin on all fours on a mat. Drop onto your left forearm and extend your right leg directly to the side.

2. Raise your right leg as high as you can and pause.

3. Lower it almost completely, without letting it touch the ground.

Repeat this action for 45 seconds (beginner) or 1 minute (intermediate), then switch by putting your right forearm on the ground and extending your left leg to the side, following the same protocol.

TOMMY TIP

A slow tempo yields the best results!

DUMBBELL PUSH-UPS

Are you feeling stronger than last time? You'd better be! This time, focus on keeping your elbows close to your side.

1. Start in a plank position, with each hand on a DB under each shoulder. I'm demonstrating from my knees here, but if you're an intermediate, you should be up on your toes.

2. Engage your core, maintain a flat back (neutral spine), bend your elbows and drop your chest to about 2 inches above the DB. Keep your elbows as close to your sides as possible.

3. Pause, then push your body up until both arms are extended.

Repeat this sequence for your allotted time: 45 seconds if you're a beginner, 1 minute if you're an intermediate.

JUMP SQUATS

This is not only a strength and cardio exercise, it's also a plyometric exercise—one designed to create peak results through quick, explosive movements. You will be moving constantly, so try and stay light on your feet. You want to be as quiet as a teenager sneaking into the house at 3 a.m., not as loud as an elephant on stampede!

1. Stand tall, with your feet shoulder width apart. Drop into a squat position, with your weight on your heels.

2. Engage your core and jump straight up so that your body is completely extended. As you land, return to the squat position you started from.

Repeat this sequence for your allotted time: 45 seconds if you're a beginner, 1 minute if you're an intermediate.

TIME FOR A 1-MINUTE REST.

TOMMY TIP

Do not "overjump." The point is to be fully extended on the jump and then land contracted in the squat position. Intermediate exercisers, hold a pair of small dumbbells (15- to 30-pound) for increased resistance.

BURPEES

And again!

1. Stand tall, with your feet shoulder width apart.

2. Bend at your knees and hips, while placing both hands on the floor.

3. Step (beginner) or thrust (intermediate) both feet back so you are in a push-up position. Then reverse what you just did, kicking both feet back in, tucking your knees and standing up (beginner) or jumping (intermediate).

Repeat for your allotted time: beginners, 45 seconds; intermediates, 1 minute.

STABILITY BALL AND DUMBBELL RUSSIAN TWISTS

This one will make you feel like a circus act, and you may even fall off the SB once or twice.

But it will make you tight through the middle. So, you ready?

1. Sit on a medium-sized SB, holding a 10- to 15-pound DB. Walk your body down the ball until your shoulder blades are in contact with the SB, and keep your feet shoulder width apart. Extend your arms straight up, holding your DB in both hands, directly above your chin.

2. Slowly rotate your body and drop the DB to the right until the outside of your shoulder is on the SB.

3. Pause, contract your abs and rotate back to the other side.

Alternate from side to side, and repeat this sequence for your allotted time: 45 seconds if you're a beginner, 1 minute if you're an intermediate.

TOMMY TIP

Go slow at the beginning and speed up as you feel more comfortable. Brace your heels into the ground and keep your hips up at all times!

DUMBBELL LOW-TOE HI-FLIES

It's time for you to be an athlete! Shoulders, core, glutes and cardio . . . that's what's in store for you with this one. If you thought the burpee was tough, well, this is its older, grumpy brother! All you need is a 10- or 15-pound dumbbell.

1. Grab a 10-pound DB and hold it in your left hand, just outside your right knee. Lift your left leg so that it hovers above the ground, keeping your weight balanced on your bent right leg.

2. With your core engaged, bend forward from your waist, lowering to a 45-degree angle.

3. Explode and jump laterally to your left leg, while lifting your left arm straight up in the air and straightening your back into an upright position. Pause, then jump back to your right leg while lowering your back to a 45-degree angle and bringing the DB back to outside of your right knee.

Repeat this sequence non-stop for your allotted time: 45 seconds if you're a beginner, 1 minute if you're an intermediate. Then switch hands and do it again.

CORE LEG DROPS

This core move will have your friends using your stomach to do their laundry. This is one of the best exercises I know for your lower abdominals—when done correctly—so pay attention.

1. Lie on a mat, flat on your back, with your hands palms down beside your hips and your legs pointing straight up at the ceiling.

2. Pin your knees together; engage your core and slowly lower your legs to within 1 foot of the floor. Keep your shoulder blades on the ground at all times.

3. Pause, then return your legs to the 90-degree starting position.

Repeat this sequence for your allotted time: 45 seconds if you're a beginner, 1 minute if you're an intermediate.

AND THAT'S A WRAP . . . FOR YOUR FIRST SET. TAKE A MINUTE TO CATCH YOUR BREATH AND GRAB SOME WATER, THEN REPEAT. AFTER YOUR THIRD SET, ADD A STABILITY BALL ROLLOUT. GO!

TOMMY TIP

The more slowly you raise your legs back up, the more you use your lower abdominals.

STABILITY BALL ROLLOUTS

Shred, shred, shred. This one is all about a hard, defined, hot stomach.

1. Grab an SB and place your forearms on top of it, with your hands clasped. Extend your legs back, so that you are on your toes. Keep your body in a straight line at all times.

2. Push your elbows forward so that the SB is rolled away from your body.

3. Pause, then return to the starting position. The only things that should be moving are your arms; do not rock your body.

Repeat for your allotted time: beginners, 30 seconds; intermediates, 50 seconds.

COOL-DOWN

Time for your cool-down! You probably walked in, and if you don't do your cool-down today, you'll likely limp out. Don't skip this one, as it has been quite the week. For that very reason, we are going to cool down for 15 minutes today.

STATIC STRETCHES

Once you have finished, it's time for you to do your static stretches:

SPINAL TWISTS

1. Lie on the floor, with your arms extending outward in a T position. Put your right foot on your left knee.

2. Using your left hand, gently pull your right knee toward the floor, twisting your spine and keeping your left arm straight out, hips and shoulders on the floor. Hold for 30 seconds.

Repeat, using the right hand and left knee.

QUADRICEPS/HIP FLEXOR STRETCHES

1. Starting in a standing position, take a big step forward with your left leg, then place your right knee on the ground.

2. Maintaining this posture, shift the entire body slightly forward from the hip. You should feel this stretch down the front of your quad and hip flexor. Exhale and hold the stretch. Don't arch your back.

Hold for 30 seconds, then gently release and switch legs.

HAMSTRING STRETCHES

1. Lie down on your back, with a slight bend in both legs.

2. Lift your right leg straight up and grab it behind your calf. If you are flexible enough, grab your ankle (or even your toe). Gently pull your right leg toward you, keeping your back straight.

Hold the stretch for 30 seconds. Repeat with the left leg.

HIP STRETCHES

1. Lie down and cross your left foot over your right knee.

2. Clasp your hands behind your right knee. Gently pull your right leg toward you, keeping your back straight.

Hold the stretch for 30 seconds.
Repeat with the left leg.

DON'T FORGET TO HYDRATE YOURSELF. YOUR BODY IS PROBABLY STRAINING UNDER INCREASED DEMAND AND WILL ONLY FUNCTION PROPERLY IF YOU ARE DRINKING YOUR REQUIRED WATER. TRAVEL WITH A LARGE WATER BOTTLE IF THAT WILL MAKE IT EASIER FOR YOU.

DAY 20 MEAL PLAN

Chow down and fuel up.

BREAKFAST 3/4 cup low-fat yogurt; 1/4 cup granola; 1/4 cup All-Bran cereal; 1/2 cup strawberries; 1-1/2 cups skim or soy milk.

SNACK 1 mango; 20 almonds.

LUNCH Chicken pita: Stuff 1 whole-wheat pita bread with 3 oz. leftover chicken, 1 cup lettuce, tomato, onion and mustard mixed with 1/4 tsp. honey.

SNACK 1/2 cup edamame.

DINNER Beef fajita: Stir-fry 4 oz. lean steak, 1 cup sliced peppers and onion in 1 tsp. olive oil. Serve in 1 large whole-wheat tortilla with 3 tbsp. salsa. **Cook-ahead option:** Cook an extra 3 oz. of beef and 1 cup of peppers and set aside for tomorrow's lunch.

DAY 21
Active Rest

TOMMY RULE #21: IF TODAY IS "ONE OF THOSE DAYS," HIT THE RESET BUTTON AND MAKE TODAY THE BEST DAY EVER!

So, today is the day your habit kicks in. It's a pretty interesting concept, don't you think? We're all the victims of our own habits, whether we're smokers, procrastinators, day-dreamers, heavy drinkers, self-pitiers, chronic oversleepers—whatever. It seems sometimes that we're not in control, that we just kind of stumble from one thing to another, just fol-lowing our familiar patterns.

But today is the day you fully realize that it doesn't have to be that way. We all have good habits, too, and what's great about them is that we can be in control of them. In fact, as you've just proven, we can create them out of thin air (and a whole lot of effort). You want to be something? Be it. You want to be the kind of person who gets out of bed in the morning and takes on the world on your own terms? Be that person. It's as easy (and as hard) as that.

And today is the day you begin to reap the rewards for the sweat and sore muscles you've been enduring. Today you are the person you set out to be three weeks ago. You stuck with the plan, and now the plan is going to stick with you. You're not in the habit of hoovering down a bowl of chips while you're sitting in front of the TV—you're in the habit of satisfying yourself with the kind of healthy fuel your body has been asking for all along. You're now in the habit of listening to your body's natural insistence that you use it—by running, biking, swimming, skipping or whatever it is your body wants to do to stay active. Feels good, doesn't it?

The hardest part is over. To be honest, the real challenge isn't your daily cardio or resistance training, and it is not the adjustment that comes with a new way of eating; the hard part is sticking with the plan and convincing yourself to do what's right when it would be so easy to go back to your old ways. The hard part is mental. Well, my friend, that part is over. Your old ways are gone. So there is no more fighting to do every day. Now you're in the habit of doing the things you've been telling yourself for three weeks that you had to do. So congratulations on getting here. Now you can enjoy not only the rest of the 10PS, but the years of fun-filled physical activity and healthy eating that lie ahead of you.

Notice I didn't say "sit back" and enjoy the rest of the 10PS. You don't sit back anymore, do you? That's not your habit anymore. And that is true even when you're resting. Trust me: Just sprawling out on the couch or hammock is no way to rest. I'm not saying you're never going to relax again. But I am saying that the best time to move around a little is when you feel like it the absolute least. I know this from personal experience—I've had my share of sore muscles! I couldn't begin to tell you how many times I've been sore after a game, stunt or workout. Deep inside, I just wanted to grab a huge mattress and curl up like a baby. Come to think of it, if someone had shown up with a man-sized pacifier, I might not have stood a chance! But that's when that little voice inside you has to pipe up, bullhorn and all, ready to kick your ass back into gear.

Following 21 days of the 10PS can be a grind. That's as it should be, since anything worth doing is, by definition, going to be hard. You've had a tough week; I know that. You may be feeling sore, cranky or just kind of sluggish. On the other hand, you may be energetically charged and ready for more. (After all, that's what exercise does for you. It doesn't cost energy—it gives you energy.) Whichever one it is, the best solution for your problem is a recovery method called active rest or active recovery.

You've already been doing it, so you already know that some sort of low-intensity exercise after workouts gets the blood flowing through your system and reduces soreness in your muscles by reducing lactate levels in your body. On previous days in the 10PS, I've mentioned walking, running, riding and a bunch of other things. Well, that's the way the new you rests.

Another way of putting it is that the soreness in your muscles is not your body's way of telling you to flop onto the couch. It's your body telling you to get moving.

So what's it gonna be? How are you going to kick your ass into gear right now, on this 21st habit-building day? You're going to feel great tomorrow on Day 22. You're going to want to run through walls and beat down stability balls—I made that one up myself. Whatever you decide to do, go and do it now while you're fresh and focused. We've got 10 more days to make some big changes.

Good luck!

DAY 21 MEAL PLAN

You're only as strong as your weakest link. Make sure your weak link isn't nutrition!

BREAKFAST Fruit smoothie: Blend 3/4 cup of low-fat yogurt, 1 cup mixed frozen berries, 1/4 cup orange juice (optional) and 1/2 scoop protein powder; serve with 1/2 English muffin with 1 tbsp. natural peanut butter; 1-1/2 cups skim or soy milk.

SNACK 1/2 bran muffin; 1 oz. light cheese.

LUNCH Turkey sandwich: Layer 3 oz. turkey breast with tomato, mustard and lettuce on 2 slices of whole-grain bread.

SNACK 1/2 cup edamame.

DINNER Grilled salmon: 4 oz. salmon, 1/2 cup brown rice, 1-1/2 cups asparagus. You can use up to 1 tsp. olive oil for grilling either the salmon or the asparagus.

DAY 22
Motivation Day!

TOMMY RULE #22: WORRYING DOESN'T DO YOU ANY GOOD AT ALL—WORK IS WHAT MAKES A DIFFERENCE. WHAT YOU DO IN THESE FINAL FEW DAYS WILL PUT A LASTING STAMP ON YOUR 10PS JOURNEY. WE BUILD FOUNDATIONS, AND THEN WE REALLY GROW!

You've passed the 21-day stage, so your healthy habits should be ingrained at this point. From here on in, we will build on your solid foundation and push you to new levels of success. I know it has been a grind, but you're still here, aren't you? And that means you're pushing ahead.

Motivation is something you will have to create at times. I know as well as anybody that there are those days when you wish you were somewhere else—days when it just seems too difficult to continue. Everything seems too hard to bother with. Yeah, I've been there. Happens all the time.

And I know how to get through that, too. You've probably figured it out yourself if you're still here. Visualization helps immensely during times like that. Knowing where you want to be is going to help you put one foot in front of the other. Sure, stretching a resistance band or rolling around on a stability ball may not seem especially interesting at any given moment. But I'd be willing to bet that your sculpted new body and your new high-energy lifestyle are going to be pretty interesting to you no matter where you are or what you're doing.

So if you're finding it hard to get psyched up to go to the gym, or you're in the middle of your second set of plié squats and you find yourself wishing with all your heart that you were somewhere else (like on the couch), don't let your mind dwell on how boring the squats are—think about that delicious burn in your hips and thighs, and visualize that rock-hard athletic body that is taking shape at that very moment.

Sometimes you are going to have to talk to yourself to get past the pain and discomfort you are feeling. Every day, when you wake up, you have the ability to determine how you are going to do that day. That's up to you. It's the purest kind of power. You can choose to be down on yourself, or you can say "Bring it on!"

Over the last 21 days, I've shared a few success stories with you about amazing feats and transformations to be celebrated. We all come from different places mentally and physically. Following a healthy lifestyle and losing inches and pounds should not be a miserable slog—it should be an amazing journey, during which you face challenges head-on and succeed. Sometimes you will not see the light at the end of the tunnel, but you just have to soldier on, knowing that everything is going to be okay. Hard to believe? Here's some more proof.

Meet Sophia, a truly phenomenal lady and the definition of a warrior. She is another one of my shining stars, and she has become a very good friend. Her journey is nothing short of miraculous, and getting to know her has touched my life and completely changed my outlook. Her story is quite moving, and the obstacles she has overcome will show you that the mind is a very powerful thing. If life has ever dealt you a devastating blow, if you ever doubt your abilities, if you often say to yourself, "I can't," then listen up. Once you hear Sophia's story, you will be unstoppable. Here is the story of my ultimate warrior, Sophia:

My story starts well enough. I was fit, active, strong and on top of the world—about to get married and just starting in my career. Then, I met my nemesis: cancer.

Talk about a sucker punch. Years of treatments, new diagnoses and numerous surgeries took their toll. Somewhere in there, a lupus diagnosis (which for me manifests itself in joint pain and severe skin rashes) only worsened my already low morale. I was depressed, miserable and close to 300 pounds. It was like I had fallen asleep for eight years, and in my moments of wakefulness was seeking escape in food and inactivity.

As I sat on the couch watching TV one afternoon, I remember thinking that being inactive was not alleviating my pain, so maybe I should get up and do something. That day, I began walking. Then I got a pedometer and I started to play a game with myself; being a very competitive person, I played that game to win. Each day, I had to get more steps than the day before. I began to think about what I was eating, and made small changes like cutting out white bread or decreasing sodium intake. Walking turned to running, and soon I had lost 40 pounds. I got sick again, but after my recovery I joined a "biggest loser" contest at work and lost another 35 pounds in four months (winning $900 in the process).

It was during this time that I joined a Bootcamp class. Although it was agonizingly painful, I stuck with it because I was seeing results. But it was slow going and I was curious to see how far I could take my fitness level. I knew I needed a trainer—someone with expertise and the strength to push me. That is when I discovered Tommy.

Working with Tommy has been one of the most pivotal experiences of my life. I rate it up there with having my baby and getting married. Tommy heard my story, took one look at me, and I just know he was thinking, "Oh, I'm going to have myself some fun with this one!"

Workouts were intense from the get-go. He taught me that the best cardio was intense interval training—his ass-kicker hill and sprint intervals are amazing. I remember the first time I finished a cardio session. I got off the treadmill and sent him a text message: "I just kicked the ass right outta yer 'ass kicker'!" My endurance was improving daily. The full-body functional-type movements he incorporated into the workouts gave me unparalleled results in strength, and I began to see big changes in my body shape. The importance of resistance training was another long-overdue lesson Tommy taught me. The importance of changing my body composition and the benefits of increased muscle mass in the form of a higher metabolic rate were new to me—and they have been revolutionary in terms of helping me get to the correct weight.

I had always thought that as long as I was active, I didn't need to worry too much about my diet. Maria Thomas helped me change my mind quickly! My normal pattern was to not eat much of anything before 1 or 2 p.m. Then I would have a little snack, like a latte and muffin, and dinner when I got home around 9. I would also snack continually (usually on popcorn) till bedtime. When I first saw what my new diet would look like, I freaked out! Eating five times a day? I told Maria

I'd never lose any weight eating that much and that often. She told me to trust her—so I did.

I think people would be shocked to know how much you have to eat (and how often) in order to lose weight. I had always restricted my intake severely in order to drop pounds. Well, I came to the conclusion that I needed to be putting just as much thought, planning and energy into my nutrition as I was into my exercise and activity. You cannot maximize the benefits of one without the other—they go hand in hand.

During the four weeks, I lost 13 inches and 21 pounds. And I am 7 to 10 pounds lighter now than I was then. To date, I have lost almost 130 pounds. People ask me all the time (after they finally recognize me), "What's your secret?" Here is my answer: There is no secret, no gimmick and no shortcut. It's about eating right, sweating a lot and pushing past your limits (in fact, they're not "limits" at all, since they're only in your mind; you can push right past them).

Although it is simple, it is not easy. Baby steps to a new you. "I can't" resides in the mind, not the muscles. I finally decided I was no longer going to be a victim of life's circumstances and sit on my fat ass watching life pass me by. Transformation begins on the inside, and we all have within what it takes to transform the "with-out." We will prioritize what we value and we'll get after what we want. How bad do you want it? Are you experiencing the best you there is? If not, don't rip yourself off, and don't shortchange the rest of the world, either.

Although I was on my own way to uncovering and unleashing that inner strength, Tommy helped me see that whatever quality I possessed that made me survive cancer so many times could also help propel me forward. I am a nine-time "thriver"—not just a cancer "survivor." I have cancer, but it does not have me, and although we will likely cross paths again, I will not lie down and wait. As long as I have life to live, I will live it.

This experience inspired me to become a personal trainer, Bootcamp instructor and nutrition counsellor so that I can do my part to empower others to find within themselves the path to transformational change. As my next fitness goal, I am contemplating training for a figure competition—Wow! Who would've guessed that two years ago? I have a real sense of accomplishment to know that I've lost the weight, but I have a deeper sense of pride that I've gained the respect of my trainer. Tommy and I share a mutual admiration, and I consider him a mentor and friend.

Thanks, Tommy!

How does that one grab you? I don't know about you, but I am forever grateful for my encounter with Sophia, who is now one of my sources of inspiration, as well as a very good friend. Through it all, Sophia's husband, Dean, and their daughter, Kennedy, have been her biggest cheerleaders and support system, and they live every day to the fullest.

So what's your excuse now? You should enjoy the day, and even go out for a light run, hike, ride or whatever makes you tick. Day 23 is tomorrow—the start of the last week of the 10PS, but the beginning of the "new you." I'll see you in the trenches!

DAY 22 MEAL PLAN

Try to take the time to really enjoy today's meals—healthy eating gives you the pleasure not just of taste, but also of the knowledge that you're giving your body what it really needs. Eat up!

BREAKFAST 2-egg omelette (with 1 oz. light cheese and mushrooms); 2 slices whole-grain toast with 2 tsp. margarine; 1 orange; 1-1/2 cups skim or soy milk.

SNACK 1 cup grapes; 20 almonds.

LUNCH Beef wrap: 3 oz. beef, 1 cup peppers, 2 tbsp. salsa in 1 large fajita.

SNACK Granola bar.

DINNER Soup and salad: 1-1/2 cups chicken noodle soup, 2 cups mixed-green salad (lettuce, onion and peppers) with 2 tbsp. each of slivered almonds and dried cranberries. Mix with a dressing made from 1 tbsp. balsamic vinegar and 1 tsp. olive oil.

Bet that was easier to stick to than ever before—congrats on your new healthy habits.

And here are your meals for the week. Make sure your last week of the 10PS is a huge success by stocking up and planning.

MEAL PLAN #4

DAY 23	DAY 24	DAY 25	DAY 26	DAY 27	DAY 28	DAY 29
Breakfast	**Breakfast**	**Breakfast**	**Breakfast**	**Breakfast**	**Breakfast**	**Breakfast**
Toast, boiled egg, orange and a glass of milk	Yogurt with granola, All-Bran cereal, strawberries and a glass of milk	Fruit smoothie, English muffin with natural peanut butter and a glass of milk	Toast with natural almond butter, orange and a glass of milk	Yogurt with granola, All-Bran cereal, peaches and a glass of milk	Scrambled eggs, back bacon, toast, grapes and a glass of milk	Fruit smoothie, English muffin with natural peanut butter and a glass of milk
Snack	**Snack**	**Snack**	**Snack**	**Snack**	**Snack**	**Snack**
Blueberries and yogurt	Mango and almonds	English muffin with natural peanut butter	Strawberries and yogurt	Watermelon and almonds	Blueberries and almonds	Bran muffin and light cheese
Lunch	**Lunch**	**Lunch**	**Lunch**	**Lunch**	**Lunch**	**Lunch**
Tuna wrap	Chicken leftovers with yam and mixed-green salad	Grilled turkey and cheese sandwich with snap peas	Curried beef leftovers and mixed-green salad	Chicken Caesar pita	Soup and rye crackers with salmon and baby carrots	Turkey wrap
Snack	**Snack**	**Snack**	**Snack**	**Snack**	**Snack**	**Snack**
Granola bar	Hummus with grape tomatoes and rye crackers	Hummus with rye crackers and snap peas	Granola bar	Edamame	Granola bar	Hummus with rye crackers and broccoli
Dinner	**Dinner**	**Dinner**	**Dinner**	**Dinner**	**Dinner**	**Dinner**
BBQ chicken breast with yam and mixed-green salad	Prawn stir-fry	Curried beef with mixed-green salad	Chicken Caesar salad	Salmon and potatoes with spinach salad	Open-face turkey burger with mixed-green salad	Pasta with meat sauce

DAY 23
HITZ Resistance #10

TOMMY RULE #23: THERE IS NO SUCH THING AS "I CAN'T." YOU EITHER WILL OR WILL NOT!

You'll notice that, at this point, there is no real difference between the rep times for beginner and intermediate exercisers. That's right, ex-beginners: You've caught up. Intermediates, are you feeling more like experts? Well, there's only one way to prove it: If your rep times this week aren't quite tough enough, try adding 10 seconds and see how that goes.

You're all 23 days in, and you've already built proper habits. Now it's time to roll on to what may have seemed mission impossible 23 days ago. This is your last resistance week in the 10PS, but just the tip of the iceberg in your transformation. Everything that lasts has a solid foundation, and that's what we have built here: a solid foundation. This week is going to challenge you mentally and physically and propel you to new heights. Can't wait to hear about it—but first, you're gonna be about it!

Gulp . . . you better be ready, because as my friend Russell Peters would say, "Somebody gonna get a hurt!"

TODAY'S WORKOUT

FOCUS	EQUIPMENT	REPETITIONS	SETS
Today (I've got a coy grin on my face right now) all I need to say is **HIGH-INTENSITY TRAINING ZONE!**	A pair of 15- to 20-pound dumbbells (DBs) and a 10- to 20-pound DB, a stability ball (SB) and a skipping rope.	One minute.	Crank it up to three sets today—get ready for a challenge.

HERE WE ARE, IN THE FINAL WEEK OF THE 10PS. I KNOW YOU'RE GETTING STRONGER AND FITTER. SO GUESS WHAT? I'M MAKING YOUR WORKOUTS HARDER. TIME TO GET YOUR GAME FACE ON AND GET OUT THERE. CHECK OUT WHAT I'VE GOT FOR YOU TODAY:

Warmup
Dynamic Stretches
HITZ Resistance #10

• SKIPPING • DUMBBELL CORE ROWING • STABILITY BALL HAMSTRING CURLS • CORE SLIDERS
• STABILITY BALL AND DUMBBELL ONE-ARM FLIES
1-minute rest . . . grab some water!

• SKIPPING • CORE SIDE PLANK DIPS • DUMBBELL SQUAT PRESSES • STABILITY BALL JACKKNIFES
• DUMBBELL WOOD CHOPPERS

How did you like them apples? Well, there's more where that came from . . . Grab some water, 'cause there are two more sets to do.

I know you'd be disappointed if I didn't make you do a **CORE PLANK** until failure after your final set, so I'd better throw one in.

Cool-Down
Static Stretches

WARMUP

Jump on a bike or treadmill for your 10-minute warmup. If you are training outdoors, you should be jogging or riding a bike.

For the first five minutes, work at an intensity of Level 4 on the PES. You should be sweating a little, but still be able to speak comfortably.

For the last five minutes, work at an intensity of Level 5. You should be just above comfortable, sweating more and still able to speak comfortably.

DYNAMIC STRETCHES

After your warmup, I've got three dynamic stretches:

DYNAMIC SUMO SQUATS

1. Stand tall (shoulders back), with your feet close together. Take a large lateral step to the right and drop into a deep squat (think of a sumo wrestler). Pause, then return to the starting standing position.

2. Now take a large lateral step to the left and drop into a deep squat. Pause, then return to the starting position.

Perform 5 repetitions on each side.

DYNAMIC QUAD STRETCHES

1. Stand tall (shoulders back), with your feet shoulder width apart. Lift your left foot behind you and grab your ankle (or foot) with your left hand.

2. Gently push your left hip forward, while keeping a straight line with your body and maintaining your balance on your right heel. Hold for 3 seconds, then release your left ankle.

Repeat this sequence with your right leg. Perform 5 repetitions on each leg.

DYNAMIC CHEST AND BICEP STRETCHES

1. Stand tall (shoulders back), with your feet shoulder width apart. Slowly move your arms out to the sides, slightly behind you, with your thumbs up (just like The Fonz).

2. As your arms go back, rotate your thumbs down and back until they are pointing to the wall behind you. Pause, then return to the starting position. You should feel this one in your chest and biceps.

Perform 10 repetitions.

WARMED UP? OKAY, GO!

SKIPPING

You should be a pro at this by now . . .

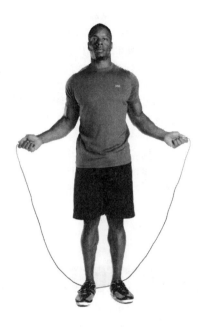

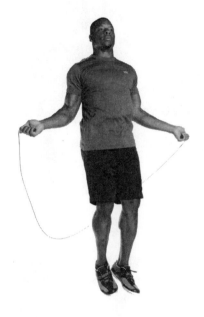

1. Place your skipping rope on the ground and stand in the middle of it. Grab the handles, which should reach about 6 inches below your collarbone when you pull the handles straight up.

2. Start to rotate the rope. The rotation should come from your wrists. To increase the speed of the rotations, increase the tightness of the circles that your wrists are making.

Skip for 2 minutes.

DUMBBELL CORE ROWING

Remember this one? Get ready to shred your core.

1. Place two 10- to 20-pound dumbbells on a mat, shoulder width apart. Position yourself so that you are lying horizontal and face down. To avoid tilting, form a wide base with your legs.

2. Grab the handles of the DBs directly under your shoulders and extend your arms so that they are straight and you are in the plank position. Keep your elbows as close to your sides as possible.

3. Engage your core, maintain a flat back (neutral spine) and row (pull) one dumbbell up toward your hip; you will be stabilizing your body with the other arm. Pause and repeat with your other arm.

Repeat this sequence for 1 minute.

STABILITY BALL HAMSTRING CURLS

Keep those hips up, even as you pull the ball in. Don't cheat yourself, because I'm watching . . . I'm always watching!

1. Lie on your back on a mat (or the floor), with your arms flat beside you. Place both your legs on an SB—your calves and heels must be in contact with the SB at all times.

2. Lift your hips up so that your butt is off the ground. Contract your core and squeeze your glutes.

3. While keeping your hips high, pull the SB toward your butt with your heels, pause, then return to your starting position (hips up at all times).

Repeat this sequence for 1 minute.

CORE SLIDERS

Let's kick that muffin top or spare tire to the curb!

1. Lie on your back, with your feet on the ground and your knees bent. Put your hands flat by your sides and raise your head 3 inches or so off the ground, while looking up toward the ceiling.

2. Keep both hands in contact with the mat at all times, and reach and slide your left hand forward toward a spot between your feet. Make sure you slide far enough to challenge yourself.

3. Pause and repeat the same slide with your right hand.

Follow the same action for 1 minute.

TIME FOR A 30-SECOND REST. JUST ENOUGH TO CATCH YOUR BREATH AND GRAB SOME WATER.

STABILITY BALL AND DUMBBELL ONE-ARM FLIES

This exercise will attack those "chicken cutlets" that reside on the top sides of your armpits. Feel the burn and contract your chest throughout the exercise to gain the most benefit.

1. Sit on a medium-sized SB, holding a DB in your right hand. Walk your body down the ball until your shoulder blades are in contact with the SB. Your feet should be shoulder width apart.

2. Extend your arm straight up, holding the DB so that it is directly over the middle of your chest. Keep your weight on your heels and keep your hips up.

3. Slowly lower the DB directly to your right side until the DB is 3 inches above your chest; pause, then return to the starting position.

Repeat this sequence 1 minute, then switch to your left arm for 1 minute.

TOMMY TIP

Your core must be engaged and your hips must always remain high. Maintain a slow and steady speed, especially on the descent. Your palms should always be up.

SKIPPING

Need I say more? Get off your butt and let's go for two!

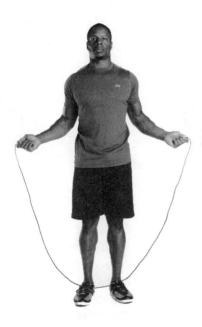
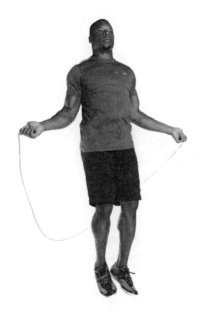

1. Place your skipping rope on the ground and stand in the middle of it. Grab the handles, which should reach about 6 inches below your collarbone when you pull the handles straight up.

2. Start to rotate the rope. The rotation should come from your wrists. To increase the speed of the rotations, increase the tightness of the circles that your wrists are making.

Skip for 2 minutes.

CORE SIDE PLANK DIPS

If you've ever done a side plank, then great. If not . . . even better. This is an amazing exercise to burn your obliques while working your overall core. You won't have to wait to get that burning sensation—I'd say it will appear within 15 seconds of starting the exercise. So when you say you'd do anything to have a tight midsection, you should be careful what you wish for!

1. Lie on the ground on your left side, with your body completely straight. Your weight should be resting on your left forearm, with your left elbow directly under your left shoulder. Stack your feet directly on top of each other. (Beginners, you can have your bottom leg bent with your top leg straight.)

2. Raise your hips as high as you can so that the only things on the ground are your left forearm and your feet (or knee, if you're a beginner). Now pause and hold for 30 seconds.

3. Drop your hips so that they are about 2 inches above the ground.

Repeat this up-and-down sequence for 30 seconds, then repeat it on your right side for a 30-second-hold, plus 30 seconds of dips.

TOMMY TIP

You can speed through these as fast as you like, but ensure that your elbow position is perfect! Dig your feet into the ground and focus on your core throughout the entire movement.

DUMBBELL SQUAT PRESSES

It's time to push the pace with this full-body exercise. It's an explosive movement that will force you to have some coordination and technique. You will feel this one through your entire body. The key to making it to 1 minute is to let your legs assist you in the shoulder press. You ready? Of course you are. Now get to it.

1. Grab a pair of 15- to 30-pound DBs and hold them at shoulder height. Stand tall and make sure that your feet are slightly wider than shoulder width apart.

2. Squat so that your thighs are parallel to the floor.

3. Pushing through your heels, use your glutes to "explode" back up to the starting position, while at the same time pushing the DBs straight up over your head by extending your arms. Then drop back into your squat position and return the DBs to just above your shoulder.

Repeat this sequence for 1 minute.

TOMMY TIP

Keep your weight on your heels and have a slight bend in your knees. This is an explosive movement, so it should be done quickly with proper form.

STABILITY BALL JACKKNIFES

Ready to scream "Six-pack, here I come"? I want perfect form only on these jackknifes.

Once your knees point to the ground . . . it's over!

1. Place your hands on the floor in push-up position.

2. Place one shin on a medium-sized SB, now the other shin.

3. Engage your core and pull your knees up toward your chest. Pause, then return to the starting position.

Repeat this sequence for 1 minute.

DUMBBELL WOOD CHOPPERS

The wood chopper is an awesome core exercise that will attack your obliques like no other.

The twisting action will remove the thickness that your abdominals are hiding under.

1. Stand tall, with a 10- to 20-pound dumbbell cupped in your hands. Make sure that your feet are slightly wider than shoulder width. Put a slight bend in your knees, with your hips slightly pushed back.

2. Contract your abdominals from top to bottom. Then, with your arms straight, squat down and rotate your body toward the outside of your left knee. Do not round your lower back, and make sure you keep your head and chest up.

3. Raise your body, twist and swing upward to the outside of your right shoulder, as if you had a baseball bat in your hands (swinging for a high pitch). Pause, then return to your original position.

Repeat the movement for 30 seconds and then switch sides, so that you are low on your right side and high over your left shoulder.

TIRED? I DIDN'T THINK SO! YOU'VE GOT TWO MORE SETS TO DO. GRAB SOME WATER, THEN GET THEM DONE. DONE ALL THREE? GIVE ME A CORE PLANK!

CORE PLANK

Do this after your last set and hold it until failure!

1. Begin on all fours (hands and knees) on a mat.

2. Extend your legs so that your entire body is flat, in a straight-arm plank position, then go down to your forearms.

3. Raise your hips so that your body is in a straight line and your weight is on your elbows and toes. Beginners, you may need to be on your knees. That's fine for now—just ensure that your hips are down, with your core engaged. This should be hard work.

Hold the plank position until you can't hold it anymore! You have only a single set of this one, so make it count.

COOL-DOWN

Nice work. Are you about worn out? You'd better be! Now it's time to breathe in . . . breathe out. You've earned the right to a proper cool-down today, so I've got five stretches for you:

STATIC STRETCHES

I've got five stretches on deck today. Here they are:

HIP STRETCHES

1. Lie down and cross your left foot over your right knee.

2. Clasp your hands behind your right knee. Gently pull your right leg toward you, keeping your back straight.

Hold the stretch for 30 seconds.
Repeat with the left leg.

CHEST COMPLEX TRIPLE STRETCHES

1. For the first stretch, stand next to a wall or door frame. Extend one arm and bend at the elbow, so that your arm forms a right angle, with your upper arm parallel to the ground and your forearm sticking straight up. Place your forearm against the wall or door frame. Now, twist your whole body away from the wall, with a special emphasis on pushing your chest through the turn, so that you feel a gentle stretch in your chest. Hold this for 10 seconds.

2. For the next stretch, step away from the wall so that, instead of your forearm, only your hand is on the wall. The arm still forms a right angle from your body, but this time your hand and shoulder are at the same level. Make the same twist, pushing your chest into the turn, to stretch the chest in the new position. Hold this for 10 seconds.

3. For the third and final variation, step further from the wall and extend your arm straight, so that the entire arm is parallel to the ground. Place your hand on the wall, then twist again into the stretch. You should feel the tension in your chest. Hold this for 10 seconds.

Switch arms and repeat this sequence.

SPINAL TWISTS

1. Lie on the floor, with your arms extending outward in a T position. Put your right foot on your left knee.

2. Using your left hand, gently pull your right knee toward the floor, twisting your spine and keeping your left arm straight out, hips and shoulders on the floor. Hold for 30 seconds.

Repeat, using the right hand and left knee.

QUADRICEPS/HIP FLEXOR STRETCHES

1. Starting in a standing position, take a big step forward with your left leg, then place your right knee on the ground.

2. Maintaining this posture, shift the entire body slightly forward from the hip. You should feel this stretch down the front of your quad and hip flexor. Exhale and hold the stretch. Don't arch your back.

Hold for 30 seconds, then gently release and switch legs.

HAMSTRING STRETCHES

1. Lie down on your back, with a slight bend in both legs.

2. Lift your right leg straight up and grab it behind your calf. If you are flexible enough, grab your ankle (or even toe). Gently pull your right leg toward you, keeping your back straight.

Hold the stretch for 30 seconds. Repeat with the left leg.

INCREDIBLE WORK TODAY. REST UP—TOMORROW'S GOING TO BE YOUR HARDEST HITZ CARDIO YET.

DAY 23 MEAL PLAN

You're in the home stretch—keep just as focused on what you eat as how you work out, and I guarantee you'll be pleased on Day 31.

BREAKFAST 2 slices whole-grain toast; 1 boiled egg; 2 tsp. non-hydrogenated margarine or butter; 1 orange; 1-1/2 cups skim or soy milk.

SNACK 1 cup blueberries; 3/4 cup low-fat yogurt.

LUNCH Tuna wrap: Mix 1 oz. canned tuna with 1 tbsp. light mayonnaise and mustard. Spread on a large whole-wheat wrap, then top with spinach, tomato and cucumber with 1 oz. light cheese.

SNACK Granola bar.

DINNER BBQ Chicken breast: Grill 4 oz. chicken breast with BBQ sauce; 1/2 cup baked yam (peel the yam, then cut it into cubes, drizzle with 1 tsp. olive oil and bake at 350°F until tender). Serve with 2 cups mixed-green salad and 1 tbsp. light dressing. **Cook-ahead option:** Barbecue an extra 3 oz. chicken breast and bake an extra yam for tomorrow's lunch.

DAY 24
HITZ Cardio #7

TOMMY RULE #24: PUSH YOURSELF AS HARD AS YOU CAN TODAY, BECAUSE I WANT YOU TO BE ABLE TO LOOK IN THE MIRROR AND SAY "I DIDN'T HOLD BACK TODAY. MY TANK IS EMPTY!"

I've got to warn you: Today is going to be a tough one. HITZ Cardio #7 is going to push you to new levels. My HITZ medley is sure to rattle your cage, so good luck with it. I've planned this for you to be in the gym, as you are going to be using the treadmill, bike and elliptical trainer. However, the 10PS is something you can do just about anywhere. So if you do not belong to a gym, pick three different cardio exercises—for example, running hills, skipping and swimming—and just follow the Tabata method you'll see explained in the bike section on page 296. The important thing is that, whether you're in the gym or not, you'll be alternating between bursts of serious exertion and recovery phases.

This will take you about 30 minutes total to complete, and you'll need a stopwatch for portions of it, although most of your cardio equipment should have a timer on it. If you just ate . . . good luck!

TODAY'S WORKOUT

FOCUS	EQUIPMENT	TOTAL TIME
Mixing it up to stretch your endurance.	Ideally, treadmill, bike and elliptical—but any three cardio methods will do.	About 30 minutes.

HERE'S WHAT'S ON DECK:
Warmup
Dynamic Stretches
HITZ Cardio #7
Cool-Down
Static Stretches

WARMUP

For 5 minutes, work at an intensity of Level 4 on the PES. You should be sweating a little, but feeling good and still able to carry on a conversation effortlessly.

DYNAMIC STRETCHES

All warmed up? Good. Now perform the following three dynamic stretches:

DYNAMIC GLUTE AND HAMSTRING STRETCHES

1. Stand tall (shoulders back), with your feet shoulder width apart. Lift your left foot and grab just below your left knee with both hands.

2. With both hands, gently pull your left knee up, while maintaining your balance on your right heel. This will activate your butt and the backs of your legs. Hold for 3 seconds, then release your left leg.

Repeat the same sequence with your right leg. Perform 5 repetitions with each leg.

DYNAMIC QUAD STRETCHES

1. Stand tall (shoulders back), with your feet shoulder width apart. Lift your left foot behind you and grab your ankle (or foot) with your left hand.

2. Gently push your left hip forward, while keeping a straight line with your body and maintaining your balance on your right heel. Hold for 3 seconds, then release your left ankle.

Repeat the same sequence with your right leg. Perform 5 repetitions on each leg.

DYNAMIC SUMO SQUATS

1. Stand tall (shoulders back), with your feet close together. Take a large lateral step to the right and drop into a deep squat (think of a sumo wrestler). Pause, then return to the starting standing position.

2. Now take a large lateral step to the left and drop into a deep squat. Pause, then return to the starting position.

Perform 5 repetitions on each side.

HITZ CARDIO #7

After your dynamic stretches, get some water and get ready to attack HITZ Cardio #7. If you need to increase or decrease the speed or incline, do it, but remember that you don't have anything to save it for. I want you to leave it all out there, all right? Now let's go!

Time	Description	Perceived Exertion Scale (PES)	Speed (mph)	Incline
1 min.	Nice and easy. Let's start to stretch those legs out by hitting your stride at about 60% of your max.	Level 5–6	At least 5	3%
1 min.	Open it up. This should be tiring—you're working at 80% of your max.	Level 7–8	At least 6.5	5%
1 min.	If you have a hill or heavy shorts handy, use them! I want you to increase the resistance and keep your speed. You'll be at 80–85% of your max intensity/ability.	Level 8	At least 5.5	10%
2 min.	Gear down to 60%.	Level 5–6	At least 5	0%

Time	Description	Perceived Exertion Scale (PES)	Speed (mph)	Incline
1 min.	Time to speed up to 80% of your max.	Level 7–8	At least 7	10%
1 min.	Drop the speed, but increase the resistance—70% is good here.	Level 6–7	At least 5.5	10%
1 min.	Give 'er on this one. Think college here—it's almost last call at the bar and you're 10 minutes away. This is a speed you can muster up for special occasions—yup, about 80 to 90%.	Level 8	Your max speed	2%
2 min.	Nice work! You made last call at the "juice bar." Gradually slow to 50% and get ready for the bike!	Level 5–6	At least 5	5%

ARE YOU WARM NOW? YOU'VE GOT A 2-MINUTE BREAK FOR WATER.

SPIN BIKE

For your spin-bike portion, you are going to ride for 10 minutes. If there are toe straps, use them. You will be performing a 4-minute Tabata-bike sprint blast; this means that your intervals will be at a 2:1 work-to-recovery ratio. For your work phase, go all-out, and I mean all-out! Come on, it's just 4 minutes in total. The second phase is a recovery pace, going at 40% of your maximum effort. It's gonna look something like this: 20 seconds hard blast (this is your work phase), followed by 10 seconds of a "coasting" recovery phase. That would be one set.

So remember, just eight sets, for a total of 4 minutes. Non-stop action!

Use your stopwatch or the timer on the bike, and use a moderate tension. The resistance should not be easy, nor should it be too hard. Now, that's enough chatter—get to work!

Finished yet? Are you still with me? Was 4 minutes that bad? Yup, it was. Trust me, I know!

TAKE A 2-MINUTE BREAK AND GET READY FOR YOU LAST STATION IN THE MEDLEY.

ELLIPTICAL TRAINER OR SKIPPING

Time	Description	Perceived Exertion Scale (PES)	Resistance
1 min.	Time to get loose. You should be working at 50% of your maximum ability.	5	Level 4–5
1 min.	Pick up the pace, working up to 80%.	8	Level 9–11
1 min.	Drop it off a bit to 70%.	6–7	Level 7–8
2 min.	Gradually raise to 80%. Push the pace every 15 seconds.	7–8	Level 8–10

COOL-DOWN

You can stay on the treadmill or simply go for a nice, slow walk, head up and eyes open. Stay at a low intensity for a minimum of 10 minutes—Level 3 on the PES. You should be nice and comfortable; this cool-down is designed to slowly bring your heart rate down, so go easy with it.

STATIC STRETCHES

Finished? Okay, time for you to do your static stretches. Perform the following four:

SPINAL TWISTS

1. Lie on the floor, with your arms extending outward in a T position. Put your right foot on your left knee.

2. Using your left hand, gently pull your right knee toward the floor, twisting your spine and keeping your left arm straight out, hips and shoulders on the floor. Hold for 30 seconds.

Repeat, using the right hand and left knee.

QUADRICEPS/HIP FLEXOR STRETCHES

1. Starting in a standing position, take a big step forward with your left leg, then place your right knee on the ground.

2. Maintaining this posture, shift the entire body slightly forward from the hip. You should feel this stretch down the front of your quad and hip flexor. Exhale and hold the stretch. Don't arch your back.

Hold for 30 seconds, then gently release and switch legs.

HAMSTRING STRETCHES

1. Lie down on your back, with a slight bend in both legs.

2. Lift your right leg straight up and grab it behind your calf. If you are flexible enough, grab your ankle (or even your toe). Gently pull your right leg toward you, keeping your back straight.

Hold the stretch for 30 seconds. Repeat with the left leg.

HIP STRETCHES

1. Lie down and cross your left foot over your right knee.

2. Clasp your hands behind your right knee. Gently pull your right leg toward you, keeping your back straight.

Hold the stretch for 30 seconds. Repeat with the left leg.

AND NOW YOU ARE FINALLY DONE! GREAT JOB. MAKE SURE YOU GOT A PROPER COOL-DOWN TODAY, BECAUSE WE ARE RIGHT BACK IN THE FIREPIT TOMORROW. I LOVE THE MEDLEY BECAUSE IT FORCES YOU TO GET USED TO A VARIETY OF EXERCISES IN THE SAME SESSION, PLUS YOU WON'T GET BORED. NOW GET OFF YOUR FEET AND GO EAT!

DAY 24 MEAL PLAN

You're going to be starving after a workout like today's, but don't give in to the urge to break your plan. Your meals today are essential, so stick with the plan!

BREAKFAST 3/4 cup low-fat yogurt; 1/4 cup granola; 1/4 cup All-Bran cereal; 1/2 cup strawberries; 1-1/2 cups skim or soy milk.

SNACK 1 mango; 20 almonds.

LUNCH 3 oz. leftover BBQ chicken; 1 cup yam; 1 cup mixed-green salad.

SNACK 1/3 cup hummus; 1 cup grape tomatoes; 2 rye crackers.

DINNER **Prawn stir-fry:** De-vein and peel 10 to 12 raw prawns, and stir-fry them with 1 tsp. olive oil, 2 tbsp. chopped onion and 1/4 cup red pepper until almost pink. Add 2 cups bok choy and 2 tsp. hoisin sauce, and cook until tender. Serve over 1/2 cup buckwheat noodles or whole-wheat spaghettini.

DAY 25
HITZ Resistance #11

TOMMY RULE #25: YOUR ONLY LIMITS ARE THE ONES YOU SET FOR YOURSELF, SO AIM HIGH.

The fact that you are at this point shows me that you are driven to excel and want to make positive changes to your lifestyle. You are doing amazing, and I expect nothing less for your workout today. You've got a few more days until you can write your own success story, and in the meantime, we must finish strong. So bear down and get ready to roll—Day 25 starts now.

TODAY'S WORKOUT

FOCUS	EQUIPMENT	REPETITIONS	SETS
Every single muscle in your body—literally.	A pair of 10- to 15-pound dumbbells (DBs) and two 15- to 25-pound DBs, a stability ball (SB) and a bar for pull-ups.	One minute—beginners and intermediates.	Three sets in total.

TODAY'S ANOTHER MOUNTAIN TO CLIMB, AND I'VE PUT TOGETHER ANOTHER MOUNTAIN OF A WORKOUT ROUTINE FOR YOU. I DON'T CARE IF YOU NEED ROPES AND PULLEYS TO GET YOU TO THE TOP THIS TIME, BUT HOPEFULLY YOU WON'T NEED AN OXYGEN MASK WHEN IT'S ALL DONE. YOU FEELING READY? THEN CHECK OUT WHAT I'VE GOT IN STORE FOR YOU.

Warmup
Dynamic Stretches
HITZ Resistance #11

- HIGH-KNEE RUNNING · DUMBBELL SCAP SQUATS · PULL-UPS · STABILITY BALL AND DUMBBELL CHEST PRESSES · CORE HEEL SCRAPERS
1 minute to refocus and rehydrate.

- HIGH-KNEE RUNNING · CORE X-BODY MOUNTAIN CLIMBERS · DUMBBELL LATERAL SIDE LUNGES · CORE LATERAL LEG DROPS · DUMBBELL TWISTING SHOULDER PRESSES

You know the routine: go get some water, refresh your mind and get after two more sets!

What's that? You say you want to do a **CORE PLANK** after your final set? Well, don't worry, I was getting to that. Now, hit it!

Cool-Down
Static Stretches

WARMUP

Jump on a bike or treadmill for your 10-minute warmup. If you are training outdoors, you should be jogging or riding a bike.

For the first five minutes, work at an intensity of Level 4 on the PES. You should be sweating a little, but feeling good and able to carry on a conversation effortlessly.

For the last five minutes, work at an intensity of Level 5. You should be just above comfortable, sweating more and still able to talk easily.

DYNAMIC STRETCHES

After your warmup, here are your dynamic stretches:

DYNAMIC BACK SWINGS

1. Stand tall (shoulders back), with your feet shoulder width apart. Lift and hold both arms up to the side at shoulder height. Twist as far as you can to the right, so that you can feel a good stretch in your mid- to lower back.

2. Pause, then twist to the left (you should resemble a propeller as you twist).

Repeat for 10 revolutions.

DYNAMIC QUAD STRETCHES

1. Stand tall (shoulders back), with your feet shoulder width apart. Lift your left foot behind you and grab your ankle (or foot) with your left hand.

2. Gently push your left hip forward, while keeping a straight line with your body and maintaining your balance on your right heel. Hold for 3 seconds, then release your left ankle.

Repeat this sequence with your right leg. Perform 5 repetitions on each leg.

DYNAMIC CHEST AND BICEP STRETCHES

1. Stand tall (shoulders back), with your feet shoulder width apart. Slowly move your arms out to the sides, slightly behind you, with your thumbs up (just like The Fonz).

2. As your arms go back, rotate your thumbs down and back until they are pointing to the wall behind you. Pause, then return to the starting position. You should feel this one in your chest and biceps.

Perform 10 repetitions.

DYNAMIC SUMO SQUATS

1. Stand tall (shoulders back), with your feet close together. Take a large lateral step to the right and drop into a deep squat (think of a sumo wrestler). Pause, then return to the starting standing position.

2. Now take a large lateral step to the left and drop into a deep squat. Pause, then return to the starting position.

Perform 5 repetitions on each side.

READY FOR THAT MOUNTAIN? I THOUGHT SO. LET'S GET MOVING!

HIGH-KNEE RUNNING

You can do it. Visualize the ground being on fire—that's how high I want your knees on this one.

1. Stand tall, with your feet shoulder width apart. Run on the spot, lifting your knees as high as possible and pumping your arms vigorously. Ideally, your knees will be coming up to waist height.

2. You must remain tall at all times. Do not slump.

Keep going for 1 minute.

DUMBBELL SCAP SQUATS

Keep your core engaged and lift your arms as high as possible for maximum effect—and maximum results!

1. Stand tall, with your feet shoulder width apart, and hold a 5- to 15-pound DB in each hand, letting the DBs at your sides. Get into a half-squat position, keeping your weight balanced on your heels.

2. Tilt forward so that your upper body is at a 45-degree angle.

3. Extend and lift both arms behind you (holding the DBs) as high as you can. Then return to the starting position.

Keep your arms and core braced, and squat continuously all the way up, and then down, for one minute.

TOMMY TIP

Do not use heavy dumbbells; 5 to 15 pounds will be plenty.

PULL-UPS

Here we go again with one that you'll love to hate. Keep that head neutral! You don't get to skip it if you don't have a bar (nice try!)—just substitute dumbbell rows to work the same muscle groups.

1. Set a bar at about hip height. If you're in the gym, you can use a Smith machine, squat rack or other bar. If you're not in a gym, you can use a bar stretched between two chairs, like I did! Lie down on your back so that the bar is directly above your chest.

2. Extend your legs (bent knees for beginners, straight legs for intermediates). Grab the bar using an overhand grip that is slightly wider than shoulder width.

3. Focus on your upper back/lats and row (pull) your body up to the top position (the bar should graze your chest). Pause, then return to the starting position.

Repeat this sequence for 1 minute.

STABILITY BALL AND DUMBBELL CHEST PRESSES

This one is going to require you to engage your core, glutes, arms and chest. Use a lighter weight for the first set, so that you will know how to adjust up or down for the remaining sets. The eccentric (descent) phase is just as important as the concentric (push) phase—don't let gravity cheat you out of a solid burn.

1. Sit on a medium-sized SB, holding two 12- to 30-pound DBs on your thighs. Walk your body down the ball until your shoulder blades are in contact with the SB. The DBs should now be slightly above your chest, and your feet should be shoulder width apart, with your weight on your heels and your hips raised.

2. Contract your chest and press the dumbbells straight up above your chest (so that they meet in the middle).

3. Pause, then lower the DBs until your arms are at a 90-degree angle (DBs will be about 3 inches away from your chest).

Repeat the sequence for 1 minute.

TOMMY TIP

Do not bounce on the ball, and do not bang the weights together (unless you, too, want to join the "no neck" crew).

CORE HEEL SCRAPERS

Remember to go slow, and your flat stomach will appear much sooner.

1. Lie flat on your back (use your mat if you have one). Without tucking your chin, raise your head off the ground and look up at the ceiling. Then lift your heels off the ground while bending your knees, so that your thighs are at a 90-degree angle to the mat.

2. Lower both legs from the hip until your heels graze the ground.

3. Now push your heels out until both legs are straight. As you extend your legs, push your lower back into the ground for support. Beginners, you can have a slight bend in the knees—for now. Pause, then return your legs and head to the starting position.

Keep going for 1 minute.

TAKE A 1-MINUTE BREAK BEFORE CONTINUING WITH . . .

HIGH-KNEE RUNNING

Get 'em up! Let's go! One minute!

1. Stand tall, with your feet shoulder width apart. Run on the spot, lifting your knees as high as possible and pumping your arms vigorously. Ideally, your knees will be coming up to waist height.

2. You must remain tall at all times. Do not slump.

Keep going for 1 minute.

CORE X-BODY MOUNTAIN CLIMBERS

A rock-hard stomach does not come easy. It takes work and effort on your part. This core move delivers one hell of a punch when done correctly. You can challenge yourself further by placing your forearms on an SB—are you game?

1. Place both hands on a mat, with your hands directly under your shoulders. Walk both feet back so that you are in a push-up position.

2. Brace your abs and lift your left leg 1 foot off of the ground.

3. Drive your left knee toward your right elbow. Pause, then return to the starting position.

Repeat this action, with your right knee driving toward your left elbow. Alternate sides for 1 minute.

TOMMY TIP

Do not let your hips sag. Keep your abs braced at all times.

DUMBBELL LATERAL SIDE LUNGES

Power off of the ground to make this exercise more ballistic—this is your second time through.

1. Standing tall, with your feet shoulder width apart, cup your hands and hold a 15- to 30-pound DB between your legs.

2. With your left leg, take a large lateral (sideways) step as far as you can to the left—you need to bend your left knee while keeping your right leg straight.

3. Pause, then push off from your left foot to your original standing position. Repeat this action to the right.

Alternate from side to side for 1 minute.

CORE LATERAL LEG DROPS

Keep your legs squeezed together, especially on the way up, and you will realize the power of this one . . . once again.

1. Lie flat on your back on a mat, with your hands palms down, making a wide base with your upper body, then raise your legs so they're pointing straight up.

2. Pin your knees together, engage your core and let your legs drop to the right side without letting them touch the ground.

3. Pause, then repeat on the left side.

Repeat this action for 1 minute.

DUMBBELL TWISTING SHOULDER PRESSES

This exercise will challenge your balance and stabilizing muscles, targeting your shoulders and core. Move in a slow, fluid motion to truly receive the benefits of this particular shoulder press, and do not use a DB that is too heavy—10 to 15 pounds should do it.

1. Grab a 10- to 15-pound DB and hold it in your right hand at shoulder height. Step and turn your left foot outward at a 90-degree angle (your feet should resemble the letter L). Your upper body should be facing forward in the same direction as your right foot, with all your body weight on your left heel.

2. Lift your right foot off the ground and twist your body toward your left foot, while at the same time pressing the DB straight up, driving your right knee to a 90-degree angle.

3. Hold in this position for one second (you should resemble the Statue of Liberty) and then return to the starting position.

Repeat this sequence for 1 minute. Turn around and repeat the sequence for 1 minute with the DB in your left hand and your weight balanced on your right heel.

TOMMY TIP

Think of the following sequence: step, twist and press! The DB should be straight up in the air at all times. You must engage your core and go slow for this exercise.

CORE PLANK

Hold this one until failure after your third and final set!

1. Begin on all fours (hands and knees) on a mat.

2. Extend your legs so that your entire body is flat, in a straight-arm plank position, then go down to your forearms.

3. Raise your hips so that your body is in a straight line and your weight is on your elbows and toes. Beginners, you may need to be on your knees. That's fine for now—just ensure that your hips are down, with your core engaged. This should be hard work.

Hold the plank position for as long as your poor abs will let you!

COOL-DOWN

Nice one. Feeling shredded? Nothing like going until you've got nothing left, is there? That's the way we do it around here. Now let's breathe a bit and cool down. You know the drill. Ten nice and easy minutes should do it today.

STATIC STRETCHES

Surprise! You're not done yet. Today was a big day, so I've got five stretches on deck for you:

HIP STRETCHES

1. Lie down and cross your left foot over your right knee.

2. Clasp your hands behind your right knee. Gently pull your right leg toward you, keeping your back straight.

Hold the stretch for 30 seconds.
Repeat with the left leg.

CHEST COMPLEX TRIPLE STRETCHES

1. For the first stretch, stand next to a wall or door frame. Extend one arm and bend at the elbow, so that your arm forms a right angle, with your upper arm parallel to the ground and your forearm sticking straight up. Place your forearm against the wall or door frame. Now, twist your whole body away from the wall, with a special emphasis on pushing your chest through the turn, so that you feel a gentle stretch in your chest. Hold this for 10 seconds.

2. For the next stretch, step away from the wall so that, instead of your forearm, only your hand is on the wall. The arm still forms a right angle from your body, but this time your hand and shoulder are at the same level. Make the same twist, pushing your chest into the turn, to stretch the chest in the new position. Hold this for 10 seconds.

3. For the third and final variation, step further from the wall and extend your arm straight, so that the entire arm is parallel to the ground. Place your hand on the wall, then twist again into the stretch. You should feel the tension in your chest. Hold this for 10 seconds.

Switch arms and repeat the sequence.

SPINAL TWISTS

1. Lie on the floor, with your arms extending outward in a T position. Put your right foot on your left knee.

2. Using your left hand, gently pull your right knee toward the floor, twisting your spine and keeping your left arm straight out, hips and shoulders on the floor. Hold for 30 seconds.

Repeat, using the right hand and left knee.

QUADRICEPS/HIP FLEXOR STRETCHES

1. Starting in a standing position, take a big step forward with your left leg, then place your right knee on the ground.

2. Maintaining this posture, shift the entire body slightly forward from the hip. You should feel this stretch down the front of your quad and hip flexor. Exhale and hold the stretch. Don't arch your back.

Hold for 30 seconds, then gently release and switch legs.

HAMSTRING STRETCHES

1. Lie down on your back, with a slight bend in both legs.

2. Lift your right leg straight up and grab it behind your calf. If you are flexible enough, grab your ankle (or even your toe). Gently pull your right leg toward you, keeping your back straight.

Hold the stretch for 30 seconds. Repeat with the left leg.

GET A FULL NIGHT'S SLEEP TONIGHT—TOMORROW'S YOUR LAST HITZ CARDIO, AND LET'S JUST SAY THAT I'M NOT GOING TO LET YOU OFF EASY.

DAY 25 MEAL PLAN

You're seeing huge results now, I know, but resist the urge to reward yourself with a treat—the real treat will come on Day 31, when you look down at that scale, so keep focused!

BREAKFAST Fruit Smoothie: Blend 3/4 cup low-fat yogurt, 1 cup mixed frozen berries, 1/4 cup orange juice (optional) and 1/2 scoop protein powder; serve with 1/2 English muffin and 1 tbsp. natural peanut butter; 1-1/2 cups skim or soy milk.

SNACK 1/2 English muffin; 1 tbsp. natural peanut butter.

LUNCH Grilled turkey and cheese sandwich: Assemble a sandwich of 1 oz. light havarti cheese and 1 oz. sliced turkey between 2 slices of whole-grain toast. Spread the outsides of the sandwich with 2 tsp. margarine, then grill until the cheese melts. Serve alongside 1/2 cup snap peas.

SNACK 1 cup snap peas; 1/3 cup hummus; 2 rye crackers.

DINNER Curried beef: Fry 3 oz. cubed sirloin with 1/2 tsp. olive oil, 1/2 to 1 tsp. curry paste (depending on how spicy you like things) and 1/2 cup tomato or pasta sauce. Let simmer for about 40 minutes until tender. Serve with 1/2 cup brown rice and 2 cups mixed-green salad with 1 tbsp. light salad dressing. **Cook-ahead option:** Make an extra 3 oz. of beef and 1 cup of rice for tomorrow's lunch.

DAY 26
HITZ Cardio #8

TOMMY RULE #26: THERE ARE ONLY TWO WAYS TO APPROACH TODAY'S CHALLENGE. FELLAS, SOME OF YOU ARE GOING TO HAVE TO MAN UP, AND TO MY LADIES . . . TIME TO LEAVE THE SKIRTS AT HOME, BECAUSE WE'VE GOT WORK TO DO!

Can you believe that this is the last cardio workout of the 10PS? We've had quite the journey up to this point, and you've set the path for the rest of your life. All of the HITZ Cardio workouts were designed to work you thoroughly, and give you the kind of variety that will keep things challenging and fun. Okay, stop swearing—maybe they weren't that fun, but look down and notice how much smaller your physique is. There we go . . . I knew I could get a smile out of you.

I really hope you've enjoyed the cardio workouts, because I had fun putting them together for you, and on Day 28, you'll see how you can piece together your own workouts to avoid doing the same thing day in, day out.

Today's workout is best done on a treadmill. It's a HITZ burst session, and that means you'll be working hard for 4-minute intervals and then you'll get a few minutes to recover. If you're at home, or you prefer to be outside on a bike, the basic philosophy stays the same. The whole point is to get yourself going just about as hard as you can—that's right, I'm talking 8s and 9s on the PES, so your lungs are burning and your legs are begging for mercy. But don't worry, because mercy is exactly what you're going to give them (at regular intervals). You're going to get revved up for 4 minutes, then coast for 2. It's a lot more demanding than going out for a leisurely jog, but then, you get a lot more out of it. Ever wonder where athletes get their explosive speed and ability to keep doing it for a whole game? Well, you won't be wondering after a burst session.

TODAY'S WORKOUT

FOCUS	EQUIPMENT	TOTAL TIME
Pushing it farther than ever with your longest workout yet.	Your choice.	About 50 minutes.

HERE'S WHAT'S ON DECK:
Warmup
Dynamic Stretches
HITZ Cardio #8
Cool-Down
Static Stretches

WARMUP

As always, first we've got to warm up!

For five minutes, work at an intensity of Level 4 on the PES. You should be sweating a little, but feeling good and able to carry on a conversation effortlessly.

DYNAMIC STRETCHES

After your warmup, perform the following three dynamic stretches:

DYNAMIC GLUTE AND HAMSTRING STRETCHES

1. Stand tall (shoulders back), with your feet shoulder width apart. Lift your left foot and grab just below your left knee with both hands.

2. With both hands, gently pull your left knee up, while maintaining your balance on your right heel. This will activate your butt and the backs of your legs. Hold for 3 seconds, then release your left leg.

Repeat the same sequence with your right leg. Perform 5 repetitions with each leg.

DYNAMIC QUAD STRETCHES

1. Stand tall (shoulders back), with your feet shoulder width apart. Lift your left foot behind you and grab your ankle (or foot) with your left hand.

2. Gently push your left hip forward, while keeping a straight line with your body and maintaining your balance on your right heel. Hold for 3 seconds, then release your left ankle.

Repeat the same sequence with your right leg. Perform 5 repetitions on each leg.

HITZ CARDIO #8

All warmed up? After your dynamic stretches, get some water and get to it!

Time	Description	Perceived Exertion Scale (PES)
4 min.	Slowly increase your speed, incline and/or resistance until you're working at an intense pace. You should be working very hard, but able to hold this pace for 4 minutes.	Level 8–9
2 min.	Reduce speed to a very light pace to fully recover.	Level 3–4
4 min.	Giddyup! Increase your speed, incline and/or resistance until you're working at an intense pace.	Level 8–9
2 min.	Reduce speed to a very light pace to fully recover.	Level 3–4
4 min.	Gulp, here we go again! Increase your speed, incline and/or resistance until you're working at an intense pace.	Level 8–9
2 min.	Reduce speed to a very light pace to fully recover.	Level 3–4
4 min.	Need I say more? Increase your speed, incline and/or resistance until you're working at an intense pace.	Level 8–9
2 min.	Reduce speed to a very light pace to fully recover.	Level 3–4

Time	Description	Perceived Exertion Scale (PES)
4 min.	You're more than halfway through now—keep on going. Increase your speed, incline and/or resistance until you're working at an intense pace.	Level 8–9
2 min.	Reduce speed to a very light pace to fully recover.	Level 3–4
4 min.	It's all downhill from here . . . Increase your speed, incline and/or resistance once again until you're working at an intense pace.	Level 8–9
2 min.	Reduce speed to a very light pace to fully recover.	Level 3–4
4 min.	Two more bursts to go. Don't try to sprint; just keep doing what you're doing. Increase your speed, incline and/or resistance until you're working at an intense pace.	Level 8–9
2 min.	Reduce speed to a very light pace to fully recover.	Level 3–4
4 min.	Last one, I promise . . . Increase your speed, incline and/or resistance until you're working at an intense pace.	Level 8–9
2 min.	Reduce speed to a very light pace to fully recover.	Level 3–4

COOL-DOWN

You know what time it is! To cool down, stay on the treadmill at a low intensity for a minimum of 10 minutes. (If you're not on a treadmill, just keep doing what you're doing.) You should be at an intensity of Level 3 on the PES. You should be relatively comfortable, so go easy with it.

STATIC STRETCHES

Once your heart rate is down and your 10 minutes are up, it's time for you to do your static stretches:

HIP STRETCHES

1. Lie down and cross your left foot over your right knee.

2. Clasp your hands behind your right knee. Gently pull your right leg toward you, keeping your back straight.

Hold the stretch for 30 seconds.
Repeat with the left leg.

SPINAL TWISTS

1. Lie on the floor, with your arms extending outward in a T position. Put your right foot on your left knee.

2. Using your left hand, gently pull your right knee toward the floor, twisting your spine and keeping your left arm straight out, hips and shoulders on the floor. Hold for 30 seconds.

Repeat, using the right hand and left knee.

QUADRICEPS/HIP FLEXOR STRETCHES

1. Starting in a standing position, take a big step forward with your left leg, then place your right knee on the ground.

2. Maintaining this posture, shift the entire body slightly forward from the hip. You should feel this stretch down the front of your quad and hip flexor. Exhale and hold the stretch. Don't arch your back.

Hold for 30 seconds, then gently release and switch legs.

HAMSTRING STRETCHES

1. Lie down on your back, with a slight bend in both legs.

2. Lift your right leg straight up and grab it behind your calf. If you are flexible enough, grab your ankle (or even your toe). Gently pull your right leg toward you, keeping your back straight.

Hold the stretch for 30 seconds. Repeat with the left leg.

I WANT TO THANK YOU FOR GIVING IT YOUR ALL TODAY. AFTER DOING THOSE HITZ BURSTS YOU WILL CONTINUE TO BURN CALORIES INTO THE NIGHT. MAKE SURE YOU HYDRATE, BECAUSE THAT SESSION WAS A LONG ONE AND I'M SURE YOU'LL FEEL IT LATER! NOW, GET OFF YOUR FEET AND GO EAT!

DAY 26 MEAL PLAN

You deserve a day full of amazing meals, so here you go! Today's delicious meals:

BREAKFAST 2 slices toast; 2 tbsp. natural almond butter; 1 medium orange; 1-1/2 cups skim or soy milk.

SNACK 1 cup strawberries; 3/4 cup low-fat yogurt.

LUNCH Curried beef leftovers: 1 cup curried beef (approximately 2 oz.); 1 cup brown rice; 1 cup mixed-green salad with 1 tbsp. light dressing.

SNACK Granola bar.

DINNER Chicken Caesar salad: Toss 4 oz. grilled chicken breast with 3 cups romaine lettuce, 1 tbsp. light Caesar dressing and 1/2 cup croutons. Top with 1 tbsp. light Parmesan. **Cook-ahead option:** Grill an extra 2 oz. of chicken breast to set aside for lunch tomorrow.

DAY 27
HITZ Resistance #12

TOMMY RULE #27: PRESSURE BUSTS PIPES—DON'T LET IT BURST YOU. FIGHT THE URGE TO RATCHET UP THE PRESSURE ON YOURSELF AND JUST DO WHAT YOU'VE GOTTA DO.

Ah, Day 27 . . . You have battled through the last 26 days and it has brought you to the point where you have all the tools you need to carry on. This is your last resistance workout in the 10PS, and as you go forward into life, great things are sure to come. Doesn't it feel good to see something through to completion, to finish a seemingly impossible task, to lose weight and inches without depriving yourself of a normal life? Now the only remaining question is: What will you do from this point forward?

Now, before you get all nostalgic on me as you think back over the 10PS, take a look at the workout I've got in store for you today. You're going to be glad when this one is over! But as you know, not much in life feels better than the way your body is humming after a workout. So let's savour the burn on this one for old times' sake and enjoy that cool-down glow when the moment comes.

Today you will need that inner voice in your head to push you past your comfort zones. Ladies, "woman up" for this one; guys, grab your jockstraps. You're going into battle today, but I know you are ready for it.

TODAY'S WORKOUT

FOCUS	EQUIPMENT	REPETITIONS	SETS
It's your last HITZ Resistance—nothing will be spared.	A pair of 10- to 20-pound dumbbells (DBs), one 20- to 30-pound DB and a bar for pull-ups.	1 minute.	Three gruelling sets.

COME ON, LET'S DO THIS TOGETHER ONE LAST TIME!

Warmup
Dynamic Stretches
HITZ Resistance #12

· SKATERS · DUMBBELL SPIDERMAN PUSH-UPS · DUMBBELL LUNGE CURLS · CORE AB POPPERS
· STABILITY BALL AND DUMBBELL ONE-ARM ROWING
1 minute to refocus and rehydrate.

· DUMBBELL LOW-TOE HI-FLIES · CORE LEG DROPS · RESISTANCE BAND LAT PULL-DOWNS
· GLUTEUS MEDIUS HIP RAISES · DUMBBELL STATIC ONE-ARM CURLS

Two more sets to go, and then you and I are gonna do a chest bump!

I know you want it: Let's do a **CORE PLANK** until failure after your last set.

Cool-Down
Static Stretches

WARMUP

Jump on a bike or treadmill for your 10-minute warmup. If you are training outdoors, go for a jog or hop on your bike.

For the first five minutes, work at an intensity of Level 4 on the PES. You should be sweating a little, but feeling good and able to carry on a conversation effortlessly.

For the last five minutes, work at an intensity of Level 5. You should be just above comfortable, sweating more and still able to talk easily.

DYNAMIC STRETCHES

All warmed up? Great. Now let's perform the following four dynamic stretches:

DYNAMIC QUAD STRETCHES

1. Stand tall (shoulders back), with your feet shoulder width apart. Lift your left foot behind you and grab your ankle (or foot) with your left hand.

2. Gently push your left hip forward, while keeping a straight line with your body and maintaining your balance on your right heel. Hold for 3 seconds, then release your left ankle.

Repeat this sequence with your right leg. Perform 5 repetitions on each leg.

DYNAMIC CHEST AND BICEP STRETCHES

1. Stand tall (shoulders back), with your feet shoulder width apart. Slowly move your arms out to the sides, slightly behind you, with your thumbs up (just like The Fonz).

2. As your arms go back, rotate your thumbs down and back until they are pointing to the wall behind you. Pause, then return to the starting position. You should feel this one in your chest and biceps.

Perform 10 repetitions.

DYNAMIC SUMO SQUATS

1. Stand tall (shoulders back), with your feet close together. Take a large lateral step to the right and drop into a deep squat (think of a sumo wrestler). Pause, then return to the starting standing position.

2. Now take a large lateral step to the left and drop into a deep squat. Pause, then return to the starting position.

Perform 5 repetitions on each side.

DYNAMIC BACK SWINGS

1. Stand tall (shoulders back), with your feet shoulder width apart. Lift and hold both arms to the side at shoulder height. Twist as far as you can to the right, so that you can feel a good stretch in your mid- to lower back.

2. Pause, then twist to the left (you should resemble a propeller as you twist).

Repeat for 10 revolutions.

YOU READY? YOU BETTER BE! LET'S GO.

SKATERS

This exercise will need your maximum effort. Yes, it will burn, and yes, you will want to stop, but you've made it this far, so stick with it!

1. Stand tall on your (slightly bent) right leg with your foot hovering above the ground. Keep your head and chest up.

2. Push off your right foot and jump laterally (sideways) as far as you can to your left foot. Avoid letting the other foot touch the ground as you jump across.

3. Pause, then jump back across to your right foot.

This is a continuous-movement exercise that you must maintain for 1 minute.

DUMBBELL SPIDERMAN PUSH-UPS

It's time to shred away, and the DB will add the extra punch that you need. You remember the Spiderman push-up, don't you? Well, this is pretty much the same thing, only harder. Your Spidey senses tingling yet? They should be. Grab a DB in the 10- to 20-pound range, and let's get going.

1. Start in a plank position, with a 10- to 20-pound DB in each hand, positioned directly under your shoulders. Your head and hips should be neutral and in line with your toes (if you're still struggling a bit, try the push-up from your knees until you get stronger).

2. Engage your core, then step forward with your right hand (holding the DB) and your left knee. As you put the DB to the floor, bend your elbows and lower yourself so that your chest is within a couple of inches of the ground.

3. Pause, then push your body up and return your right hand and left leg to the starting position.

Repeat this action on the opposite side, moving your left hand forward and driving your right knee to meet your right elbow. Keep going for 1 minute, alternating hands.

TOMMY TIP

Never let your back sag. The closer your elbows are to your sides, the more you will work your triceps muscles; the wider you have them, the more you will work your chest. Keep your head neutral (flat) and focus on lowering your chest, not your chin. If you cannot do a push-up from your knees, then stand up and use a wall.

DUMBBELL LUNGE CURLS

Remember, this is a compound exercise that tackles your legs and biceps—which means you get max results.

1. Stand with your feet shoulder width apart, while you hold a pair of 5- to 20-pound DBs.

2. Take a large lunge step forward with your right leg, while bending both knees until your right thigh is parallel to the ground and your left knee is pointing down at the ground. At the same time, curl both DBs up and ensure that your weight is supported on the heel of the right (front) foot while balancing on the left (rear) toe.

3. Push off your right heel to return to the upright starting position. As you stand up, slowly lower both DBs to your side.

Repeat the sequence, stepping with your left leg. Alternate lunge steps for 1 minute.

CORE AB POPPERS

Your beer belly's nemesis. Really give this one all you've got.

1. Lie on your back on a mat (or the floor), with your arms flat on the mat beside you. Then raise both your legs straight up in the air. Lift your head off the ground, looking up at the ceiling; do not tuck your chin.

2. Engage your core and lift your butt off the mat. If you're on the right track, your heels should be moving directly above you.

3. Pause, then lower slowly to the mat.

Repeat this sequence for 1 minute.

STABILITY BALL AND DUMBBELL ONE-ARM ROWING

Are you ready to challenge yourself even further this time? If you're game, follow the same instructions, but try not to hold on to the SB (keep it close so as not to fall).

1. Place your left hand on a medium-sized SB and hold a 15- or 20-pound dumbbell in your right hand.

2. Brace your abdominals and lift your right leg so that it is straight (parallel with your back).

3. Pull (row) the dumbbell up toward your right hip, pause, then return to the starting position.

Keep going for 1 minute.

TIME FOR A 1-MINUTE BREAK. REMEMBER TO GRAB SOME WATER!

DUMBBELL LOW-TOE HI-FLIES

Now that you're this deep into the 10PS, *explode* should have a whole new meaning. Really hit this hard.

1. Grab a 10-pound DB and hold it in your left hand, just outside your right knee. Lift your left leg so that it hovers above the ground, keeping your weight balanced on your bent right leg.

2. With your core engaged, bend forward from your waist, lowering to a 45-degree angle.

3. Explode and jump laterally to your left leg, while at the same time lifting your left arm straight up in the air and straightening your back into an upright position. Pause, then jump back to your right leg while lowering your back to a 45-degree angle and bringing the DB back to outside your right knee.

Repeat this sequence non-stop for 1 minute. Then switch hands and repeat on the other side.

CORE LEG DROPS

I love this combo, don't you? Perfect practice makes perfect . . . so be perfect!

1. Lie on a mat, flat on your back, with your hands palms down beside your hips and your legs pointing straight up at the ceiling.

2. Pin your knees together; engage your core and slowly lower your legs to within a foot of the floor. Keep your shoulder blades on the ground at all times.

3. Pause, then return your legs to the 90-degree starting position.

Repeat this sequence for 1 minute.

RESISTANCE BAND LAT PULL-DOWNS

Back ass? What back ass? Finish kicking that back fat to the curb with more lat pull-downs.

1. Attach your resistance band to an elevated bar or other solid structure and hold on to the handles with a wide overhand (thumbs-down) grip. Drop into a squat position—you should be leaning forward at a 45-degree angle.

2. Using your lats as the primary mover, shrug down and then pull your elbows down toward your hips.

3. Pause, then fully extend your arms.

Repeat this action for 1 minute.

GLUTEUS MEDIUS HIP RAISES

Burn, baby, burn—it's that time again!

1. Begin on all fours on a mat. Drop onto your left forearm and extend your right leg directly to the side.

2. Raise your right leg as high as you can and pause.

3. Lower it almost completely without letting it touch the ground.

Repeat this action for 1 minute, then switch by putting your right forearm on the ground and extending your left leg to the side, following the same protocol.

DUMBBELL STATIC ONE-ARM CURLS

Round two on this one—focus on perfect reps, keep that static arm at a 90-degree angle and
away from your body . . . and go for a heavier weight if you're game!

1. Hold two DBs at your side
while standing tall, with your
feet shoulder width apart.

2. Lift the DB in your left hand,
bending your arm until it's at
a 90-degree angle (hold that
position). Then lift your left leg
with your knee bent (also at a
90-degree angle).

3. Curl the DB in your right
hand up toward your shoulder
and then lower it back to the
90-degree angle.

**Repeat for 1 minute, then
switch sides. (That is, hold the
DB in your right hand, lift your
right leg up to a 90-degree
angle and begin to curl the DB
with your left hand.)**

**...AND ANOTHER SET IS DONE. TAKE A 1-MINUTE BREATHER, GRAB SOME WATER, THEN REPEAT TWICE MORE.
AFTER THAT? ANOTHER CORE PLANK!**

CORE PLANK

Hold this one till failure after your third and final set!

1. Begin on all fours (hands and knees) on a mat.

2. Extend your legs so that your entire body is flat, in a straight-arm plank position, then go down to your forearms.

3. Raise your hips so that your body is in a straight line and your weight is on your elbows and toes. Beginners, you may need to be on your knees. That's fine for now—just ensure that your hips are down, with your core engaged. This should be hard work.

Hold the plank position until your abs send up a white flag of surrender.

COOL-DOWN

You did it! All the way through. Every last exercise. And I couldn't be prouder. We'll celebrate in a minute, but for now, let's keep you from fainting. This shouldn't be a surprise, but take 10 minutes to bring your heart rate down.

STATIC STRETCHES

Next up, perform the following five stretches:

HIP STRETCHES

1. Lie down and cross your left foot over your right knee.

2. Clasp your hands behind your right knee. Gently pull your right leg toward you, keeping your back straight.

Hold the stretch for 30 seconds.
Repeat with the left leg.

CHEST COMPLEX TRIPLE STRETCHES

1. For the first stretch, stand next to a wall or door frame. Extend one arm and bend at the elbow, so that your arm forms a right angle, with your upper arm parallel to the ground and your forearm sticking straight up. Place your forearm against the wall or door frame. Now, twist your whole body away from the wall, with a special emphasis on pushing your chest through the turn, so that you feel a gentle stretch in your chest. Hold this for 10 seconds.

2. For the next stretch, step away from the wall so that, instead of your forearm, only your hand is on the wall. The arm still forms a right angle from your body, but this time your hand and shoulder are at the same level. Make the same twist, pushing your chest into the turn, to stretch the chest in the new position. Hold this for 10 seconds.

3. For the third and final variation, step further from the wall and extend your arm straight, so that the entire arm is parallel to the ground. Place your hand on the wall, then twist again into the stretch. You should feel the tension in your chest. Hold this for 10 seconds.

Switch arms and repeat the sequence.

SPINAL TWISTS

1. Lie on the floor, with your arms extending outward in a T position. Put your right foot on your left knee.

2. Using your left hand, gently pull your right knee toward the floor, twisting your spine and keeping your left arm straight out, hips and shoulders on the floor. Hold for 30 seconds.

Repeat, using the right hand and left knee.

QUADRICEPS/HIP FLEXOR STRETCHES

1. Starting in a standing position, take a big step forward with your left leg, then place your right knee on the ground.

2. Maintaining this posture, shift the entire body slightly forward from the hip. You should feel this stretch down the front of your quad and hip flexor. Exhale and hold the stretch. Don't arch your back.

Hold for 30 seconds, then gently release and switch legs.

HAMSTRING STRETCHES

1. Lie down on your back, with a slight bend in both legs.

2. Lift your right leg straight up and grab it behind your calf. If you are flexible enough, grab your ankle (or even your toe). Gently pull your right leg toward you, keeping your back straight.

Hold the stretch for 30 seconds. Repeat with the left leg.

STAND UP AND PAT YOURSELF ON THE BACK—YOU'VE COMPLETED THE LAST HITZ RESISTANCE DAY OF THE 10PS! CONGRATULATIONS—YOU SHOULD BE EXTREMELY PLEASED. AS I'VE MENTIONED BEFORE, THIS IS ONLY THE BEGINNING FOR YOU. OVER THE NEXT THREE DAYS, YOU WILL HAVE SOME TASKS AND EXERCISES TO DO, BUT FIRST STOP AND ENJOY THIS MOMENT—YOU'VE EARNED IT.

DAY 27 MEAL PLAN

Don't be tempted to cut back on your food as you approach the weigh-in on Day 31—you're still going to need all this fuel!

BREAKFAST 3/4 cup low-fat yogurt; 1/4 cup granola; 1/4 cup All-Bran cereal; 1/2 cup sliced peaches; 1-1/2 cups skim or soy milk.

SNACK 1 cup watermelon; 20 almonds.

LUNCH Chicken Caesar pita: 2 oz. chicken breast, 1 cup romaine lettuce tossed with 1 tbsp. light Caesar dressing and 1/2 cup croutons, stuffed in a whole-wheat pita.

SNACK 1/2 cup edamame.

DINNER Salmon and potatoes: Boil 3 to 4 small (1 in.) potatoes until soft, but not completely cooked. Drain, and toss with 1/2 tsp. olive oil, 1 tsp. light Italian dressing and a dash of lemon juice. Place in an ovenproof container alongside 4 oz. salmon arranged on foil. Bake at 375°F for about 20 minutes. Serve with 2 cups spinach salad and 1 tbsp. light dressing.

DAY 28
HITZ Cardio Workshop

TOMMY RULE #28: YOU'VE SEEN, YOU'VE PERSPIRED, YOU'VE CONQUERED!

You did it! You worked your way through the 10PS, and now you're probably wondering "What do I do now?" Well, today we are going to figure that out. We'll set up an interval cardio day, and then you are going to do it. After all, it's only Day 28 and you've got a few more days to go until you take your final measurements and do your fitness test for the second time.

But you're going to be designing your own workouts soon, so let me tell you a little bit about how I put together the 10PS for you, and how I look at training in general. Then you'll have the tools to keep shredding well into the future.

As you noticed during the cardio days in the 10PS, I'm all about interval training. That is how I came up with my High-Intensity Training Zone functional training system. I've been doing interval training since my days playing football, and just like you . . . I hate running.

Let me clarify. I hate *slow* running, because the results take so much longer to achieve, and that takes up way too much time. So when you are choosing an exercise to do, try to pick one that safely uses the largest muscle groups in your body at a fast pace. Do you remember all that high-knee running you did? Well, ta-da, that's a way to boost your workout intensity and put yourself on the fast track to permanent weight loss.

We're not trying to isolate one muscle—it's faster and better to work them all at once. That's the way your body wants to work, so it feels good. And it makes your workout more intense and satisfying.

Now, what exercises are you going to include for your intervals?

Let me give you a few ideas: sprinting, spinning, stairs and hills will force you to use your entire body. All those knee drives aren't just pumping your legs—they're packing a real punch on your abs, too. Just as an example, let's use sprinting for your exercise and workout today.

You've probably also noticed that we don't do intervals every day. When you're planning your interval cardio workouts, give yourself a day in between, because you'll be working at much higher levels. Workouts that go for hours are a waste of time as well, so yours should be one hour at the absolute longest. Even that can be too much of a good thing, especially if you're on a tight schedule. Don't worry: 20 to 40 minutes is plenty.

How many intervals should you do? I suggest starting off with 5 to 10 rounds, and then you can build up from there. Each round would consist of one burst and one recovery interval.

How long? That all depends on you. We've used different time intervals in the 10PS—today we will work with 45 seconds, and as you get better conditioned, I would recommend dropping your interval periods to somewhere between 20 and 30 seconds. The shorter times will also mean shorter rest times, but awesome results. You can always play with this number to make it effective for you.

Stay with a 1:1 ratio, meaning that you should work for an equal time period on your burst and recovery. If we use one minute as an example, each round would consist of one minute at 80%, followed by one minute at 50%. If you find that too difficult, then you can use a 1:2 ratio, which would mean one minute at 80%, followed by two minutes at 50%.

Now let's put this puppy together and set up your workout for today. You're going to sprint on a treadmill or run outdoors, and we are going to use 30-second intervals for 10 rounds. See, it's not that hard. Let's get you moving—after all, you're still on my time!

And yes, we are going to start with your warmup—that's another habit that should be ingrained by now. Let's get to it. You know the drill: five minutes at Level 4 on the PES. Then your dynamic stretches. Why don't you get ready with a hamstring stretch, a quad stretch and a sumo squat. C'mon—you know how to do it.

Let's put some of our theory into practice. Take a look at the table on the next page, and you'll see what I was talking about. See how the workout alternates between Level 8 and Level 5 on the PES? Whether you're on a treadmill or in the park, those numbers aren't going to change. And when you're a lean, mean running machine, they're not going to change, either. You'll just be running faster to hit those numbers. Because when you do these intervals, you're building both your explosive strength and your cardio capacity. So, you'll find you're able to go faster and longer.

But enough talk. Make sure you've got some water on hand. If you're on a treadmill, keep the incline at 3 degrees. And if you're in the park, enjoy the fresh air. Have fun!

SAMPLE HITZ CARDIO INTERVAL WORKOUT

Time	Perceived Exertion Scale (PES)	Description	Incline
30 sec.	Level 8	80% of your max	3%
30 sec.	Level 5	50% of your max	3%
30 sec.	Level 8	80% of your max	3%
30 sec.	Level 5	50% of your max	3%
30 sec.	Level 8	80% of your max	3%
30 sec.	Level 5	50% of your max	3%
30 sec.	Level 8	80% of your max	3%
30 sec.	Level 5	50% of your max	3%
30 sec.	Level 8	80% of your max	3%
30 sec.	Level 5	50% of your max	3%
30 sec.	Level 8	80% of your max	3%
30 sec.	Level 5	50% of your max	3%
30 sec.	Level 8	80% of your max	3%
30 sec.	Level 5	50% of your max	3%
30 sec.	Level 8	80% of your max	3%
30 sec.	Level 5	50% of your max	3%
30 sec.	Level 8	80% of your max	3%
30 sec.	Level 5	50% of your max	3%
30 sec.	Level 8	80% of your max	3%

COOL-DOWN

There you have it: You've completed your own interval program. Now you can put one together anytime you want, and adjust the variables accordingly.

◆◆◆

Today you've jumped a big mental hurdle—being able to take the training wheels off and plan your own workouts. It's a big step, a key one for making the 10PS an everyday part of the rest of your life. Nice work. Now you just have to follow your meal plans for the day and get ready for tomorrow, when we will put a resistance circuit workout together! But first, the all-important cool-down. You know how to do that, right? Just spend at least 10 minutes at Level 3 on the PES, and you'll be ready for your static stretches—let's do a spinal twist, a quad and hip flexor stretch, a hamstring stretch and a hip stretch. And after that, it's time to eat.

DAY 28 MEAL PLAN

You deserve a day full of amazing meals, so here you go! And don't forget to hydrate!

BREAKFAST 2 eggs, scrambled; 2 slices back bacon; 2 slices whole-grain toast; 2 tsp. margarine; 1/2 cup grapes; 1-1/2 cups skim or soy milk.

SNACK 1 cup blueberries; 20 almonds.

LUNCH Soup and crackers: 1 cup split pea soup; 2 rye crackers spread with 1 oz. salmon mixed with 1 tbsp. light mayo; 1/2 cup baby carrots.

SNACK Granola bar.

DINNER Open-face turkey burger: Grill a 3 oz. ground turkey patty and top with 1 oz. light cheese. Serve on the bottom half of a whole-grain bun (skip the top half) alongside 2 cups mixed-green salad and 1 tbsp. light dressing.

DAY 29
HITZ Resistance Training Workshop

TOMMY RULE #29: IT AIN'T OVER TILL IT'S OVER!

I can't begin to tell you how proud I am of you that you've made it to this point. You've shed sweat, tears and, I'm willing to bet, inches and pounds. Was it as hard as you imagined it would be? Maybe even a bit harder, I bet. And was it worth it? Of course it was!

Remember, what you have now is a solid foundation, and today you will learn how to build on it to keep your momentum going as you settle into a healthy new lifestyle.

How do you like your hard new body? Yeah, I know, you want to make it harder still, so here are some things to keep in mind as you design your own workouts.

A big part is going to be your resistance workout. My take on resistance training comes from spending more than 20 years in gyms and fitness facilities all over the world. Anyone who knows me also knows how serious I've been about staying in shape. It was a prerequisite to playing sports the absolute best that I could, as well as training people just like you. Hey, no one wants a personal trainer who can't make it up a flight of stairs without getting winded!

Fitness trends come and go, but there are a few things that remain constant. First, you must continually challenge your body. If you keep doing the same things, your body is going to figure out that it doesn't have to try as hard. And it won't. That's when you'll see your gains start to plateau. If you want to change things, you've got to keep your body on its toes. You won't bore your muscles that way, and you won't bore your mind, either.

I've found that the best way to keep things challenging is functional training. I've already told you in the Introduction why I love it; it gives your body what it really craves deep down, and that means you get great results. There are thousands of machines that come out each and every year, each of them promising some miraculous transformation. The only problem with machines is that many of them do not force you to use multiple muscle groups. That means it will take you longer to achieve the results that you want, if you get there at all. Your body wants to move around, and flex and stretch and balance and all the things that come with an active life. It does not want to pull on cables all afternoon, or push stacks of iron up and down. Give it what it wants, and it will reward you. Give it a stack of iron, and it will be bored. So get off of the machines and use exercises that force you to engage your whole body.

You have already worked through 64 different exercises in the 10PS—and that is just the tip of the iceberg. I chose those exercises because they do what machines do not. They are very demanding on the core, and when packaged right, they will give you one hell of a workout in a short period of time. And remember, the more variety you give your body, the better it will respond. I'm sure you've seen people in gyms who do the same thing every single day. And year after year, they end up looking exactly the same. Do not fall into that boredom trap. Make sure you use all the exercises I've thrown at you in the 10PS, and the results will keep coming.

What we are going to do now is set up a little circuit using some of the exercises in the 10PS, so that you will be able to set up your own workouts as you venture into your new healthy lifestyle on Day 32.

If you want to work as efficiently as possible, turn your workouts into 30- to 45-minute full-body workouts. You want to pick 8 to 10 exercises that will include all your major muscle groups, along with some core exercises. You can also throw a few cardio bursts in there to increase the intensity, just like we did on the HITZ Resistance days. Let's warm you up, then put together a resistance package for you.

WARMUP

All right, this is the last time I'm going to be here when you warm up, so let me just say for old times' sake that this part of your workout is crucial. You know that, right? Your warmup gets your blood flowing and your system firing. That means that you're not only going to perform better, you're going to burn more fat. That's a win–win, so let's do it.

You know the drill now. Ten minutes of cardio at Level 4 on the PES, followed by your dynamic stretches. From here on in, it's your call. You know what to do and what gets your juices flowing. Maybe you'll be choosing your dynamic stretches on the basis of what you feel like. Were you blasting off sets of curls yesterday? You probably feel like a nice chest and biceps stretch. Were you pushing stacks with your squats? Then you may have a hankering for the sweet pain of a quad stretch. You get the idea. It's all up to you, starting tomorrow. For today, why not go for a dynamic hamstring, a dynamic quad and a dynamic chest and biceps for good measure? Go on, now—you know the routine.

All right, then. Now onto the workout itself.

What you want to keep in mind is that the goal is to get your whole body in on the act. You've probably seen the members of the no-neck crew working the same muscle groups all afternoon. And you've probably also noticed that some of them lurch around like zombies and their clothes don't seem to fit properly. You may go into the weight room dreaming of having gigantic pipes or bulging deltoids, but if you don't work your whole body, you're just putting it out of whack. And, of course, you're missing out on the opportunity that comes with hitting all those other muscle groups. You'll be fitter and leaner for getting your whole body involved, I can promise you that.

So let's look at a sample workout.

Warmup
Dynamic Stretches
HITZ Resistance

• BURPEE PUSH-UPS • PRISONER SQUATS • DUMBBELL CORE ROWING • CORE SCISSORS • SKIPPING
• DUMBBELL LUNGE SHOULDER PRESSES • STABILITY BALL CORE REACH CRUNCHES • STABILITY BALL ONE-LEG
• BRIDGES • DUMBBELL HEEL-TO-TOE CHOPS • HIGH-KNEE RUNNING • PLANK—DON'T WORRY . . . ONE SET
ONLY, AFTER YOUR THIRD SET OF THE REST.

Cool-Down
Static Stretches

Let's actually do it. But first, let's take a quick look at why we're doing it. By now, I hope you're 100% clear on why you always start with a warmup and dynamic stretches, but understanding your resistance exercises can be harder. The burpee push-up has the knee thrusts that attack the core, quad action in the up-and-down motion and the upper-body rip of the push-up itself. Plus, it's high-tempo, which brings in an element of cardio.

And so it goes down the list. Even things like rowing, which usually just target the back, have been tweaked to attack the core. Something like the lunge shoulder press takes an exercise that traditionally beefs up your upper body and adds an element that's going to burn your lower body, too. We want you working muscles from head to toe and everything in between. Especially in between.

Just about everything we do will involve your core, and that's because a powerful core is going to make you perform better, feel better and look better. But you already know that, don't you? You've no doubt noticed that your balance has improved, that things just seem easier nowadays, that you're tightening your belt a few notches more than you were a month ago. That's the magic of a strong core. So yeah, go after those arms, beef up those shoulders and work on those buns of titanium. Do it all. Just make sure you keep working that core.

Alright, enough admiring the sample session. Let's do it! You know how this works. You're going to perform three sets of the complete circuit, and you will be at each station for 1 minute. After each complete 11 minute circuit, you will get a 2-minute rest.

Go time!

◆ ◆ ◆

How was that? Now it's up to you to choose what you want to use for the cool-down today—as it will be from here on in. Just go at a nice and relaxed pace for about 10 minutes, and don't forget to do your static stretches. Let's try a spinal twist, a quad/hip flexor and a hamstring stretch. Great work today!

Who said you have to be in the gym for two hours to get a solid workout? Now you have an idea of how to put together your own sessions, and if you want a little extra push, hire a trainer for a session once or twice a week—or month, or whatever suits your budget or needs. Just make sure you don't end up with a "machine trainer," because that will just be a waste of cash!

DAY 29 MEAL PLAN

Same rules as always: Fuel up the right way, and get lots of water.

BREAKFAST Fruit smoothie: Blend 3/4 cup low-fat yogurt, 1 cup mixed frozen berries, 1/4 cup orange juice (optional) and 1/2 scoop protein powder; serve with 1/2 English muffin with 1 tbsp. natural peanut butter; 1-1/2 cups skim or soy milk.

SNACK 1/2 bran muffin; 1 oz. light cheese.

LUNCH Turkey wrap: 2 oz. turkey breast; lettuce, tomato, cucumber and mustard mixed with 1/4 tsp. honey; served in a large whole-wheat wrap.

SNACK 1/2 cup broccoli; 1 cup hummus; 2 rye crackers.

DINNER Pasta with meat sauce: Brown 3 oz. extra-lean ground beef, then drain the fat. Mix with 1/2 cup pasta sauce, tomato, onion and peppers and let simmer. Meanwhile, cook 1/2 cup whole-wheat spaghettini. Drain, then toss with 1 cup spinach. Add the sauce to the pasta and enjoy.

That's the last meal plan we have for you on the 10PS. Tomorrow, we'll give you all the tools you need to start building your own meals.

DAY 30
Nutrition Workshop

TOMMY RULE #30: HOW YOU FUEL YOUR BODY IS JUST AS IMPORTANT AS HOW HARD YOU WORK IT.

Eating right isn't rocket science. Somehow, for thousands of years, our ancestors managed to stay lean and fit, and didn't have to read books or watch TV shows to figure out what to have for supper. But then, they didn't have to walk down the aisles of massive supermarkets filled with fat-laden processed foods; they didn't have drive-thrus. Plus, they were used to being hungry some of the time, anyway.

But the fact is, today you have to know how to eat. You have to learn how to drive, how to use your new phone, how to exercise—well, you have to learn how to eat, too. That's one thing our ancestors had going for them, even if they couldn't get avocados whenever they felt like it—they had traditions. That's right: Traditional meals are a kind of diet. Look around the world; wherever people eat the way their cultures have for centuries, they're lean and healthy. Wherever they eat a "modern" diet of processed food, they're fat. The pattern is not hard to figure out. If you just eat whatever comes your way, you're going to be fat. If you stick to a plan, you're going to be healthy. Simple as that.

Right. So now you just need a quick lesson in how to eat, since I'm not going to be here for you on Day 32. One thing you can do (and I recommend this) is to go back and look at the meal plans you've been eating for the past month. In fact, you could even just reuse them. But at some point you're going to want to mix it up a bit, try new foods, swap things in and out. And that's great—just don't swap out a portion of cauliflower for a portion of a supersized combo at your local grease restaurant (unless you want to be supersized yourself).

The most common excuse I hear is "I don't have the time" (or energy or knowledge) to eat right. Well, guess what? You don't have that excuse anymore. Now that you've made it this far, you do have the energy, you've shown you have the time, and we're taking care of the knowledge part right now. So you can scrap your last reason for not eating right. I want to tip my hat to Maria one more time, since her meal plans are an important part of the 10PS. So what is behind her ass-kicking regimen? First off, she's already sorted out the calories for you. As you go forward, follow her lead. For the last 29 days, you've been consuming 1,500 to 1,600 calories per day. If that's working for you, I probably don't have to tell you to keep it up.

I'm guessing that you've figured out already that the food you eat is like an investment. So, just as eating too much is going to make you unhealthy, so is eating too little. Those calories you take in are the same ones that fuel your muscles when you're working out. And if you're not working out, you're not burning fat. And if you're not burning fat, you're staying fat. See what I mean? You need to eat to lose weight. So don't be tempted to accelerate your diet. It's not going to work.

I'm going to leave you with a few ground rules to keep in mind as you plan your future meals. Seriously, file these away, live by them, and you won't go wrong. I'm not saying that you have to tattoo them on your forearm as a reminder never to eat French fries, and I don't want you scolding your friends when they scarf down a few appetizers at an office party. I'm just saying that you should think of these as something like the traffic rules you abide by every day. You may bend them (or break them) from time to time in small ways, but everything works better if you don't—and the people who break them all the time tend to come to a bad end. But no one is going to give you a ticket if you have a second piece of cake on your birthday.

My training company is called 13HITZ, so here are your top 13 nutrition tips straight from our favourite expert, Registered Dietitian Maria Thomas. Play by these rules, and you'll be shredded:

1. Keep servings of grains (rice, potatoes, noodles, bread) to 1/2 cup at dinner.
2. Combine protein with carbohydrates at meals and snacks. That will make the energy last longer and keep you from getting hungry.
3. Fill half your dinner plate with vegetables. It's all a matter of real estate—assign the best property to the stuff your body really wants: fibre, vitamins and healthy carbs.
4. Don't eat within three hours of bedtime. Remember, food is an investment, so put it to work. If you don't, it's going to go into your savings account—and that's just another word for fat.
5. Eat every three hours. The whole point of being healthy is to be clear-eyed and energetic, so keep that body fuelled up.
6. Read labels and check online for calorie-counting websites. I'm not saying you have to be neurotic about it; I'm just saying you need to be aware. A lot of processed foods claim to be healthy, or low-calorie, or high-fibre, or whatever. But there is no label police to keep them honest. So when in doubt, check the nutritional table on the side of the package. That's where you'll find the truth. They say the proof of the pudding is in the eating, but that's too late for us. The proof is also on the side of the box, so check it.
7. Set specific goals. A goal without a plan is really just a wish, so set a realistic, yet specific, goal that you will work toward.
8. Don't hesitate to give yourself a reward when you achieve that goal!
9. Clear your cupboards of foods you snack on when bored, tired or "nibblish." You can't eat junk food you don't have.
10. Never overeat! (That's right. I said never. But don't worry, you won't enjoy overeating, anyway, so it's not like you're missing out on anything.)
11. Take a multivitamin.
12. Keep a journal. You will be more successful if you keep track of your food and beverages daily.
13. Remember, it takes about three weeks to form a habit, so stick with your plan for at least three weeks! You've gotten into the habit of eating well, but now you have to establish the habit of doing it without the 10PS meal plan. I know you can do it.

That's not so hard, is it? Follow those rules, and you'll be unstoppable. But then, you already know that. You're probably already shopping for new clothes, since your old, pre-shred clothes no longer fit. You know that the holy trinity of cardio work, resistance exercises and a healthy diet will yield incredible results. So keep it up!

Of course, one month of healthy eating is not going to make you into a food expert. There are certain nutritional combinations that will assist you in losing weight quickly and getting you in the best shape of your life. Specific quantities of proteins, carbohydrates, fats, amino acids and so on must be consumed with each meal. But you've been doing it for a while, so you should have a good idea of how to put them together. Be confident and have fun—and just remember that food is not your enemy.

Hey, why not strap on your shoes and get some exercise right now? Today is a day of rest and reflection, so how about some yoga, or a swim? Why not take the kids out for a bike ride, or take the dog for a run? Let's get moving!

DAY 31
Results Day

TOMMY RULE #31: THERE ARE DAYS WHEN DREAMS ARE REALIZED, HOPE BECOMES REALITY AND WISHES DO COME TRUE. TODAY IS ONE OF THOSE DAYS! TAKE YOUR RIGHT HAND, PUT IT ON YOUR LEFT SHOULDER AND GIVE IT A FEW TAPS FOR ME.

Congratulations, troops: You've made it to Day 31 of the 10PS! If you're as pumped as I am, then let's get this show on the road and get your latest round of numbers. First, though, flip back to your first measurements on Day 1 (page 21) and your second measurements (page 188). Fill the first two columns with these old, pre-shred numbers. Done? Good. Now, grab your measuring tape and your scale and fill in Day 31:

	Day 1	Day 15	Day 31	Four-Week Loss
Chest/Bust. Stretch the tape around your back and your nipples—make sure it's straight.				
Waist. Use your belly button as the centre point, just like the last time. And don't suck it in—I know that trick!				
Hips. Measure the widest part of your hips, all the way around, just like you did on Day 1.				
Weight. Take your shoes off and use the same scale you did on Days 1 and 15.				

Okay, now subtract your Day 31 numbers from your Day 1 numbers, and input the difference as you four-week loss. Well, what do you think? Numbers don't lie, so I'm guessing that as long as you held up your side of the bargain and put in the hard work that was required of you, high fives are in order. Congratulations! I know it wasn't easy, but it was worth it, wasn't it?

But we're not done yet: We've still got to do your fitness test. It seems like a long time ago now, but remember Day 1, when just warming up was nearly enough to wear you out? Well, we're going to do the same thing in a few minutes, and you're going to see how far you've come. So grab some breakfast if you haven't had it yet. If you're already fuelled up, set up your stations and get your stopwatch ready. Have a look at the exercises on the list if you've forgotten them. You want to make sure you're not wasting time figuring out what to do. You want to be ready to go hard and destroy the numbers you set a month ago.

But first, it's time to warm up. You know what you're doing, right? You've done it many times now, and you've got many more warmups to look forward to. Jump on a cardio machine, or get out onto the sidewalk or running path outside your door—your 10-minute warmup awaits. And then your dynamic stretches, of course. You wouldn't forget those, would you? Not on Day 31!

Feeling ready to set a new personal best? Are you ready to surprise yourself? I would expect you to shave between 10 and 20% off your earlier numbers. If you're feeling strong and your seven stations are ready to go, then let's do this.

Remember, go as fast as you can as long as you're under control.

GO!

HITZ FITNESS TEST	REPS	MEN	WOMEN
Skipping (Double Jump Rotations)	30		
Prisoner Squats	30		
Sit-Ups or Crunches	30		
Walking Lunges	30 Steps		
Resistance Band Lat Pull-Downs	30	Strong	Medium
Dumbbell Plié Squats	30	40 lb.	20 lb.
Bench Push-Ups	30		

What was your time? _____

Well, what do you think of that? I hope you're feeling proud of yourself, because none of the changes you're documenting today would have happened without your willpower. I can jump up and down and holler at you, and Maria can make one meal plan after another, but nothing was going to change one bit until you got your ass in gear.

And you did. And look at you now.

Now here's something to blow your mind a little. Feel how much stronger you are now? Well, that's after only 13 resistance sessions. Feel all that extra stamina? You're probably feeling you could keep it up forever right now. That's after only nine cardio sessions. Just nine!

Think about that for a minute. You've barely even begun your new lifestyle, and your clothes are already falling off you. Imagine what things are going to be like once you've been living this way for a while!

Now, just in case your results aren't mind-blowing, let's put things in perspective a little. First, these 31 days were always meant to be the tip of the iceberg—just the start of a whole new life. So it's way too early to even consider being disappointed. If you're thinking that way, let me ask you: How are you feeling? If you're feeling stronger and more energetic, healthier and more positive than you were 31 days ago, then I'd say your effort has been more than worth it, and the results are right around the corner. Keep it up.

Let me also ask whether you've been a serial dieter in the past. As I mentioned earlier, a series of shock diets can seriously mess with your metabolism and make it a bit more sluggish. Again, keep at the work you've been doing this past month, and those results are sure to come. Trust me, I've seen it.

And I've seen enough to know that, usually, if the results aren't quite there on Day 31, the effort probably wasn't there on some of the days before. I'm not saying that to make you feel bad. I'm saying that to make you feel good. Think about it: Your opportunity for the change you want so badly is still waiting for you. So keep at it.

But why am I dwelling on all that? If you're here on Day 31, I'm willing to bet you're pleased with your results. If you've got some before and after photos you're proud of, I'd love to see them. Your comments would be welcome, as well. I have to admit, it's a great feeling to see the results of those people I work with, who started with short-term goals and turn them into life-altering achievements.

But this isn't even close to the end of the process you started a month ago—so what's next?

If you're feeling like you could still use some guidance, that's totally fine. Hey, you can always go through the 10PS again. Not a bad idea at all. One thing, though: I would suggest that, as you hit your HITZ Resistance days, you do each day of exercises in the reverse order. Remember, if you want your body to respond, you've got to throw something new at it. Believe it or not, your body has already started to figure out the 10PS. Reversing the order is just the kind of surprise tactic you need to keep your body on its toes. This will give you a whole new feeling of burn.

But the 10PS was never really just about the exercises or the meal plans, was it? Sure, you can't get the job done without the right tools. And I've made certain I've given you not only the right tools but also the best tools. But having the tools isn't even close to being the only thing you need. If you walked into a dentists' convention and handed them the proper tools to work on your car, chances are you still wouldn't want them fixing your brakes. That's right: The tools are only useful if you've learned how to use them. And, of course, once you know how to use them, you can use them any time you want.

So you haven't just got a smaller waist and a stronger core; you now have knowledge. You've built an impressive toolbox of workouts and effective ways to train. Your food choices and portion sizes are now under control. And knowledge is freedom. See? Now that you have the knowledge it takes to be the kind of person you set out to be a month ago, you are free to become that person. More than ever, it's all up to you now.

That should give you great optimism. Because success requires even more than tools and the knowledge to use them; it takes the desire to use them. I don't care if you're a professional football player, or a volunteer at the local foodbank, or a mother getting up on a cold winter morning to get the kids to school on time; it's the desire to get things done that makes the world go around. Many people think they have just enough of that desire to get through the day—they just don't seem to have that little bit more it takes to change their lives.

But you've learned a couple of things in the past month that will probably turn out to be more important than how to do a proper squat or how many calories you should consume in a day. You've learned that your desire and your energy are not limited. You can dig down and get more, whenever you need to. It's not easy, but you know now that you can do it.

And you've learned that those reserves of desire, or willpower, or competitive juices, or whatever you want to call them, are enough to change your world. Maybe just a few pounds or inches at first. But that's just the beginning, right? It's a bit like pushing a railroad car. It may be pretty tough to get it going, but once it's rolling, look out, because it's going to be hard to stop.

So, what about those goals we were talking about a month ago? Those old jeans, or that outfit you wanted to wear to that special occasion. Or that 5K you wanted to run. Or walking 18 holes instead of riding in a cart. How did that turn out for you?

I'm guessing you probably made it, didn't you? I'm not surprised. I wouldn't be surprised by another thing, either: I'll bet you already have another, more ambitious goal. Maybe it's another 10 pounds. Maybe it's a 10K run. Could be anything, really, couldn't it? Teenagers sail around the world and 80-year-olds run marathons. You see what I'm getting at here? Anything really is possible. You probably wouldn't have believed me a month ago, but I'm guessing you probably know it for a fact now.

You've just completed the first part of a transformation that is as big as you want to make it. Remember back at the beginning, when I said that the 10PS is more about leading than following? Well, that's even more true now. Your progress has depended on your commitment all along. But now that the tools and knowledge are in your hands, your desire is going to have to see you through the challenges ahead. No one is going to tell you what to eat or how to work out now. It's up to you.

That may sound like a big job, but it's actually great news for you. If there's one thing that's true of all high-level sports, whether it's pro football or Ping-Pong, it's the axiom that the player or the team that "wants it more" usually wins. You've probably seen underdogs rise to the occasion in a big game, or a player go head to head with someone bigger and more talented and still come out on top. That's because desire and hard work are what make winners—nothing else.

Why is that good news for you? Because the only person who can stop you now is you, and you've already proven that you have the desire and the will to do the hard work. If you didn't, you wouldn't be here right now, on Day 31.

So, what are you going to do? If I know you—the new you—you're going to get out there and do something. Flex those muscles, get that heart pumping and those lungs burning a little. Just get out there and enjoy some of the things you couldn't do a month ago—and let yourself dream about the things you'll soon be doing.

Maybe I'll see you out there.

ACKNOWLEDGEMENTS

What an amazing feeling! My words have been put to paper and then onto your table. I feel blessed to be in this position, and I am grateful to those who have inspired and influenced me.

To all the teammates I've ever had, to all the coaches who have taught me, to all the clients I have worked with, to all the fitness professionals I've learned from, to all of my fellow Gaiters and "flemo" boys, thank you. In some way, you have made a difference in my life.

I want to give a shout out to The Eyes and to Slice for believing in me and jump-starting this whole new fantastic career. Thanks to the entire *LTP* and *Bulging Brides* team— "Miss Dogg," you rock!

Special thanks to coaches Lindsey, Russell, Gretes, Breck, Allen, Kim and Jacques Chapdelaine, Steve Ramsbottom, Dave Ritchie, Mike Talic and L. Browne. All of you have been instrumental in my growth, because you never let me settle for average, but pushed me to be the best that I could be.

To Curtis Russell, Nick Garrison, Kate Cassaday and the HarperCollins team, thank you for "feelin' my vision" and shaping an amazing book. You guys made writing my first book experience very enjoyable. Your input was appreciated and very helpful. THANK YOU.

Special thanks to Maria Thomas, RD, at www.urbannutrition.com—you are awesome! Your meal plans are top-notch, and they make a difference. We have helped 98 contestants on *The Last 10 Pounds Bootcamp* lose hundreds of inches and pounds over the last five years; I look forward to many more success stories. I can't wait to read your book when it comes out!

To my wife and daughter, mother and father, thank you so much for your input, love and support. Thank you for keeping me focused. A special thank you to my mom—you made some tough decisions for me as a youngster, and those lessons have brought me to this point.

INDEX OF EXERCISES AND STRETCHES

Note: Because the stretches occur so frequently throughout the book, page numbers are given for only the first instance of each stretch.

Spiderman push-ups, 71, 146
squats
    dumbbell plié, 30, 95, 197
    dumbbell scap, 145, 308
    jump, 249
    prisoner, 26, 70
stability ball
    core reach crunches, 203
    hamstring curls, 75, 276
    jackknifes, 120, 282
    mountain climbers, 149
    one-arm rowing, 94
    one-leg bridges, 228
    push-ups, 225
    reverse hyperextensions, 99
    rollouts, 151, 254
    Supermans, 69
stability ball and dumbbell
    chest presses, 310
    one-arm flies, 278
    one-arm rowing, 341
    Russian twists, 251
stability ball with dumbbell reverse fly, 201
static lunges, 93
walking lunges, 28
walkouts, core, 123
x-body mountain climbers, core, 313

STRETCHES
chest complex triple stretches, 50
dynamic back swings, 40
dynamic chest and bicep stretches, 23
dynamic glute and hamstring stretches, 39
dynamic quad stretches, 23
dynamic sumo squats, 24
hamstring stretches, 33
hip stretches, 32
quadriceps/hip flexor stretches, 33
spinal twists, 34